Cois Fharraige & Spiddal
A History

John J Keady

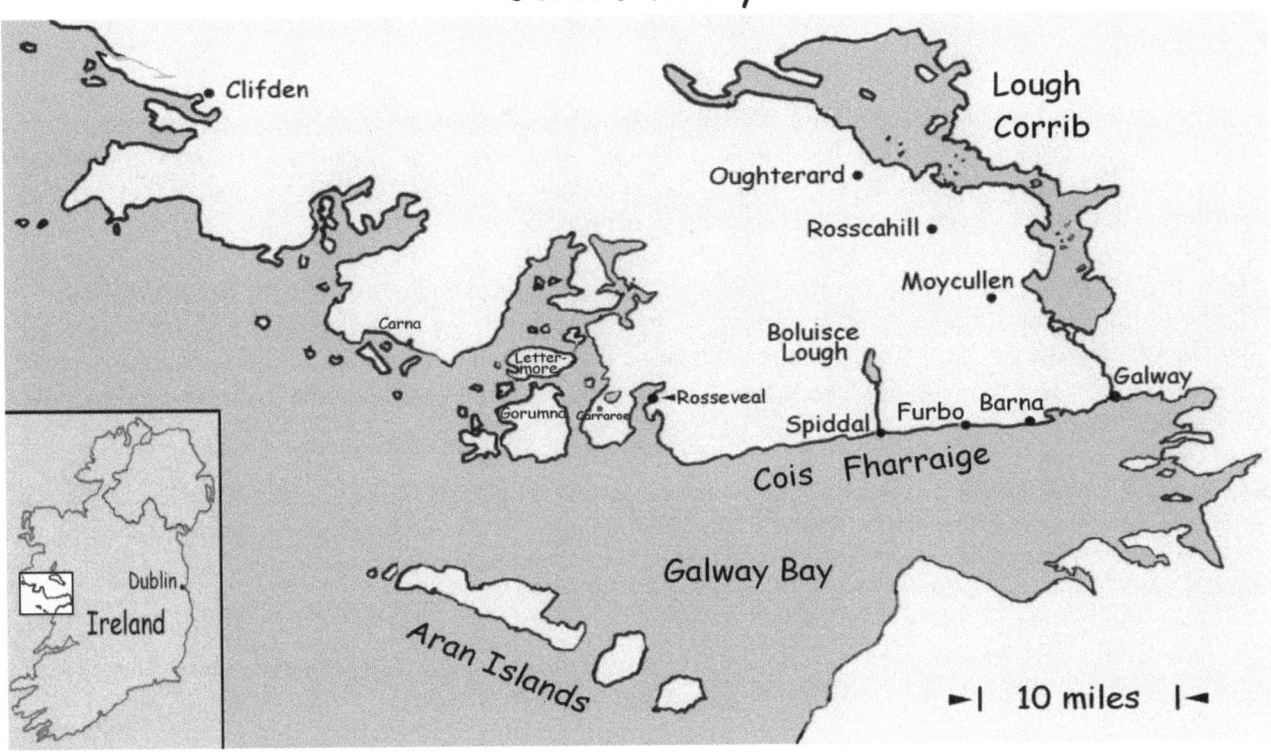

3rd Printing
(with minor corrections)

Copyright © John J Keady 2021-2024

Published by Casco Bay Celtic Press. Maine publisher specialized in publishing Celtic history, literature and genealogical works.

Editorial and Sales Offices:
Casco Bay Celtic Press
PO Box 1388, Waldoboro, Maine 04572
www.cascobaycelticpress.com

Manufactured in the United States of America

Preface

I mí Iúil na bliana 1698, scríobh John Lodge, oifigeach de chuid Chaisleán Bhaile Átha Cliath, faoi thailte a bhí tearc i ndaoine in Iar-Chonnacht, ar an taobh thiar de Loch Coirb agus Abhainn na Coirbe. Bhí sé ag cur síos ar eastát (roinnt tailte i gceantar an Spidéil san áireamh), a bhí curtha le chéile ag Richard Nimble Dick Martin, faoi Acht Lonnaithe na bliana 1662. Bhain Lodge úsáid as an bhfrása "hainous lands", sé sin, drochthailte agus é ag cur síos ar an gceantar agus thug sé le fios go raibh deacrachtaí ag Nimble Dick tionóntaí a earcú.

Fós féin, dhá chéad bliain ina dhiaidh sin, tugadh "Ceantar Cúng" ar roinnt mhaith de na tailte in Iar-Chonnacht, go háirithe ceantair in aice an chósta. Tugtar Cois Fharraige ar cheantar an chósta ó Bhearna siar go dtí an Chloch Mhór (ó dheas de Ros a' Mhíl). Tá an ceantar seo suite ar an taobh ó thuaidh de Chuan na Gaillimhe, áit a bhfuil glúnta de mo chuid sinsear i gcré na cille.

Maíonn roinnt mhaith daoine i gCois Fharraige a bhfuil spéis acu ina gcuid préamhacha gur as Gaillimh Thoir a gcuid sinsear. Tá ráite faoi dhuine de mo shinsir mháthartha gur as Baile Átha an Rí a tháinig sí go hIar-Chonnacht agus í ar a teitheadh. Thuig an dream a tháinig nach raibh rompu ach an talamh tearc bocht. Bhí tionchar mór ag Conradh Luimnigh maidir le díshealbhú daoine - daoine a raibh orthu imeacht as tailte maithe torthúla siar go Cois Fharraige.

Fágtar muid le roinnt mhaith ceisteanna gan freagraí agus muid i mbun staidéir ar stair áitiúil. Ní bhíonn sé follasach amach is amach maidir le heachtraí, eagraíochtaí agus fiú mionsonraí faoi na daoine a mhair ag an am sin. Tá cuimhneamh maith soiléir ar roinnt daoine, cuimhneamh doiléir ar chuid eile agus tá roinnt daoine eile ligthe I ndearmad. Déanaim iarracht mistéir nó dhó a réiteach.

Déanaim iarracht freisin eolas níos leithne a chur ar fáil maidir leo siúd a bhfuil cuimhneamh doiléir orthu agus a gceart a thabhairt chomh maith dóibh siúd atá ligthe i ndearmad.

In July 1698, a Dublin Castle official, John Lodge, wrote of sparsely populated lands in Iar-Connacht, west of Lough Corrib and the Corrib River. He was writing about an estate (including some "Spiddle" lands), assembled by Richard *Nimble Dick* Martin, via the 1662 Act of Settlement. Describing the area, Lodge employed the phrase "hainous lands," and indicated that Nimble Dick had some difficulty recruiting tenants.

Yet two centuries on, significant parts of Iar-Connacht, especially the coastal areas, met the legal definition of the "Congested District." Cois Fharraige (*By the Sea*), is the North Galway Bay coastal area running west from around Barna to the Cloghmore South vicinity (south of Rosseveal), where rest generations of my ancestors.

Those along Cois Fharraige interested in their roots, when asked whence their ancestors came, often answer 'East Galway.' A maternal ancestor of mine is said to have arrived in Iar-Connacht from Athenry, on the lam. Few came into Cois Fharraige because they thought the grass greener. Retribution following the Treaty of Limerick likely enhanced the influx into Cois Fharraige.

In looking into the local history, one finds a mystery or two, as well as individuals, institutions, and events, all significant in their day, now remembered with various degrees of clarity. There are the well remembered, the vaguely remembered, and the forgotten.

What follows are attempts to solve a mystery or two, along with efforts to better document some of the vaguely remembered and resurrect some of the forgotten.

Table of Contents

Table of Contents (continued)

Abbreviations

great^2 = great great,   great^3 = great great great,   aka = also known as,   Bart.= Baronet

d.s.p. = descessit sine parole: died without issue, GV = Griffith's Valuation,

J P = Justice of the Peace,   RC or C = Roman Catholic,   P = Protestant,

RCB=Representative Church Body (Anglican),   ICM = Irish Church Missions (Anglican),

RIC = Royal Irish Constabulary,   OS = Ordnance Survey(s),   RM = Resident Magistrate,

VOB = Valuation Office Books, NAI = National Archives of Ireland

MP = Member of Parliament,   LED = Landed Estates Database,

CDB = Congested Districts Board,   DS = Down Survey   NB = Nota Bene

Acknowledgments

For various suggestions and information, I am especially indebted to Colm Pat Colm Keady, Jerry Darby Keady, Cáit Fitzpatrick, Noreen Kennedy, Noel Conneely, Kathleen Devaney, Mike P Ó Conaola, Seán Ó Neachtain, Lochlainn Ó Tuairisg, Ronnie O'Gorman, Stiofán Ó Cúláin, Bartley Conneely, Joe Folan, Dr Susan Hood, Steve Donohoe, Barbara Hergett, Redmond Morris, and Tim Schmelzer.

I'm grateful to Séamas Ó Máirtín for his as Gaeilge translation of the preface. I am deeply indebted to the late Timín Joe Tim Curran.

That being said, the document's shortcomings accrue to me.

Introduction

Over time I've collected snippets: oral history, newspaper articles, court reporting etc, that provide insight about life along the north Galway Bay coastal area known as *Cois Fharraige* (*by the sea, the coast*). In Italian, this would be: *in riva al mare, la riviera.* Ours is a very different *la riviera.* The snippets etc are gathered here, in a series of topics. Within a topic, the narrative is more or less chronological. The first two topics provide a sort of orientation.

Articles in a local newspaper were reprinted in other newspapers across Ireland and Britain, increasing the odds an article survived in one archive or another. This syndication network was used to potentially influence the authorities, by arousing public indignation, and was used for fund-raising. Some Spiddal area clergy were adept at both.

Much of the secular press had their Protestant or Catholic sympathies. In the Ulster or Dublin press, something might be characterised as 'Romish' or 'Popish.' You have your clue. Accounts of a particular event, in various independent newspapers, seldom were entirely consistent. While one might expect some biased or exaggerated reporting, some reporting was fiction.

The Chancery Court transcripts (including the subsidiary Estates Court) provide great insight into the Anglo-Irish Ascendancy, who were fond of litigating against each other, even brother against brother.

Deciphering the proceedings reminded me of remarks associated with Shaw and Wilde about the Americans and the British, paraphrased as 'two peoples separated by a common language.'

The summaries, and especially the parliamentary Hansard transcripts, are often obtuse, at least to me. Never say in ten words, what you can say in fifty or a hundred. Now is the pot calling the kettle black.

The gentry also used the lower Petty Sessions Court, and the newspapers, in their disputes against each other, and against their tenants. And the Petty Sessions was where the tenants pursued their grievances against each other. Often the disputes had already been vigorously contested in the fields, along the streams and roads, and up on the bog, before ending up in the Petty Sessions. As we will see, this applies to both the gentry and the peasantry.

The Petty Sessions also reveal another phenomenon: individuals who appear in the Petty Sessions, but not in other civil and church records. Without the Petty Sessions records, one wouldn't know that certain individuals existed.

The gentry figure prominently, and so some cursory gentry genealogies are included as appendices.

Cois Fharraige, and Spiddal in particular, in the province of Connacht, had interesting connections to other places. Luckily the Connachtman likes to ramble, and so we'll examine these connections by rambling over to Dublin. We'll also ramble west of Cois Fharraige, over to Canada and the USA.

An extraordinary resource in what follows has been *DIPPAM (Documenting Ireland: Parliament, People and Migration)*, containing *EPPI*, the *Enhanced British Parliamentary Papers on Ireland*, all (15,000) official papers on all aspects of the Union with Ireland. See Appendix XIV.

Cois Fharraige & Its Landowners

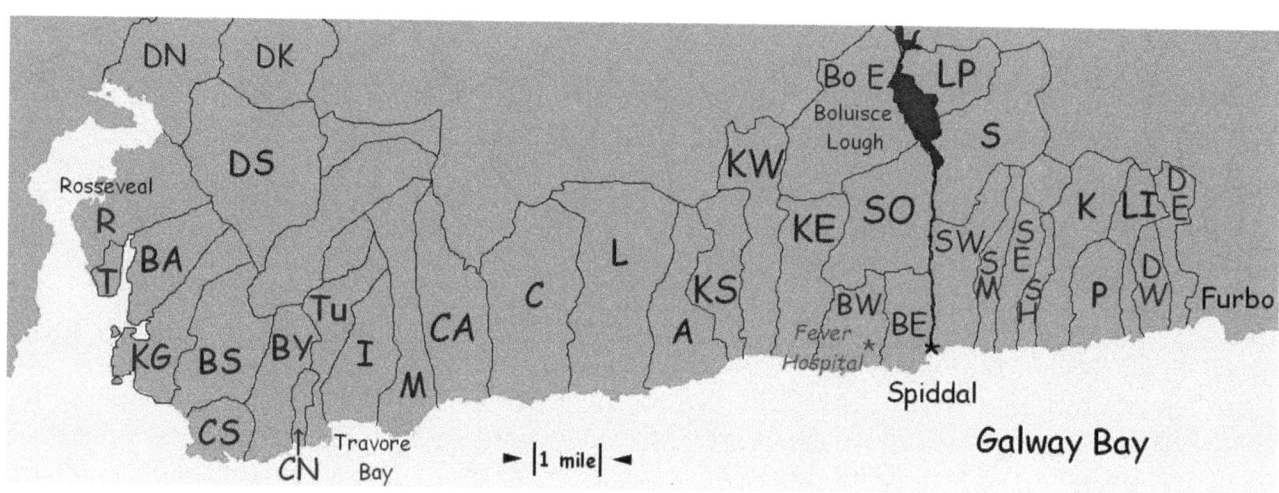

Cois Fharraige
(adapted from www.townlands.ie)

ID	Townland
A	Aille
BA	Ballintleva
BE	Bohoona East
Bo E	Boliska Eighter
BS	Banraghbaun South
BW	Bohoona West
BY	Ballynahown S.
C	Cornarone
CA	Cartronlahan
CN	Cartron
CS	Cloghmore South
DE	Derryloughan East

ID	Townland
DK	Derrykyle
DN	Derrynea
DS	Deroogh South
DW	Derryloughan West
I	Inverin
K	Killough (Coilleach)
KE	Kilroe East
KG	Keeraunnagark S.
KS	Knock South
KW	Kilroe West
L	Loughaunbeg
LI	Lippa

ID	Townland
LP	Letterpeak
M	Minna
P	Park
R	Rosseveal
S	Shannagurran
SE	Spiddal East
SH	Sheeaunroe
SM	Spiddal Middle
SO	Shannawoneen
SW	Spiddal West
T	Tonacrick
Tu	Tully

Absent a legal definition (that I know of), we'll take Cois Fharraige (*By the Sea or Beside the Sea*) to be the North Galway Bay coastal region running from Barna west to Cloghmore South (*An Chloch Mór Theas*). Our main interest is west of Furbo. Some townlands farther west, and some inland townlands technically not *beside the sea*, figure in this narrative, and thus are included in the map and table. Over many decades, enough seaweed was hauled to up to Shannagurran and other inland townlands, that they could be thought of as an honorary part of the coast.

Townland	Down Survey Owners by Year		Griffith's Valuation Immediate Lessor	Census Population by Year*	
	1641	1670	1855	1841	1851
Derryloughaun East	Patrick French (C)	Roger Flaherty (P)	Andrew W Blake	127 (20,0)	70 (10,3)
Derryloughaun West	Patrick French (C)	Roger Flaherty (P)	Andrew W Blake	91 (12,1)	69 (12,0)
Lippa	Edmund Halloran (C)	Issedorus Lynch (C)	James Browne	75 (13,3)	69 (10,2)
Park			Patrick Blake	128 (20,0)	116 (19,3)
Killough	Thomas Lynch (C)	Thomas French (C)	James Browne	191 (32,1)	132 (24,0)
Sheeaunroe	Dominick Lynch (C)	Anthony French (C)	James Browne	114 (22,0)	86 (16,0)
Spiddal East	Richard Darcy (C)	Oliver Martin (C) Anthony French (C)	Thomas Bunbury Anthony Donnellan, Thomas Naughton	141 (25,0)	217 (41,2)
Spiddal Middle	Richard Darcy (C)	Oliver Martin (C) Anthony French (C)	Peter S Comyn	79 (13,0)	66 (12,0)
Spiddal West	Richard Darcy (C)	Oliver Martin (C) Anthony French (C)	Peter S Comyn	563 (99,3)	199 (35,0)
Letterpeak	Heirs of Hugh O'Flaharty (C)	Anthony French (C)	Anthony Donnellan	27 (6,0)	15 (2,2)
Boliska Oughter	Earl of Clanricard (P)	Earl of Clanricard (P)	Edmund O'Malley	20 (8,11)	19 (3,0)
Boliska Eighter	Earl of Clanricard (P)	Earl of Clanricard (P)	Honoria O'Malley	39 (10,12)	22 (6,0)
Shannagurran	Thomas Lynch (C)	Nicholas Bourke (C)	Peter S Comyn	40 (7,0)	51 (8,2)
Shannawoneen	Lynch Blake (C)	Nicholas Bourke(C) Sir Roger Jones (P)	Andrew Blake	49 (9,2)	27 (5,3)
Bohoona East	Stephen Lynch (C)	Robert Martin (C)	Martin Morris, Ecclesiastical Comm	290 (47,1)	257 (41,2)
Bohoona West	Stephen Lynch (C)	Robert Martin (C)	Martin Morris Patrick Blake	283 (46,1)	242 (39,5)
Kilroe East	Earl of Clanricard (P)	Earl of Clanricard (P)	Patrick Blake	234 (43,0)	168 (33,0)
Kilroe West	Earl of Clanricard (P)	Earl of Clanricard (P)	Patrick Blake	203 (34,0)	179 (31,3)
Knock South	Earl of Clanricard (P)	Earl of Clanricard (P)	Francis Comyn John Martin	224 (38,0)	125 (23,0)
Aille			Francis Comyn	308 (55,0)	250 (40,1)
Loughaunbeg			Francis Comyn	256 (45,1)	393 (62,1)
Cornrarona	Robert Martin (C)	Robert Martin (C)	Francis Comyn	676 (123,1)	388 (68,0)
Cartronlahan		Sir Thomas Meredith (P)	Patrick Blake	241 (39,2)	194 (33,0)
Minna		Richard Martin (C) Earl of Clanricard (P)	Patrick Blake Eleanor Blake	169 (30,1)	87 (17,0)
Inveran	Richard Martin (C) James Óge Darcy (C) William McShane (C)	Nicholas Bourke (C)	Patrick Blake Eleanor Blake Patrick & Eleanor Blake	313 (57,2)	153 (25,2)

* Census Format: a (b,c) = population (number of inhabited houses, number of uninhabited houses)

For an enumeration of Spiddal West and Spiddal Village, as of December 1861, see Appendix II.

Townland	Down Survey Owners by Year		Griffith's Valuation Immediate Lessor	Census Population by Year*	
	1641	1670	1855	1841	1851
Tully	Martin Blake (C)	Nicholas Bourke (C) Sir Roger Jones (P)	Patrick Blake Eleanor Blake, John Wallace	137 (25,0)	38 (6,0)
Cloghmore North	Thom Lynch (C)	Walter Blake (P)	Patrick Blake	0 (0,0)	0 (0,0)
Cloghmore South	Thom Lynch (C)	Water Blake (P)	Patrick Blake	115 (24,0)	105 (23,0)
Ballynahown North	Stephen Martin (C)	Robert Martin (C)	Patrick Blake Eleanor Blake	0 (0,0)	0 (0,0)
Ballynahown South	Stephen Martin (C)	Robert Martin (C)	Patrick Blake	260 (46,0)	96 (18,0)
Cartron			Patrick Blake	0 (0,0)	4 (1,0)
Banraghbaun North	Roger O'Flaherty (C)	Robert Martin (C)	Patrick Blake	0 (0,0)	0 (0,0)
Banraghbaun South	Roger O'Flaherty (C)	Robert Martin (C)	Patrick Blake	142 (28,0)	96 (16,4)
Keeraunngark North	Earl of Clanricard (P)	Earl of Clanricard (P)	Patrick Blake	0 (0,0)	0 (0,0)
Keeraunngark South			Patrick Blake	130 (24,0)	130 (23,4)
Derrykyle	Robert Martin (C)	Walter Blake (P)	Patrick Blake	21 (4,0)	37 (6,0)
Derrynea	Dominic French (C)	Walter Blake (P)	Patrick Blake	177 (32,0)	80 (11,1)
Ballintleva			Patrick Blake	99 (15,0)	52 (9,1)
Tonacrick		Richard Martin (C) Earl of Clanricard (P)	Patrick Blake	102 (14,0)	120 (19,0)
Rosseveal	Thom Lynch (C)	Water Blake (P)	Patrick Blake	277 (47,1)	145 (30,8)
Derroogh South	Syralagh O'Flahartye (C)	Sir Thomas Meredith (P)	Patrick Blake	68 (13,0)	80 (16,0)

Census Format: a (b,c) = population (number of inhabited houses, number of uninhabited houses)

After the 1610 Ulster plantation, grievances accumulated and festered, resulting in a 1641 Catholic rebellion that became bound up with the tumult of the English Civil Wars that began in 1642. Wars that brought Oliver Cromwell to prominence, and to Ireland. After his Irish campaign, the _Down Survey_ (DS) was conducted during 1656-1658 by William Petty, surgeon-general of the English army, who laid _down_ measurements. Cromwell's men and investors were to be paid with the spoils of war; confiscated Catholic land. Hence the survey. The Catholics were to be exiled; _To Hell or Connaught,_ a remark often attributed to Cromwell. Over time, many original survey documents were destroyed. But, copies of documents travelled. The DS was largely reassembled from these surviving geographically dispersed resources.

E W Lynam, in _The O'Flaherty Country,_ stated that the 1656 Plantation scheme, in principle, involved exiling the dispossessed Catholics of Down and Antrim to the baronies of Ballynahinch, Moycullen, and the half-barony of Ross. Ca 1914, Lynam made admittedly cursory enquiries in these areas, and found few descendants of Down or Antrim people. Or perhaps he found few people willing to acknowledge their Ulster ancestry. The year 1670 is after redistribution of forfeited Catholic lands.

The 1847-1864 Griffith's Valuation (GV) provides an informative peek into mid 19th Century Irish life. A more formal name was the; "General Valuation of Rateable Property in Ireland."

It was a survey/assessment of land holdings and buildings etc, with an eye to taxing them to support the poor. Every plot and building was assessed and valued. Also cataloged was who rented what from whom. Although it's not a census, one can extract information about individuals.

The Griffith Volume for Galway was printed/published on 7 Mar 1855. At the National Archives are the Valuation Office Books (VOB), showing that the assessors were in the Spiddal area during the summer and autumn of 1853. These valuations, which I'm assuming were the starting point for the GV, were significantly modified (reduced usually) before making it into the final March 1855 compilation.

The 1841 and 1851 Census Summaries, before and after the Great Famine, show the famine's effects on individual townlands. Being summary data, for an individual townland there is no further more refined accounting of the causes of depopulation; eviction, emigration, and death from starvation and death from disease.

A number of those named in the DS and GV tables descend from Anglo-Normans who came to Ireland, many as lieutenants of Strongbow (The Earl of Pembroke) or Henry II, from 1169 on. The wealthiest person listed in the table likely was the Earl of Clanricard, a de Burgh (aka de Burgo, Burca, Bourke, Burke), whose ancestor was a lieutenant of Henry II. The Martins descend from an Oliver Martin, said to have accompanied Richard the Lion-Hearted to the Holy Land. The Blakes descend from a man named Caddell, who arrived with Strongbow, as did a Monte Maurisco, a name which morphed into Morris over time.

At their fortified Galway settlement by the mouth of the Corrib, the Anglo-Norman weaponry included the sword, the lance, the battle ax, and the institution of marriage. Thus the Irish and Anglo-Normans were fighting each other and intermarrying. Sometimes seemingly at the same time.

Some native Irish are listed in the tables. West of the Corrib, the Bourke's and Martin's nemesis was the Irish O'Flarherty sept, the ferocious O'Flaherties, who had originally occupied lands extending from the eastern shore of Lough Corrib, until they were pushed west into Iar-Connacht, where the pressure on them continued. A manuscript in the British Museum is titled; "The instrument and articles of peace with the Bourkes and Flaherties etc, made in the courthouse of Galway, June 28, 1589."

Irish sept schisms were expertly exploited. Earlier in time, the O'Flaherty sept had splintered into a number of clans, fighting each other and the Anglo-Normans. By the early 1600s, the clans had, with varying degrees of sincerity, sworn fealty to the Crown. The Moycullen clan was the weakest, given its proximity to Galway. They had to fend-off the Martins, the Bourkes, and the other O'Flaherties, especially the adjacent Lemonfield clan. This splintering was a tragedy. In 1914, E W Lynam stated;

"Had the O'Flaherties been united and held their wild country and their wilder sea as they might have held them, Iar-Connaught would still have been independent in 1602, and Hugh O'Neill's efforts for Ireland might have had a different ending."

Circa 1592, "English" Rory O'Flaherty, of the Moycullen O'Flaherties, leased land to Robert Martin, the first Martin of Ross, whose earlier seat was Dangan. Robert Martin (ca 1620 – 1700), a grandson of the first Martin of Ross, had a son Richard *Nimble Dick* Martin (1655-1731). The nickname wasn't necessarily complimentary: adept swordsman or unscrupulous lawyer, probably both. He sided with the Irish at the 1691 Battle of Aughrim, but was pardoned in 1695.

Using the Acts of Settlement, including the 1662 Act, by the end of the 17th Century he had assembled an estate of about 200,000 acres. At the National Archives of Ireland (NAI) is a document (NAI Lodge/9/117), dated July 13 1698, for the "Grant of Lands to Captain Richard Martin." Dublin Castle's John Lodge wrote about;

.........hainous lands in the remotest part of the county of Galway, called Eyre-Connaught, which with great pain and Industry he had acquired under the Acts of Settlement and which were in a manner waste, so that he could not procure Tenants without great encouragement..........

An accompanying property list included land at "Spiddle." The 185 acre (as of ca 1657) Bohoona West townland is about a mile west of Spiddal Village. In 1670, the townland belonged to Robert Martin (ca 1620-1700), grandson of the first Martin of Ross. In the DS, 12 acres were "Profitable Land." A synonym for "profitable" could be "arable." "In a manner waste" would be rock and bog.

Thus 6.5% of Bohoona West was amenable to cultivation (and/or grazing) ca 1657. The actual situation was more unfavorable, for those 12 acres were not a single unified arable tract of land, but were a significant number of smaller arable patches of land, amounting to 12 acres, scattered about the soggy southern part of the townland. Twelve acres of rundale (widely scattered plots). Not at all an unusual situation in Cois Fharraige, and for Iar-Connacht more generally. Some unprofitable land was laboriously reclaimed over time, via drainage projects and subsequent soil augmentation.

My paternal ancestor, said to be involved in the 1691 Battle of Aughrim, was possibly the first into Spiddle's Bohoona West townland ca 1700. My father was of the seventh generation there.

At the DS website, one can toggle back and forth on maps that show the Martin's holdings before and after Cromwell. The westward shift is stunning. There were few peasants in Nimble Dick's ca 1698 huge carefully organised boggy fiefdom. Not nearly enough peasants to support him and his family.

One might have thought there was an earlier infusion of Ulster refugees; Ulster Catholics, displaced after Cromwell's rampage. But, in 1914, E W Lynam stated; "The Plantation of 1656 effected, as far as I can discover, very little change in the population of Iar-Connaught." Capt Richard Martin's perhaps desperate ca 1698 "great encouragement," to sign-up voluntary tenants, might have involved lies, bribes, and desperate people.

Ninble Dick's first born son was Robert "The Brave." By some accounts he was impetuous. He was murdered in 1705, according to Archer Martin's genealogy, by "the sept of the O'Flaherties." It's said he was ambushed, while about to avenge a supposed insult to his mother made by Sir John O'Flaherty of Lemonfield. On 10 October 1707, the Lord Lieutenant of Ireland issued a proclamation naming the accused as Brian Flaherty, Edmond Flaherty, Patrick Flaherty, and John Joyce. The ringleader, likely one of the above Flahertys, was said to be an illegitimate son of Sir John. It's not clear they were apprehended. The authorities knew not to venture too far into Iar-Connacht.

The 1641 DS entry for the ownership of Letterpeak references the heirs of Hugh O'Flaherty (d.1631). This was a Moycullen O'Flaherty. The heir was a son Roderick (Rory), who being an infant when his father died, became a ward of the Crown. As a child, he was considered innocent concerning the 1641 rebellion, and had, on paper at least, an estate of 1000 acres (500 acres in other accounts), that was his upon reaching majority. Later he was concerned that, as a Catholic, the estate might be taken from him under the Penal Laws. Nimble Dick exploited this apprehension, by proposing, ca 1667, a sham legal conveyance (no money would change hands) of the estate from Roderick to Nimble Dick, to deceive the authorities.

Roderick (Rory) O'Flaherty (1629 – ca1717), the last Moycullen O'Flaherty chieftain, ended up impoverished in Park, just east of Spiddal Village. Roderick's son, Michael O'Flaherty, took Nimble Dick to court in 1717, around the time of Roderick's death, claiming the conveyance cheated his father. Nimble Dick claimed money had changed hands. In 1725 Michael O'Flaherty won his case.

Ca 1718, Michael O'Flaherty married the widow Annabel Fitzpatrick of the Aran Fitzpatricks. Eventually he *d.s.p. (descessit sine parole; died without issue),* and left the estate to his stepson Richard Fitzpatrick, the first Fitzpatrick of Moycullen. Annabel Fitzpatrick's father was Nimble Dick Martin. Michael O'Flaherty sued Nimble Dick and won, married Nimble Dick's widowed daughter, and left his estate to Nimble Dick's grandson. One has the trappings of an opera.

Among Nimble Dick's great grandchildren was Richard 'Humanity Dick' Martin of Ballynahinch and Dangan. The Martins of Ballynahinch descend from the Martins of Ross and Dangan.

The Oliver Martin co-owning the Spiddal West, Spiddal Middle, and Spiddal East townlands in 1670, was from East Galway. His family's early seat was Dunguaire Castle, Kinvara. By 1670, the family's main holdings shifted east, ranging from Ardrahan to Gort, with the seat being in Tullyra (aka Tillyra).

Oliver Martin and his brother Peter opposed the English in the Williamite War, which included the 1691 Battle of Aughrim. In the eighth year of the rule of Queen Anne (see Appendix XIV), Oliver Martin was exempted from the Anti-Catholic retribution that followed the Treaty of Limerick, for being a person "who behaved himself with great moderation, and was remarkably kind to numbers of protestants in distress....." Oliver's brother Peter lost his lands, and died in exile in France. Oliver's exemption came in 1709, just in time to benefit his heirs, as Oliver Martin died ca 1709.

Part of Cois Fharraige, just east of Furbo, is Barna. By 1852, the extensive 100,000 acre estate of Arthur Lynch, that stretched from Barna to Moycullen, was an Encumbered Estate. It was purchased by Lord John Campbell, Lord Chief Justice of England, also a director of the Law Life Assurance Society of London. Apparently Arthur Lynch was a tolerant landlord. The new landlord, not so much. In late April 1852, the *Galway Packet* referred to Lord John Campbell as "the great exterminator."

The *Galway Vindicator* reported that on Saturday 10 April 1852; "184 evictions took place on Lord Campbell's West Barna estate, in the vicinity of Moycullen," stating that the exact number of displaced individuals hadn't yet been ascertained, but that the incident was reported to the Guardians. The *Galway Mercury* stated that, at the Guardian meeting on or about 16 Apr 1852, Mr Griffin reported over 800 people were evicted from Lord Campbell's Barna estate.

A rebuttal, written on 4 May 1852 by tenant Thomas Fitzgerald of "Moycullen Lodge," published in the *Galway Mercury* on 8 May 1852, stated no such Barna estate eviction occurred. Fitzgerald was renting hundreds of acres from Lord Campbell, and was obviously somewhat beholden to him. Given that a legal eviction required a process server and had to be reported to the authorities, there are quarterly summaries available. For April through June 1852, the official report is, for "Galway West," that Lord Campbell evicted 136 families comprising 951 individuals.

Also, in April 1852, yet another dispatch reports six families being evicted from Lord Campbell's Barna estate illegally, as no report was filed with the district's relieving officer, Mr Morgan Darcy. There was some talk of prosecuting Lord Campbell, opposed by some Guardians, including James Blake of Tully. Remember that name. The Galway Guardians had no stomach for taking Lord Campbell to court.

Early in 1853, some potential purchasers of the bankrupt Martin of Ballynahinch estate dispatched the surveyor Thomas Colville Scott to Connemara, to evaluate the estate. Scott was told of extensive evictions on Lord Campbell's lands. Once the cottage was rendered uninhabitable, the evicted tenant received <u>ten shillings</u>, to facilitate their passage to America.

Ca 1852, what did it cost to get to the Americas? In May 1852, the *Munster News* was advertising steerage fares, from Limerick to Quebec for £2 17s 6d. Children under 14 years of age were half-price, infants under 12 months were free. Add in a few bob to get to Limerick from Galway, and we're at £3 (60 shillings), for one adult to go from Galway to Quebec.

About this time, advertisements appeared for the Packet 'Senator', making the Liverpool to New York run, under the able command of Capt Coffin. Not a coffin ship, but Coffin's ship. Earlier, in June 1847, the *Dublin Evening Post* quoted £4 10s steerage fares, from Liverpool to New York. This included "one pound of good Navy Bread or Bread-stuff daily." I'm not sure I'd want "Bread-stuff." Perhaps it's similar to the difference between 'cheese' and 'cheese food product.' The transatlantic fare might have been 5s or so less, from Moville (near Derry) or Queenstown (Cobh). In March 1850, the *Black Star Line* advertised free passage from Derry to Liverpool, for subsequent travel (with them) onto New York, Philadelphia, or Boston.

For steerage, from £3 up to £5 or so (60-100 or so shillings), depending on the destination, was needed to get to the Americas from Galway. A family of five might require ca £15, depending. So a Barna estate family is evicted because they can't meet the ca £5 rent, but they need ca £15 to get to America. Lord Campbell's ten shillings wouldn't get one very far. Perhaps to a new start in Liverpool. From 13 January to 20 April, 1847, the British authorities <u>documented</u> 133,069 Irish arrivals in Liverpool. The authorities were concerned because, seemingly, these Irish weren't on their way to the Americas.

Later, the English Quaker James Hack Tuke organised an assisted immigration program. As did the Irish-American (Arch)Bishop John Ireland, assisted by the Liverpool priest James Nugent. In the 1880s, one sees half-price "assisted passage" fares of around £3 advertised, for healthy agricultural labourers and female domestic servants. The *quid pro quo* was unstated.

Ca 1853, the prominent Spiddal area gentry were; Blake (Furbo), Blake (Gortnamona and Tully), Bunbury, Comyn, Lynch, Martin, and Morris families. These families weren't in quite the same class as the Clanricards or Lord Campbell, with regard to status and wealth (including landholdings).

The Blakes of Gortnamona and Tully, especially the famine-time incumbent Patrick Blake, and his Uncle James Blake, who resided at Inverin, surpassed the second Marquess Clanrickard and Lord Campbell in cruelty. In late 1847, the already infamous Blakes conducted the Tully evictions.

The Morris family was probably the most highly regarded (by the tenants) of the Spiddal area gentry. From the mid-19th Century on, Martin Morris's sons, Michael and George, probably made the family the most politically influential of Cois Fharraige gentry. I found no accounts of them conducting evictions. The family also had Galway residences in Lenaboy (Salthill), Wellpark, and Dominick Street, as well as in Dublin and London. Spiddal was a sort of western outpost for them. A 17th Century marriage with a FitzPatrick woman of Aran likely provided the Spiddal holding as a dowry.

For Cois Fharraige landowners, one sees that in 1853 Peter Sarsfield Comyn owned the townlands of Spiddal Middle, Spiddal West, and Shannagurran, (aka the "Spiddal Lands") while his older brother Francis had the townlands of Knock South (most of it), Aille, Loughaunbeg, and Cornarone.

Francis Comyn's combined holdings west of Spiddal were referred to as "Sellernamore." I got interested in ascertaining how the Comyn brothers obtained these properties. An 1861 Landed Estates Court case opinion, dated 18 April 1861, shows that the GV enumeration of who owned what, and who rented (leased) what around Spiddal ca 1853, was more complicated than it appeared.

The brothers Comyn inherited the Spiddal and Sellernamore properties from their father Laurence Comyn, after his 1820 death, according to the terms of his 1815 Will. John and Francis got the Sellernamore lands, while Peter got the Spiddal lands.

What the brothers inherited was a single lease (on the residue) of 999 years on the Spiddal and Sellernamore lands. The annual rent was £380. Laurence Comyn left his sons a debt, as an annual payment was due on the lease. In his will, he directed that £11,000 of government securities from his personal assets be set aside, with the annual dividend used to pay the rent. The 3.5% dividend yielded £385 per annum. The remaining £5 was for miscellaneous expenses.

It seems a bit odd that two rather geographically separated parcels of land were under a single lease. Strife came in 1861, when Peter Sarsfield Comyn petitioned the Landed Estates Court to apportion (split) the rent for the two distinct parcels. His legal representatives were James Murphy and Michael Morris (eventually the 1st Lord Killanin). Later, that £11,000 also became the object of litigation.

Francis Comyn opposed the petition. Brother against brother. The property owner Andrew Martyn intervened in opposition as well. From Justice Mountifort Longfield's judgment;

In this case the petitioner [Peter Sarsfield Comyn] has obtained a conditional order for Judgment, an apportionment (to bind the landlord) of the rent payable by him, out of the portion of a lease, of which he has obtained an order for sale in this Court. Cause against making the order absolute has been shown by the landlord Andrew Martyn, and by Mr. Francis Comyn, the owner of the residue of the lease hold interest. The case has been very ably argued on all sides; and I think all the facts and arguments have been fully and clearly stated.

The lands now held by the petitioner, and by the respondent Francis Comyn, were demised in 1777, by Oliver Martyn, to a person of the name of Lynch, at a rent of £380, late currency. Laurence Comyn, at the close of the last century, purchased the tenant's interest for a sum of £4250. He bequeathed separate portions to his sons. The petitioner is now the absolute owner of one portion, and has obtained an order for sale; and now seeks for an order, under the 72nd section of the Landed Estates Court Act, to have the rent apportioned. The head-rent is £380, late currency; the Ordnance valuation about £800; the gross rents about £1200, and the value of the petitioner's interest is £246 a-year.........

After Edward Martyn, the incumbent of Tullyra and Spiddal, died in 1836, I believe the bulk of the Tullyra estate went to his first born son John, while Andrew Martyn inherited the Spiddal lands. According to the court testimony, for twenty-three years prior to 1861, the Comyns made on-time annual lease payments to Andrew Martyn. It seems that Peter Sarsfield Comyn got his way.

For an enumeration of the properties in Spiddal West, see Appendix II. Many Spiddal area gentry traded in long-term leases. In the GV, enumerating the ownership chain would have been very helpful, but would have complicated the document greatly.

The Griffith bureaucrats understood there was an ownership or lease chain, for they used as a heading not "Lessor", but "*Immediate* Lessor." For the Spiddal Lands, the chain was: Oliver Martin obtained them (with Anthony French), ca 1660. In 1777, Oliver Martyn (a grand nephew of the 1670 Oliver Martin, page 7) then leased to a Lynch, and ca 1799, Laurence Comyn acquired the lease for the sum of £4250. When Laurence Comyn died in 1820, his sons were minors. Once Laurence's will was 'proved', and Peter Sarsfield Comyn reached his majority ca 1827, he came into possession of the *Spiddal Lands.*

Factoring in the tenants, the situation resembles a pyramid scheme, except the person at the very top isn't the one raking in the money. In good times, the Comyns had the best of all possible worlds. Their father's estate paid the fixed £380/year rent to Andrew Martyn (and to Edward Martyn before Andrew), while ca 1860 the Comyns are collecting ca £1200/year rent from the tenants. Of course these lands were only part of their holdings.

When a gentleman is said to have *owned* a townland, he may actually have owned a lease. A lease of 999 years (typically), or some residue of that 999 years.

The Blakes of Furbo (Forbough), prominent in the area, had their fair share of *Sturm und Drang.*

Lt. Col. John Blake (d. 1836) and Maria Blake (née Galway, from Cork) of Furbo had, among their children, Andrew, and his younger brother, John Henry. The magistrate and gentleman fisherman Andrew Blake, as we'll see, was prominent in the Spiddal Village area. For a time, John Henry Blake was the agent for his parents in Furbo. These weren't the original Blakes of Furbo. The original Blakes seem to have come to Furbo out of Oranmore. In 1764, the Blakes of Furbo heir, Thomas Blake, *d.s.p.*, as they say. The line transitioned to Thomas' cousin John Blake, son of Andrew Blake of Ballymanagh (southeast of Craughwell).

During the 1852 and 1857 parliamentary elections for Galway, there was an outcry about vote buying. A royal commission was formed to investigate and report back to parliament. At the top of the commission were the usual suspects; a retired military officer, a gentleman of leisure, a couple of archbishops, followed by the ordinary clergy. The Rev John O'Grady, the Rev Francis Kenny, and the Rev Patrick Lyons, all well known in the Spiddal area, were on the parliamentary commission.

For the 1852 election, the <u>commission</u> identified one John Henry Blake (among others) as guilty of vote buying. For the 1852 election vote buying, it's not clear what the consequences were for John Henry Blake. Apparently other <u>elections</u> were exciting affairs. The Galway election of <u>19 June 1826</u> had mayhem and death. Numerous Connemara supporters (tenants) of Col Richard (*Humanity Dick*) Martin MP <u>arrived</u> in town via boat for the election, and were canvassing the Galway streets on behalf of their man. They voted early and often. Free (stolen) whiskey, the best kind, fueled the rioting.

In the 1830s, John Henry Blake moved over to East Galway becoming the agent for his infant nephew. Eventually he become the agent for the 2nd Marquess of Clanricarde, probably the most hated landlord in Ireland. Admittedly there were a fair number of worthy candidates across Ireland. From 1841 to 1871, the population of the Clanricarde estates fell from roughly 22,000 people to fewer than 10,000 people.

Reference to the Down Tables (pages 7 & 8) shows that, ca 1670, the (then) Earl of Clanrickarde had significant Spiddal area holdings: up by Boluisce Lake, at Kilroe, Knock South, Minna and out near Rosseveal. It seems these holdings were either leased out, or otherwise disposed of by 1853.

Upon hearing of threats on his agent's life, the 2nd Marquess Clanrickarde told his agent something along the lines of: *Assure the scoundrels that your death will in no way intimidate me.* With an absentee landlord, the Marquess's agent John Henry Blake of Rathville became the object of the tenant's wrath. I found the following account in a parliamentary report.

On 29 June 1882, John Henry Blake and his wife Harriette (née Lynch) were proceeding to Loughrea. About a mile outside of Loughrea an ambush occurred. John Henry Blake and his coachman Thady Ruane were shot dead. Mrs Blake's right hip was lacerated by a bullet (her left thigh in another account). The horse was wounded too. Harriette (Harriet) recovered and lived in Loughrea until 1917, when she died.

In the parliamentary report, Harriette was listed as 28 years old, while John Blake was 75 years old. They were married in St Andrew's Catholic Church, Westland Row Dublin, on 27 January 1874. The age difference suggested that perhaps it was not John Blake's first marriage. But the registration stated that John Henry Blake was a bachelor and a *Gentleman,* while Harriet was a spinster and a *Lady.*

As an account of Cois Fharraige, it's interesting how many times St Andrew's Church, of Westland Row Dublin, appears in this narrative. You'll see. It appears, disguised, in a famous narrative. Leopold Bloom had a passing through familiarity with St Andrew's, although in *Ulysses*, James Joyce refers to the place as *All Hallows*.

Back in East Galway, arrests were made, but no prosecutions were undertaken.

John Henry Blake was interred in the family chapel in Furbo. At his 1882 death, he left behind two sons, Edmond Martin Blake (1876-1944?), aged 6, and Henry Francis Blake (1878- ?) aged 4.

In the *Police Law and Crime (Ireland) Accounts and Papers*, is a listing of the Awards (compensation) made by the Lord Lieutenant of Ireland, under the Crimes Act, for the period of 5 February – 14 August 1884 (Vol 63). An unidentified personal representative of Thady Ruane, presumably his widow Bridget, is listed to receive £400 compensation in three installments. A considerable sum. Likely it was appreciated, as Thady Ruane left behind eleven children.

Being of the gentry, Harriette's compensation was more substantial: £1200 for her personal injuries, and £3000 for the death of her husband, according to the 2 May 1883 edition of the *Dublin Daily Express*.

In 1946, a Blake descendant, Edmond Blake, commissioned the artist Evie Hone to design 14 gouache Stations of the Cross for the Church of SS Peter and Paul, Kiltullagh, near Athenry. In the summer of 2013, six of the gouaches were stolen from the church. The remaining stations were removed for safekeeping.

John Henry Blake's older brother Andrew Blake inherited the Blakes of Furbo estate, and appears numerous times in this narrative. He was a gentleman fisherman, a Spiddal Petty Sessions magistrate, who had his quarrels with his fellow gentry, the clergy, and my ancestors.

The Spiddal Catholic Parish(es)

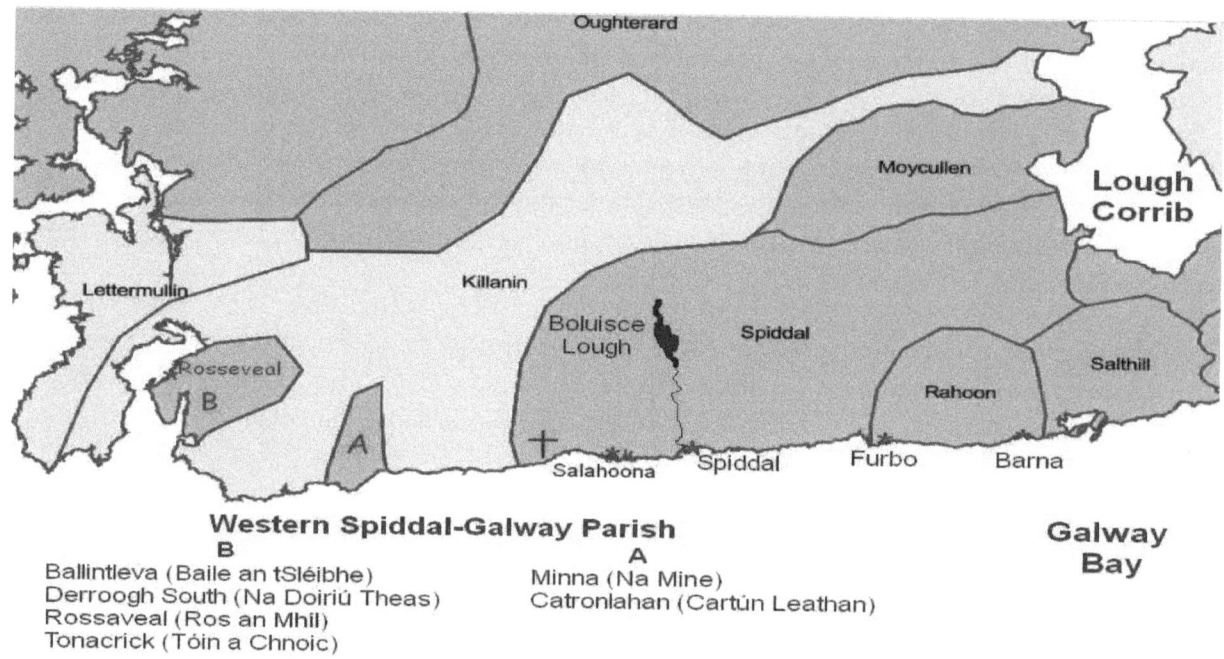

Western Spiddal-Galway Parish

B
Ballintleva (Baile an tSléibhe)
Derroogh South (Na Doiriú Theas)
Rossaveal (Ros an Mhíl)
Tonacrick (Tóin a Chnoic)

A
Minna (Na Mine)
Catronlahan (Cartún Leathan)

Galway Bay

Pre-1840 Spiddal RC Parish Map—Annotated.

This undated map resides at the National Library of Ireland (NLI). The Oughterard Heritage Website has an article, *The Shape of the Killannin Parish*, by Hilary Kiely, explaining the geopolitical contortions, going back centuries, involving metaphorical and physical brawling. I don't believe the mapmaker thought Lettemullin was actually located where the name appears. Rather, they meant that, administratively, it was in the same jurisdiction as that area.

In 1891, a swap of lands, between the Diocese of Galway and Archdiocese of Tuam, resulted in canonical litigation in Rome and conventional litigation at the Queen's Bench and the Court of Appeal. One of the priests reluctantly drawn into the dispute was Father Mark Conroy (of Rosmuc). The dispute ended only when the aggrieved priest of the parish of Killannin (west of Moycullen), Patrick Coyne, died in 1899. Mark Conroy escaped the turmoil by becoming the Spiddal Village parish priest in 1897.

The annotations of village place names, and annotations of Boluisce Lough and River, are mine. The darker tint (surrounding "Spiddal") represents parishes in the Diocese of Galway, the lighter tint (around "Killanin") represents parishes in the Diocese of Tuam. With a cross, I've noted the approximate location of the Knock Church, which was under construction between 1838 and 1844.

The current Spiddal-Galway RC parish boundaries differ from the above map. The distinct parcels labeled (by me) A and B seem to be unchanged over time. But now, the western boundary of the parish's main body is Boluisce Lough and River. It seems likely that, as the Knock Chapel approached completion in 1844, the townlands of Bohoona East, Bohoona West (containing the villages of Salahoona and Creduff), Kilroe East, Kilroe West, and Knock South, were removed from the Spiddal-Galway Parish and absorbed into the Spiddal-Tuam (aka Knock) parish.

Most everything in dark tint west of the Boluisce Lough and River (except for Regions A and B) went to Knock (Spiddal-Tuam). For those interested in the area genealogy, this adjustment had unfortunate consequences. Old Spiddal Village Parish (aka Spiddal-Galway) records have survived, while no old Knock (aka Spiddal-Tuam) records seem to exist.

Some Cois Fharraige Catholic Clergy

There were a number of notable Roman Catholic clergy in and around Spiddal over the years. At the National Library Ireland (NLI), the surviving Cill Éinde baptism/marriage/mortuary <u>registries</u> have been digitised. There is a handwritten <u>list</u> of Spiddal Parish priests going back to 1836.

The history of Cill Éinde and the parish, published at the 2007 centenary, has on page 88, a list of Spiddal parish priests going back to 1820. Perhaps the list can be extended back in time a bit. Lord Walter FitzGerald visited the Spiddal graveyard, took notes, and published them in 1898;

<u>Association for the Preservation of Memorials of the Dead in Ireland</u>

(Vol 4, pg 59-60, 1898). From his notes about one grave marker in particular:

I. H. S.
Pray for the soul of PATRICK KINELY PRIEST
who died 9th February 1759.

Perhaps the Spiddal parish priest, one of the earliest. For the historical English language name variations for Ó Conghaile, one possible sequence is: Conneely ↔ Kenneally ↔ Kinely.

Lord FitzGerald's narrative also has Michael 'Drynane' (d. ??) and his spouse (d. 1775). In Irish, for Michael, it would be 'Ó Droighneáin.' From about the mid-19th Century on, in the English records, it appears as Thornton. Ó Loideáin would be Lydon. Early in the 19th Century the English was 'Liddane' or 'Lyddane.'

In an early April 1840 issue of the *Castlebar Telegraph* came two clerical announcements. In one, the Archbishop of Tuam had "promoted the Rev. James O'Grady, late Roman curate of Turlough, to the parish of Spiddal....." Then followed: "The Rev P Fahey, R.C.C. of Galway, has been appointed, by the Right Rev. Dr. Browne, parish priest of that portion of Spiddal in his lordship's diocese."

There is the Archdiocese of Tuam and the Diocese of Galway. We have two Spiddal parishes: Spiddal-Tuam (aka *Knock*) and Spiddal-Galway (aka *Spiddal*). Maddeningly, in the newspapers of the time, Spiddal-Tuam (aka *Knock*) is often referred to as just Spiddal.

The Rev Dr. Browne was Bishop of Galway, and appointed the Rev Patrick Fah(e)y to Spiddal-Galway, whose parish church is in Spiddal. The Archbishop of Tuam appointed the Rev O'Grady to Spiddal-Tuam, whose parish church was (is) at Knock. I suspect James O'Grady is really John O'Grady.

In the parliamentary *FIRST REPORT of PUBLIC INSTRUCTION, IRELAND, 1835*, is Appendix II: *ROMAN CATHOLIC BISHOP'S RETURN OF THE ROMAN CATHOLIC CLERGY*, Diocese of Tuam, containing the statement (for 1835): "Rev Thomas Loftus; succeeded by the Rev John Canavan, Parish Priest of Spiddal."

There is also a note of a chapel in Minna. The Rev John Canavan was in Spiddal in 1835, up to about April 1840, when the Rev Fahy took over. The Spiddal parish priest roster shows a Father Fahy present in 1832. Thus he may have been already familiar with Spiddal. If so, then this time, the Rev Fahy's tenure in Spiddal Village was short but interesting.

The 20 June 1840 issue of the *Kerry Evening Post* reprinted an article from the *Dublin Evening Packet*. Supposedly, this article was an account of Father Fahy assessing his Spiddal parishioners sixpence each for new vestments, by positioning the local constabulary and judicial staff at the church entrance, on 7 June 1840, to strong-arm the money out of the parishioners.

James Martin of Ross Esq JP, believed the article, and complained about the RIC's supposed assistance. An investigation revealed the Packet article's claim to be a fabrication. A magistrates' meeting in Spiddal was called, and reported on in the 23 July 1840 issue of the *Connaught Journal*. James Martin arrived, tears in his eyes, mortified and shaken that he had some part in what turned out to be a hoax. Some magistrates suggested he be given a glass of wine, others suggested a postponement. Some poitín (moonshine), likely more plentiful in the village than what masqueraded as wine, might have been more therapeutic. The Rev Fahy arrived with his legal representative, and insisted that the hearing proceed. Father Fahy and the RIC were fully vindicated.

The *Dublin Evening Packet*, the original publisher of the fabrication, reprinted the *Connaught Journal* article, prefacing it with a statement that their correspondent was "a man of strict integrity" (whose second-hand account of the Spiddal event had just been rubbished). Below the reprinted *Connaught Journal* account, the *Packet's* editors stated that their correspondent "....would be exceedingly glad to find that the conduct of the Romish Clergy stood the test of scrutiny..."
No apology, in other words.

During the July 1840 magistrates' meeting, Father Fahy cross-examined RIC Officer Kerrigan:

> What was the state of the [Spiddal Village] chapel during your time at this district?
> Kerrigan—*Unfit for divine service.*

> Did you find the chapel comfortable or not previous to your coming to the parish?
> Kerrigan—*I was often obliged to bring in two stones to kneel on.*

> Do you think the chapel creditable to the gentry connected with this part of the country?
> [James Blake Esq then interjected:] "*O, Sir, everybody knows it is in very bad state.*"

Worship in the Spiddal Village RC chapel was hard on the knees. Father Fahy's last question was rather provocative, as the gentry the Rev Fahy was referring to were sitting on the Bench, several feet away from him. It was an excellent question. In 1840, the Spiddal Village chapel was a wreck.

The *Connaught Journal* article indicates that, previously, a well-liked Father Fahy had been the Claddagh parish priest. It seems he wasn't in Spiddal long, as he moved to Moycullen soon after the Moycullen parish priest Edmund French died in June 1840. There is an account of Father Fahy's time in Moycullen. The Moycullen Heritage website has occasional interesting references to Spiddal. The Rev Fahy kept notes documenting the Great Famine's effects in Moycullen. His last entry in May 1848 was:

> "About twelve a week die. I don't know the end of it. The mortality is frightful."

On 27 May 1848, an esteemed 38-year-old Rev Patrick Fahy of Moycullen died of typhus. Father Francis Kenny, who had been the Spiddal-Galway parish priest since August 1846, was transferred to Moycullen, after the Rev Patrick Fahy's May 1848 passing, and served there until 1897, when he died at nearly 90 years of age. After Father Kenny's passing, Thomas Curran transferred from Spiddal to Moycullen, and remained there until his 1910 passing.

The Spiddal parish register page, listing the parish priests, states that the Rev John O'Grady, affiliated with Spiddal-Tuam, administered Spiddal-Galway from 1842-1844.

Oral history from the late Father Tom Kyne is that, at one point, a layperson named Neachtain, from Upper River Road, would come down into Spiddal Village and conduct a rosary service at the chapel. Seemingly indicating that Spiddal was without a parish priest for a time. The parish priest list in the registry does seem to indicate there was no resident parish priest 1842-1844.

In August 1845, the Rev John O'Grady was seeking protection from Andrew W Blake Esq of Furbo:

I recollect last Sunday week meeting Mr. Andrew Blake; I do not remember having spoken to him these four or five years; on the day of which I speak I attended a sick call after celebrating mass, and on my return home I was riding quietly along the road when I met the defendant; I said mass that day in the chapel at Meena; defendant came over to me and without the slightest provocation, he said he would get my head smashed in pieces; I made no reply whatever, but continued to ride on. He shouted and halloed after me.

John O'Grady began his testimony stating that he was the parish priest of that part of Spiddal not under the jurisdiction of the Diocese of Galway. He was the Spiddal-Tuam (aka Knock) parish priest. But then he states the he had finished a service *at Meena* (aka Minna), prior to being accosted by Andrew Blake. Minna is in the Diocese of Galway. Perhaps the Rev O'Grady's parish multitasking continued into the summer of 1845. O'Grady had implored Blake's mother, unsuccessfully, to exert a moderating influence over her son.

James Blake of Tully was present at the session, and got involved in the cross-examinations. Andrew Blake is a Blake of Furbo. James and Andrew Blake were no doubt distant cousins of some sort.

James Blake managed the Tully estate for his nephew Patrick Blake (of Tully, see pages 7 & 8). Patrick Blake's seat was in Gortnamona, by Ballinasloe. There is a reference to Mr (James) Blake's son. The son is probably Arthur Blake, a boxer and bully, according to Tim Robinson. Perhaps this can be taken as evidence for the decline of a gentry family. In a Sunday sermon, the Rev John O'Grady denounced some boxing matches that had occurred in the parish. Likely matches in which Arthur Blake would have been involved. There was bad-blood between John O'Grady and all the Blakes.

James Blake suggested that the Rev John O'Grady really was someone else. Coming from a Blake, the accusation has a certain irony. The Blake who arrived in Ireland, with Strongbow, wasn't named Blake. He was 'Caddell' (Caddle). A descendant, Richard Caddell (aka Niger, Blake: b ca 1250 - d ca 1315: Oranmore) was Sheriff of Connaught in 1306. He was said to be 'swarthy.' The surname evolved over the centuries, into variants 'Black,' and 'Blake.' Apparently some Blakes used "Caddell" as an alias.

From Caddell the various Blake branches are supposed to descend. Later, we'll encounter the third Baron Wallscourt, Joseph Henry Blake (1797-1849) of Ardfry (near Oranmore), who for a time was a Guardian of the Poor of the Galway Union. A National Galleries Scotland mezzotint portrait of his wife, Elizabeth (Locke), Lady Wallscourt, refers to the third Baron as Joseph H Black.

James Blake's line of questioning led to nothing. The Court decided there was ample evidence that Andrew Blake threatened John O'Grady, and ordered Blake to post a bond to ensure he kept the peace for the next year.

If the Rev John O'Grady kept a diary of his time along Cois Fharraige, it would be an extraordinary document. By the spring of 1847, John O'Grady had departed for East Galway. In 1848, the Rev Francis Kenny was replaced in Spiddal Village by Coleman McGragh (McGrath).

The Rev Patrick Lyons (1813-1885), is in the GV associated with the school in Loughaunbeg (*Lochán Beag*). He was attached to the Knock/Aille church (a few miles west of Spiddal). He was listed in clerical directories as a Spiddal parish priest, as the directories didn't always distinguish Spiddal-Tuam (Knock) from Spiddal-Galway (Spiddal). The newspapers were even worse at differentiating them. Patrick's younger brother Michael Lyons studied at St Jarlath's College Tuam, and was ordained a priest on 12 Dec 1853 in St Patrick's Church, New Orleans USA. He transferred to Chicago, founding a parish that eventually had an architecturally notable church.

In a clerical directory is a record of a Rev Patrick Lyons, in the Parish of Achonry in 1835. He might have been a newly minted priest. In 1846 and 1848, it seems he was the parish priest in Kilmeen, Loughrea. His transfer to Spiddal was announced in the newspaper on 23 Aug 1851. The Rev J McCullagh was transferred from Knock to Ballindine. I did find a court reference placing the Rev Lyons in Loughaunbeg in late November 1851.

In looking into the Blakes of Tully and Gortnamona, I tentatively concluded they were Protestant. Of course, within large families with many branches, there would be variations. To evade the burden of the Penal Laws, some Catholics became what we'll call *Protestants of Convenience*. But, according to Tim Robinson, the Blakes of Tully embraced and encouraged the evangelical Anglican clerics of *The Society of Irish Church Missions to the Roman Catholics*. The best evidence for religious affiliation would be a church record. There is something approximating that, a wedding announcement, in a Belfast newspaper. From the 6 June 1853 edition of the *Belfast Mercury*:

May 26, at Spiddal Church, John Church Colhoun Esq, only son of John Colhoun, Esq., of Milford, County Donegal, to Jane, second daughter of the late James Blake, Esq., of Inverin Lodge, County of Galway.

In May 1853, two churches existed in Spiddal Village. A RC chapel in bad shape, that I doubt would have been used for any gentry wedding, and the newly built St Joseph's Anglican Church, consecrated nine months earlier. I believe the "Spiddal Church" referenced above was St Joseph's Anglican Church. The St Joseph's (aka Killannin Parish) marriage register is located in the Representative Church Body (RCB) archives in Dublin, and covers the period 1852-1913. Thus it could be checked, post-pandemic. The Protestant Blakes of Tully were not *Protestants of Convenience*.

There is oral history that the Blakes of Tully tried to kill the parish priest. Part of the story is that tension arose over the situating of a proposed church. Tom Robinson mentions that the Blakes of Tully are reputed to have burned a chapel in Inverin. Perhaps the parish priest was inside the chapel when the Blakes struck. There are three candidates for being the assassination target.

Up to the spring of 1847, the long-time Knock parish priest was John O'Grady, who was replaced by John McCullagh, who then was followed by Patrick Lyons in the autumn of 1851.

McCullagh was low-key. I have little on him. While disliking Patrick Lyons, the Blakes must have loathed his predecessor, John O'Grady. I suspect O'Grady was the more pugnacious of the two. My money is on John O'Grady as being the target. The more one learns about the Blakes, the more believable the oral history becomes.

Tomás Ó Curraoin
(Courtesy of Timín Curran)

Father Thomas Curran (Tomás Ó Curraoin) was born in Cnocán Glas, about seven-hundred-fifty yards west of Spiddal Village. Those interested in the local genealogy owe Thomas Curran a debt of gratitude. In 1884, and then in 1895, he carried out Spiddal-Galway Parish Censuses. Owing to the shelling of the Four Courts during the Irish Civil War, only fragments of various civil censuses prior to 1901 survive. (NB: some of the surviving 1821 fragments cover the Aran Islands.)

The 1884 & 1895 Spiddal-Galway Church Census results can be found at the rootsireland website. They are behind a paywall. Father Thomas Curran's 1884 and 1895 Spiddal RC Censuses, and the Rootsireland transcriptions, are invaluable. Many women in the 1884 Census married before the civil registration of marriage commenced in 1864. Very useful is that, for the married women, Thomas Curran provided their maiden names.

For those who might have Moycullen connections, the Rev Xavier Blake of Moycullen conducted a census (results at the Moycullen Heritage Website) that covered 1793-1813.

Reported by his sister Mary Kilkenny, Patrick Lyons, a fixture of the Knock area for nearly 35 years, died at 72 years of age on 10 Oct 1885, a good age for that time. In 1866, he officiated his niece's wedding in Knock. Other announcements indicate he had extended family in the area into the 20th Century. Patrick Lyons was interred within the Knock church. Some Spiddal area parish priests weren't as fortunate as Patrick Lyons:

DEATH OF THE REV. MR. HANLEY P.P.
(SPECIAL TELEGRAM)
Galway, Friday

With unfeigned regret I have to announce the death of the Rev. Malachy Hanley, P.P. of Spiddal, which melancholy event took place last night, after suffering from consumption for several months. The deceased gentleman was a pious, hard-working priest, patriotic, and devoted to his sacred calling. His remains will be interred tomorrow in the parish church, Spiddal, after solemn High Mass, at which the Lord Bishop of Galway will preside.

All the priests of the diocese will also be present. His early death is universally lamented in this city. The rev. gentleman was only 35 years of age.

Freeman's Journal
March 29, 1879

The death of the 29-year-old Spiddal parish priest, the Rev William Wilson, from a lung hemorrhage, was announced on 18 June 1880. One suspects that might have been connected to consumption. We'll see that this misfortune also extended back in time.

Cill Éinde and Earlier Churches

To the right is the Ordnance Survey (OS) map (surveyed in January 1838) for the central Spiddal Village area. The feature labelling is sometimes ambiguous. The RC chapel, in from the road a bit, was roughly where the Bridge House Hotel (aka Clancy's, now demolished) later stood. Or perhaps a bit northeast. A pub called *An Nead (The Nest)* is the very approximate modern landmark. An orphanage with that name once existed across the road. The Martin Chapel (with my name annotation), dating to July 1776, is in the graveyard.

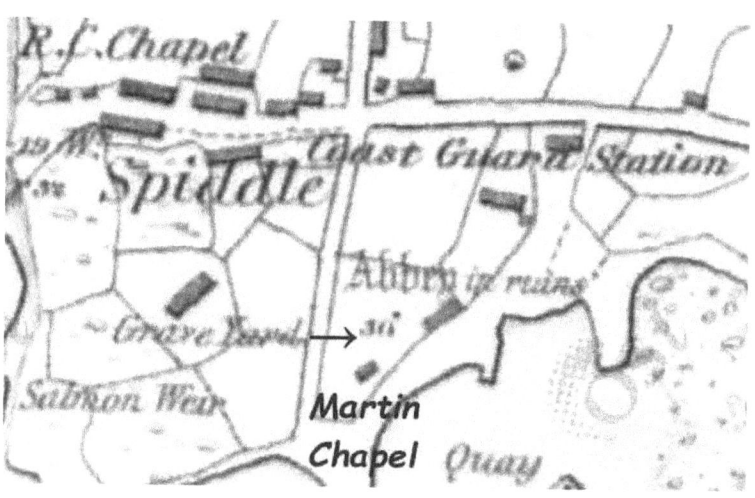

Spiddal Village 1838 OS (annotated)

Spiddal Area Valuation Office Books - 1853

Structure	Quality	Length (ft)	Breadth (ft)	Height (ft)	£	Valuation s	d
Spiddal Village RC Chapel	2C	63	22	7	3	17	7
Adjustments to Value					0	9	8
8 November 1853 Value					4	7	3
Published 1855 GV Value					2	5	

Quality Key

1	Slate roof house of stone or brick, lime mortar
2	Thatch roof house of stone or brick, lime mortar
3	Thatch roof house, of stone walls with mud mortar, or mud walls
A+	New or nearly new, built or ornamented with cut stone, superior finish
A	New or nearly new, substantial finish, without cut stone ornamentation
A-	New or nearly new, ordinary finish
B+	Not new, good repair
B	Medium age, some decay, but in good repair
B-	Medium age, more decay, not in perfect repair
C+	Old, but in repair
C	Old, out of repair
C-	Old, dilapidated, barely habitable

In 1853, the Spiddal Village RC chapel was still a wreck. Now for the "Abbey *in ruins.*"

The Old Abbey (An tSeanMhainistir) in Ruins

The left panel photo was taken from the old pier, the right panel photo, looking southeast, shows the abbey interior. A third great grandfather of mine may be in there. One sees that, in Spiddal, one doesn't have to be a famous poet to be buried in the abbey. Oral history, from the late Father Tom Kyne, has the abbey dating back to 1646. Visiting ca 1898, Lord Walter FitzGerald objected to the OS's characterization of the ruined structure as an abbey. Because of its configuration and/or size? Perhaps because there was no evidence of an associated religious order?

There are references to other Spiddal area church construction efforts. On 4 Dec 1842, John O'Grady wrote to the Galway Vindicator, acknowledging contributions towards construction of a chapel.

A Tuam clergyman and about ten Tuam area gentry contributed £7 10s. A few months later, in March 1843, the *Vindicator* quoted John O'Grady as stating the chapel had been roofless for the past six years, suggesting that construction commenced ca 1837. The *Galway Vindicator* reported, on 28 July 1844, the consecration of a new Spiddal RC Chapel. From a reprint in the 2 Aug 1844 Freeman's Journal:

CATHOLIC CHURCH
CONSECRATION OF THE NEW CHAPEL OF SPIDDLE.----

The imposing ceremony of the consecration of the new chapel at Spiddle, having been appointed for Sunday last, by his grace the Most Rev. Dr. MacHale, Lord Archbishop of Tuam, and several of the clergy of the diocese, with most of the gentry, attended on the occasion.
After the celebration of the twelve o'clock mass, by the Rev. J. O'Grady, the respected parish priest of Spiddle, his grace the archbishop ascended the altar, and taking his text from Genisis 28 chap, 17 verse delivered in the Irish language a powerful and eloquent sermon. He then proceeded to the consecration of this beautiful edifice, which reflects the greatest credit on the real and pastoral fervour of the Rev. Mr. O'Grady...........

The church is 4.7 km west of Spiddal Village. About 400 people attended, including a Rev Patrick O'Grady, of Knock Co Mayo, possibly John O'Grady's brother.

The Rev O'Grady's first project took a long time, commencing ca 1837, and finishing in mid-1844. Various factors were involved; bad weather, economic downturns, etc.

On the evening of 6 January 1839 and the next day came the cyclone that went down in Irish history as "The Night of the Big Wind" (*Oíche na Gaoithe Móire*). The Atlantic surf crested over the top of the 100-200 meter high Cliffs of Moher, and hurled huge boulders over the cliff-tops onto the Arans. Colm Keady's oral history is that the Knock church was under construction when the "Night of the Big Wind" came. This oral history is consistent with the 25 March 1843 newspaper article. The chapel must have suffered some damage. Repair of the widespread residential damage would have delayed resumption of the chapel's construction. Now for another factor. From the 1853 VOB:

Spiddal Area Valuation Office Books -- 1853							
Structure	Quality	Length (ft)	Breadth (ft)	Height (ft)	£	Valuation s	d
Knock/Aille Chapel	1A-	28.6	85.0	17.6	21	3	6
Knock/Aille Chapel Annex	1A-	14.6	21	16.0	2	9	4
Adjustments to Value					-2	-1	-1
Sept-Oct 1853 Value					20	13	9
Published 1855 GV Value					12	10	0

Compared to a standard wall of seven or eight feet in height, building walls to nearly 18 feet in height dramatically extended the construction time. Shortfalls in funding were likely an issue too. For the 1855 GV, the Knock Chapel, which some maps place in the Aille townland, is valued nearly six times more than the Spiddal Village Chapel.

Francis Comyn would have donated the land, and his support continued into the future. In January 1870, the Rev Mr Lyons P P, Spiddal (-Tuam, aka Knock):

gratefully acknowledges the Christmas Gift of a magnificently embroidered Suit of Altar Vestments for his chapel from Mr Francis Comyn, 26 Harcourt-street, presented by her son, George P Comyn Esq, his father's respected agent on the Silerna property.

The Freeman's Journal
Jan 3, 1870

Knock Chapel; St Ainnín
(Courtesy of Jerry Darby Keady)

In February 1844, about five months before the consecration of the Knock chapel, a curious acknowledgment by the Rev O'Grady appears in the '*Galway Vindicator:*'

THANKS

The Rev. Mr. O'Grady, P. P., Spiddle, kindly returns his thanks to EDMOND O'FLAHERTY, Esq. Oughterard, for his unsolicited subscription of 10s., towards the erection of his new Chapel in Spiddle---the foundation of which is to be laid on the 19th inst., by the Archbishop of Tuam. Mr. Murray, the celebrated architect, whose labours in the magnificence of the Tuam Cathedral, reflects the highest credit on Irish talent and genius, has been entrusted with the erection of the intended Chapel for the parish of Spiddle......

Galway Vindicator, and Connaught Advertiser
February 14, 1844

By March 1844, it seems the Rev John O'Grady has two ongoing Spiddal chapel construction projects. One, referenced in the 25 March 1843 article, is close to completion, and will be consecrated on 28 July 1844. As one project is approaching completion, why not start a new project? The foundation for the next chapel was to be started on 19 February 1844, for "the parish of Spiddal."

In 1844, the Rev O'Grady had significant ambitions. Mr Murray was Marcus Murray of Roscommon, who designed the final ornamentation of the Tuam RC Cathedral. His son William did the cut-stone work for the cathedral. (The original architect being Dominick Madden.) Where was this seemingly significant building to be located? In Spiddal Village, I initially thought. But, a chapel there, whose construction started in 1844, should have been completed when the GV assessors arrived in Spiddal in the summer of 1853. There is no evidence of this chapel in the 1853 VOB for Spiddal Village.

For Spiddal Village in 1853, the VOB show the existing RC chapel to be a thatch-roofed building 63 feet long by 22 feet wide, with 7 foot high walls, in poor condition. Not a facility worthy of the architect Marcus Murray. This is essentially the same building shown in the 1838 OS, and denigrated in 1840 by RIC Officer Kerrigan. An 1850 report, of the evangelical Anglican Irish Church Missions (ICM), stated that the founder of the ICM, the Rev Alexander Dallas, was in the Spiddal area:

......Mr Dallas on this day [24 June 1850] drove from Galway to Spiddal, with one of the agents of the society. After making arrangements for the establishment of a mission, they proceeded to Invern, where there was also a favourable opening for the missionary work; a building, one hundred feet long by thirty, which was intended for a Roman Catholic chapel, was presented to Mr Dallas, and is to be converted into a church when finished.......

Warder and Dublin Weekly Mail
August 17, 1850

It would have been Patrick Blake who, grudgingly I suspect, ceded some Inverin land for the RC chapel, likely with a stipulation. Namely, if the property ceased to be actively used for religious purposes, it reverted to the Blakes of Gortnamona and Tully. Construction of the RC Inverin chapel started on 19 Feb 1844, and would have ceased with the arrival of The Great Famine in 1845. In late 1846 Mr Murray died. Early in 1847, John O'Grady was transferred to East Galway. In 1850, the area was still devastated by the Great Famine. When construction stalled, I believe the stipulation was invoked, and the land with the partially constructed RC chapel reverted to the Blakes, who were then free to award the property to the ICM. The former Knock (Spiddal-Tuam) parish priest John O'Grady, over in East Galway, would have been disappointed with the outcome.

A search for this "one hundred feet long by thirty" building, as the ICM would liked to have finished it, was unsuccessful. In the VOB, there is a candidate building, an ICM schoolhouse of unspecified dimensions. It was valued at £1 5s in November 1853. The building was valued at 10s in the March 1855 GV for Galway. This modest structure wasn't "one hundred feet long by thirty."

A later newspaper report provides some insight about the 1850 structure's fate. The 21 July 1874 issue of the *Dublin Daily Express* described a "Robbery at Inverin, Connemara. -- Spiddal school-house, which is also used as a church......" An ICM school teacher had his personal possessions stolen from this school-house. Further on, the brief article refers to "the little church."

I believe the Rev Dallas' 1850 prize started out as the Rev O'Grady's RC chapel, whose foundation was started in February 1844. It was never completed as a RC chapel, nor was it completed as an ICM church. The footprint was altered (truncated likely), and the place became primarily an ICM school, and secondarily, a makeshift Anglican church.

In 1840, the Spiddal Village chapel was a wreck. The 1853 VOB and the 1855 GV for Galway have the Spiddal Village chapel still in poor condition, with a low assessed value.

It would be left to Columb McGragh to replace the old thatch-roofed Spiddal Village chapel. There is other testimony about the chapel's poor condition:

The Spiddal Chapel
A work of true charity is thus advocated by a Moycullan correspondent:---

The Rev Coleman McGragh, Parish Priest of Spiddal, is at present zealously engaged in trying to collect funds, in order to erect a chapel for the accommodation of his flock: and no wonder indeed, that he should make every effort for that purpose, for the house, or rather miserable barn, that he has been from sheer necessity, for some years past, has been obliged to offer up the holy sacrifice of the Mass in, is now in a most wretched, dilapidated state.

Its low, old, and badly thatched roof (timber and all), is in such a shaky, ruined condition that, not only does the rain pass quite freely through it, but whenever any of the usual days of devotion happens to be at all tempestuous, the poor people are actually afraid to enter it, lest the old tottering roof should tumble down upon them:..........................

The Dublin Weekly Nation
September 29, 1855

In 1855, the Spiddal-Tuam (Knock-Aille etc) parishioners had a dry place to worship, while the Spiddal-Galway (including Spiddal Village) parishioners had a wet drafty hazardous place, that was hard on arthritic knees. The Rev McGragh's purpose, in having a sympathetic newspaper correspondent dramatise the Spiddal Village chapel's decay, was to encourage contributions toward replacing it. This ploy seemed to work. In a February 16 1856 letter to the *Galway Mercury*, McGragh acknowledged a £68 donation of P S Comyn, "the kind patron of the new chapel now progressing to a rapid completion in his Town of Spiddal...." In early 1856, the chapel was still under construction. In April 1857, the Rev McGragh acknowledged that ".....Captain Bellow's charity towards the Spiddal Chapel deserves, in my opinion, to be communicated. He gave me yesterday (Good Friday), four pounds towards it." It seems the chapel wasn't quite finished at Easter-time 1857.

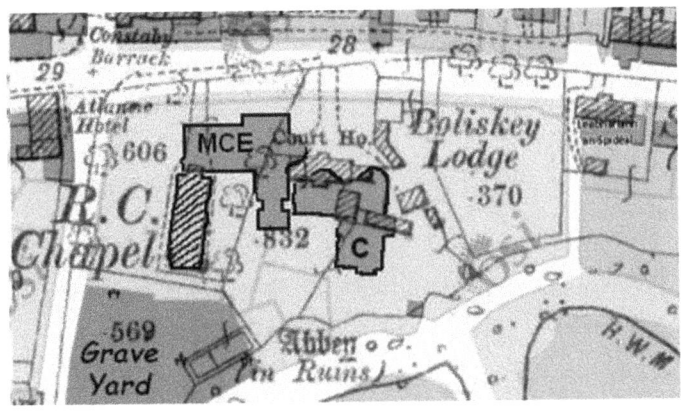

The Rev McGragh's church is shown in the 1893 Ordnance Survey of Spiddal (cross-hatched structure, left). Near the modern Cill Éinde (MCE) is a plaque about Columb McGragh's church. It seems to indicate that construction started in 1854. This is plausible as the Great Famine's effects in Spiddal lingered years beyond 1850. The parish register states the Rev McGragh died in Spiddal on 13 Dec 1860. Father Tom Kyne mentioned that Colm McGragh's church had no pews.

Composite of the 1893 OS
and Processed Satellite Imagery (from *Geohive*)

New Ross Standard -- 16 Nov 1906

An Seanséipéal
(The Old Church, from *Cill Éinde - Céad Bliain*)

Scoil Mhuire—Class of (ca) 1946
(Courtesy of Kathleen Devaney &
Margaret Coyne [back row, fourth from right])

Above left is the church depicted late in 1906, about nine months before its replacement was completed. Some time after the modern Cill Éinde was consecrated in 1907, the old building became a girls school, *Scoil Mhuire*, and later a dormitory, for overflow from the girls boarding school that the Sisters of Mercy operated a hundred or so meters farther west, in what was the old orphanage. Above, within the right panel, at the left, is the southwest corner of the modern Cill Éinde. South of that is the white-washed school, formerly Colm McGragh's church.

Father Mark (Marcus) Conroy, an uncle of the writer Seán Pádraic Ó Conaire, arrived in Spiddal, in 1897. His initial concern was about the existing decaying church, opened in 1857 by the Rev Colm McGragh. The Morris family encouraged the Rev Conroy to start fundraising for a new church. Lord Killanin's eldest son, Martin Morris, approached his friend Edward Martyn for advice about choosing an architect for the new church. Edward Martyn recommended W A Scott, who signed on.

The construction cost was £5581 17s 7d, plus £200 for accessories. The Morris family donated nearly £1300. £2725 was raised locally, while £1160 came from the US. My Shannagurran maternal great grandfathers each kicked in 10 shillings.

The church foundation was laid on 9 October 1904, while the dedication occurred on 18 August 1907.

Encouraged by Edward Martyn, in 1903 the artist Sarah Purser established an artist's cooperative, *An Túr Gloine* (*The Glass Tower*, 1903-1944, see Appendix XII). Evie Hone (page 15) was associated with *An Túr Gloine*. Cooperative members Catherine O'Brien and George Walsh, along with Phyllis Burke (b. 1930), worked on Cill Éinde's stained glass. Another cooperative member, Ethel Rhind, was born in Bengal to a Scottish father and County Antrim mother. Commissioned by Lord Killanin in 1918, she created Cill Éinde's *opus sectile* stations of the cross (1918-1928), which were installed in an unconventional sequence.

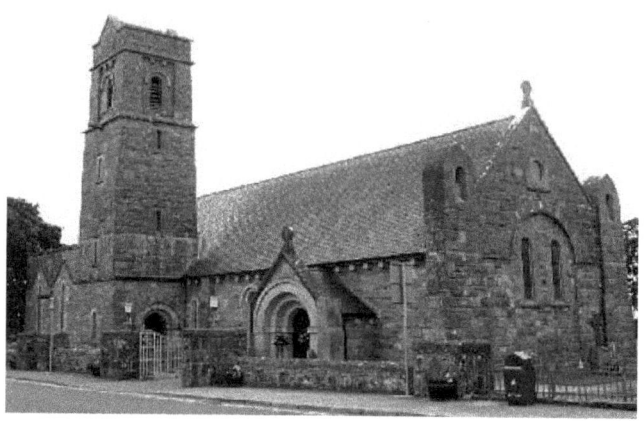

Modern Cill Éinde

In the right panel of the composite map at the top of the previous page is the footprint of the modern *Cill Éinde* (MCE). Just east, is the convent (C), whose construction began in 1923. A history (in Irish) of Cill Éinde and the parish, published at the church's 2007 centenary: *Cill Éinde – Céad Bliain*. In 1950, the third Lord Killanin, Michael Morris, reminisced about the construction of Cill Éinde, and the full discussion, which I have borrowed from, can be found at *Cumann Forbartha Chois Fharraige.*

Edward Martyn is directly related to the Martins of Spiddal. The Martyn connection to Spiddal goes back into the 17th Century, to Oliver Martyn and Cromwellian land redistribution (see page 7). Edward Martyn apparently played a role in the introduction of William Butler Yeats to Lady Gregory in 1896.

The Unionist politician Edward Carson is said to descend from Oliver Óge Martyn (on page 7 as Oliver Martin), as did Edward Martyn, which would make Martyn and Carson cousins. For a mid-20th Century appreciation of Edward Martyn, see Appendix XII.

I suspect the cemetery adjacent to the church was once more extensive. In those days, cemeteries weren't treated with a lot of respect. An example of the disrespect follows.

Convent Grounds   Steps in Detail

In behind the convent, near the low southeast corner of the lot is a gardening shed, with a set of steps for reaching it. The photograph in the left panel above, taken from the shed vantage point, shows the steps in the foreground, with part of the south wall of the convent shown in the background, in the upper right corner. Just to the left (west) of the convent, farther back, is "Cill Éinde."

The photograph in the right panel is a magnified view of the steps. One notices carving on the steps. The steps are grave markers, presumably nicked from the graveyard. Whether the steps are just one grave marker broken up, or more than one, broken up, is unclear. The significance of this depends on whether or not you suspect the marker belongs to an ancestor of yours.

1855 GV measurements were statute (not Irish) acres. The graveyard area was given as 2 roods 15 perches, ie 0.6 statute acres. The 1861 Spiddal West Townland Prospectus (Appendix II) states that the chapel *and* graveyard covered 1 acre, 1 rood, and 15 perches, that is, 1.34 statute acres.

In *Voices of Connemara*, is an interview with the Rev Tom Kyne (Tomás Ó Cadhain). Tom Kyne mentions the nuns came to Spiddal in 1909, and occupied a small house in the village. A recent but now former convent resident states they came in 1904, and in 1912 moved into a house later displaced by the new (now former) convent.

Sisters of Mercy Convent   Foundation Stone
(From Voices of Connemara)   *(Courtesy of Noel Conneely)*

The convent foundation stone inscription is: "Clochar Éinde Naomta, d'ord na Trócaire, An Spidéal 1923." Translated as: " Holy St Enda Convent of the Order of Mercy, Spiddal 1923." The August 20 1924 issue of the Freeman's Journal stated that "a beautiful and massive Carrara statue of the Sacred Heart was solemnly enthroned at the new convent at Spiddal. Nearly three thousand people were present......." The convent entry hall and main staircase are notable, with fancy floors, woodwork, and some coloured glass panels. The old furniture was removed 30 years ago. Only recently were the elderly nuns removed. When the convent's population dropped below a certain threshold, it seems a stipulation in the original ca 1923 land donation agreement caused the property to revert to the Morrises.

A picture caption, in Tom Kyne's *Voices of Connemara* article, associates the Earl of Westmeath with the convent. I suspect Boliskey Lodge was the Earl of Westmeath's summer place. The modern convent and its grounds replaced older buildings that were the Earl of Westmeath's summer compound. In the 1893 OS for Spiddal Village, in what seems to be one plot, are five buildings, and a label "Boliskey Lodge" (see pages 24 & 61). The convent and its lawn and drive are in the general vicinity of these buildings.

Appendix VIII (The Blakes of Forbough) shows the Blakes and the Earls of Westmeath connected via marriage. Ca 1853, I suspect Boliskey Lodge was known as *Goodville,* and might have been used as an auxiliary workhouse prior to 1851.

Micheal Ó Conaola (aka Mike P), remembers Ulick Sweeney of Sheeaun relating that when the convent foundation was being laid in 1923, human bones were discovered. This might have been just a one-off burial. There are other possibilities. One is that the graveyard once extended farther north. There are references to an auxiliary workhouse in Spiddal, likely located near the present-day convent. There may have been burials associated with this workhouse.

As mentioned earlier, no old Spiddal-Tuam (Knock) church records seem to have survived. What should have been Knock baptisms were occasionally recorded in the Spiddal-Galway registry. An infant born in precarious health would be rushed to the closest church to be baptised. A deceased unbaptised infant would not be buried in a consecrated graveyard, but usually ended up in a cillín, an unconsecrated burial ground reserved for the unbaptised, suicides, criminals, transients etc.

I know of two cillíns between Spiddal Village and Loughaunbeg. Some deceased unbaptised infants never made it to the cillín, and received even more informal undocumented burials.

The Martin Chapel & The Spiddal Graveyard

Martin Chapel 2004

Under the accumulated sod on the chapel roof was a tiled roof, replaced ca 2010.

Clíodhna Ní Mhurchú has added a photographic compilation of headstones for the Spiddal and Coilleach Graveyards to Find A Grave. From 1985-1995, Ian Cantwell compiled: *Memorials of the Dead; Counties Galway and Mayo (West),* containing 8000 transcriptions, including the Spiddal Village graveyard, and St Colmcille's out at Cloghmore, for memorials erected prior to 1901. His website seems to be dormant. His compilation has been transcribed in to findmypast. The most prominent memorial in the Spiddal Village graveyard would be the "Martin Chapel." Other monuments within the burial ground have interesting stories associated with them.

Before discussing the Martin Chapel, let's look into more modest monument, connected to a family in Fionnán (Finnaun, Finnane), an isolated townland northwest of Spiddal (page 47). Fionnán is the largest townland (7526 acres) in Ireland. In 1841, there were three individuals in one structure. Their name was Clancy, I suspect. In 1851 there were six individuals in one structure. In 1855, the townland is uninhabited. In the 1901 Census it was populated by one family, that of the shepherd David Walsh and his wife Sarah, their five children, and who knows how many sheep.

Finnane was in the news in the summer of 1858, via a Spiddal Petty Sessions case: *Myles Costello vs John Clancy and others.* Andrew Blake and George Morris were the magistrates. About the time Thomas Clancy of Finnane died, in 1838, £50 was spent on his vault. Not too shabby. John Clancy would be a son of Thomas, a Spiddal area resident in 1858.

Thomas Clancy's youngest son (Patrick, I think) sold his father's tomb to Myles Costello, seemingly with Thomas interred within. Then the youngest Clancy decamped for America, circa 1847.

Assuming his siblings were unaware of the transaction, Patrick's departure shortly after the transaction would have been prudent. Perhaps the transaction financed his passage to, and new start in America? The Clancy family may have only learned of the transaction in 1858, when they were taken to court.

In *Cré na Cille* , the most prestigious grave plots were in the £1 section. With a £50 monument, presumably Thomas Clancy was buried in the £1 (high ground) section of the Spiddal graveyard. Imagine his astonishment when his recently arrived neighbour informs him of the court proceeding, mentioning that the question about him to be answered, literally, was *"Cé Leis Thú !"* (*Who Owns You !*)

The Spiddal Graveyard Crypt of Thomas Clancy of Fionnán
(John J Keady)   (Courtesy of Clíodhna Ní Mhurchú)

The left panel shows the Clancy Crypt in the left foreground, the re-roofed Martin Chapel behind, with the Cill Éinde belfry in the background. The above images show what £50 got for Thomas Clancy, ca 1838. The right panel above shows the west end of the crypt, which is about 2 meters tall.

There is an inscription, mentioning Tomas(?) and Mary Clancy, running vertically, to the left of the corroded metal ring. The stonemason scribe was paid by the letter.

At the southwest corner of the top (covering) crypt slab is a difficult to access, and somewhat hard to read inscription, indicating that Thomas Clancy of Finnaun died in 1838, and that Mary, and possibly his son John, are interred within. A family crypt perhaps. Those who played on top of the crypt as children are well aware of this inscription.

In the Petty Sessions on that July day in 1858, John Clancy had forceful legal representation. It seemed the youngest Clancy and Myles Costello were on shaky legal ground. But the magistrates concluded there was a "right of property" issue. Thus they had no jurisdiction. Case dismissed.

Myles Costello seems to be resting elsewhere. The 1855 GV for Galway shows a Myles Costello renting from Andrew Blake in Cushmaigmore, over by Furbo.

Now for the Martin Chapel, erected in July 1776, at the expense of Stephen Martin, Gentleman, according to an inscription on the side of the chapel.

In the previous 2004 photograph, on the south side of the chapel, to the left of the adjacent Celtic Cross grave marker, we see the blocked up entrance, and just above the entrance, the cut rectangular memorial plaque.

Inscription 2022

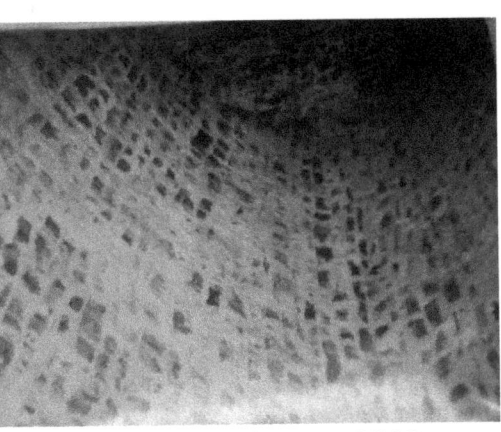

Interior Ceiling ca 2010
(Courtesy of Noel Conneely)

When Lord Walter FitzGerald visited the Spiddal <u>graveyard</u> (in 1897 or 1898) he noted:

> Standing on a bit of high ground in the churchyard is a vaulted
> mortuary chapel; over the door is a small slab on which is inscribed :---

> This Chapell was
> Built in july 1776 at The
> Expence of Stephen
> Martin Gentleman

The big mystery is: who was this Stephen Martin? In 1641, there was a Stephen Martin owning six townlands in Iar-Connacht (including two near Rosscahill), much too early in time to be our Stephen Martin. Having land in Rosscahill points to the Martins of Ross/Ballynahinch, whose genealogies for the 18th Century seem to be fairly well developed. No Stephen Martin is mentioned. There is no Stephen Martin in the Down Survey 1670 landowner list.

A combination of the Down Survey, the 1861 Chancery Court case mentioned earlier (involving Andrew Martyn), and Lord FitzGerald's ca 1898 visit to the Spiddal graveyard, points one east. The Martin Chapel entrance wasn't blocked up in 1897/1898, as Lord FitzGerald continues:

> Inside is one large limestone flag; at the upper end a coat-of-arms* is
> carved in relief, a cross, on one side of which is a half moon, and on the
> other a sun, with the motto:----Sic itur as Astra.

> Below is incised :----

> "Here lyes the Body of WILLIAM MARTIN son of FRANCIS
> MARTIN who Dyed The 26th of June 1763 Aged 34 years
> Here also is interd the Body of IANE MARTIN Als FRENCH
> Mother to WM MARTIN   She dyed the 20th of Ianvary
> 1769.   Aged 62 years"

> " *The Martin coat-of-arms is:---- A cross calvary on three grieces argent, the dexter
> arm terminating in a sun in splendour or., the sinister in a dacresunt of the second."

We have William Martin (1729-1763), aged 34 when he died, the son of Francis Martin and Jane Martin (née French, 1707-1769). We have a Martin-French matrimonial relationship. In 1670, the Spiddal townlands were owned by Oliver Martin (of Tullyra) and Anthony French.

The historian Adrian Martyn discusses an 1870 manuscript of Andrew Kirwin of Galway about *The Kirwins of Galway at the Battle of Aughrim 1691*, where the Irish suffered a great defeat. Among the Irish who fell were ".....Martin French and Dominick French, both of Spiddal, sons of Edmond French......" Thus the French family was still associated with Spiddal in 1690. Born in 1707, Jane Martin (née French, 1707-1769) is likely a descendant of Edmond French and/or Anthony French. Likely William was her first born child. I assume Stephen is also her son, and came along later.

At the NAI, the *Catholic Qualification and Convert Rolls, 1700-1845* have Francis Martin of "Spiddle" finishing the process of becoming an enrolled Anglican on 27 April 1728. About the only way for a Catholic to hold certain offices, or otherwise get ahead, while the Penal Laws were in force. James Hardiman's *The History of the Town and County of the Town of Galway*, has a Francis Martin who, early in 1764, was one of 104 members of the "common council of the town." Francis Martin of Galway died in September 1775, and got a death notice in a Dublin publication, *Saunder's News-Letter.*

Archived information about wills provides some insight into individuals. There are various indices of Prerogative Wills; the *Index of Prerogative Wills, 1811-1858*, and more generally; the *Index of Prerogative Wills, 1536-1858*. The Index is a one-line statement that a person of a certain place had a will executed or (usually) proved on a certain date. Better is an extract of the will, compiled for tax purposes. Included are the will's date, the date of death, the estate's value, the executor, the beneficiaries, etc. Of course the actual will is the most informative source. While, sadly, most prerogative wills were destroyed in the 1922 Four Courts fire, extracts of wills from registers for 1828-1839 survived.

There is a 1775 index for *Martin, Francis, Ballymanagh, W. sub. of Galway.* There is a Ballymanagh in East Galway, southeast of Craughwell. But the 1775 index seems to refer to another Ballymanagh. Are these various Francis Martins one and the same person? I suspect so.

For 2 Sept 1778, the *Catholic Qualification and Convert Rolls* show a Stephen FitzFrancis Martin, Gentleman, of Galway, becoming a registered Anglican. Fitz means "son of." The County of Galway magistrate, Stephen Martin, was in the newspapers when his unnamed son was shot in the mouth by Sheriff Netterville, on 3 June 1806. If the Stephen Martin who built the chapel was born as late as 1745 (say), then he would have been 61 years old in 1806, and could be the magistrate.

The extract of Stephen Martin's will survives. Stephen Martin of New Road died on 23 April 1823. His estate's executor was his daughter, Eliza McManus, of #28 Old Dominick St, Galway. Luckily for us, his will wasn't proved until 23 Dec 1828. Had his will had been proved shortly after his 1823 death, there would be no surviving extract. In the end, Stephen Martin's estate was valued at £1846. A note on the extract page indicates that, as executor, Eliza McManus was to pay £100. Presumably the estate tax? Stephen Martin had some land dealings with (an early) Patrick Blake of Drum, Gortnamona and Tully (see Appendix VII). I won't hold that against him. Stephen Martin had three legatees: his sons William and Anthony, and his daughter Eliza.

Stephen Martin named one of his sons William, seemingly after his own brother, who is buried in the Martin Chapel. How do we know this is Stephen Martin of Spiddal? A subsequent death notice for his daughter Eliza McManus confirms this is our man:

35

[Death] On the 29ᵗʰ instant, in Hardwicke-street [Dublin], Eliza Monimia, wife of Jas. A. M'Manus, Esq, and only daughter of the late Stephen Martin, of Spiddle House, in the county of Galway, Esq.

Freeman's Journal
April 22, 1837

I believe this is the Stephen Martin who built the Martin Chapel. I'd estimate his birth year to be ca 1745.

Ca 1776, who was the incumbent of the Martyn of Tullyra and Spiddal lands? Referring back to the Justice Mountifort Longfield's 1861 Chancery Court judgment:

The lands now held by the petitioner [Peter S Comyn], and by the respondent Francis Comyn, were demised in 1777, by Oliver Martyn, to a person of the name of Lynch, at a rent of £380, late currency.

This Oliver is a grand nephew of the Oliver Martin owning the Spiddal townlands in 1670. What do we know about this later Oliver Martyn? According to the 1882 and 1898 Burke's Landed Gentry:

OLIVER of Tillya, m. 1748, Frances, dau. of John Donnellan of Bally Donnellan Castle, and d.s.p.

I'd estimate Oliver's birth at ca 1700. In the 1898 Burke's Landed Gentry, Oliver's father was Peter. I suspect Francis Martin (the one mentioned on the headstone) and Peter Martyn were brothers, although Francis isn't in the genealogy. Oliver was succeeded by his nephew Edward Martyn. It was Edward's son, Andrew, who intervened in the 1861 Comyn Chancery Court lawsuit. The Martin Chapel in Spiddal is connected to the Martyns of Tullyra. See Appendix III.

Ca 1776, I believe this Martin family resided in "Spiddle House," as the Spiddal agents for Oliver Martyn, who quite possibly was Francis' nephew and Stephen's first cousin. This agent arrangement would not be an unusual occurrence. The Tully lands, of Patrick Blake of Gortnamona and Tully, were for decades (mis)managed by his Uncle James Blake of Inverin Lodge.

Stephen Martin's mother and brother died in the 1760s. Why did Stephen Martin wait until 1776 to build the chapel? Is it connected to the Francis Martin's September 1775 passing? I believe it is. I believe that buried in the Martin Chapel are the mother and brother of the Stephen FitzFrancis Martin mentioned in 1778. I believe he is the 1806 magistrate, and is the Stephen Martin who died in 1823.

The 1861 Chancery Court case demonstrated the Martyns still had substantial mid-19th Century land holdings in the Spiddal area, much of it leased to other local gentry. Andrew Martyn had inherited these property interests, and, from 1836, was collecting rent from the Comyns on the Sellernamore and Spiddal lands. Andrew's older brother, John, was the Martyn of Tullyra incumbent. John's son, Edward Joseph Martyn, inherited Tullyra Castle, recommended WA Scott as the architect of Cill Éinde, founded Dublin's Palestrina Choir, and was the first president of Sinn Féin. Edward J Martyn d.s.p..

Prior to 1816, some Martin lands (including Spiddal House) were acquired by Sir Robert Staples, who held them until his September 1832 suicide. Not too long after his suicide, his holdings east of Spiddal Village were acquired by the Bunburys. Then Spiddal House started to be called Manor House.

Up through the 1860s, Bohoona Lodge was sometimes referred to as Spiddall Lodge. By the latter 19th Century (ca 1893), in the OS map, Bohoona (Spiddall) Lodge is referred to as Spiddal House, while a building across from the present-day Spiddal Library was called Spiddle Lodge. Capisce?

According to Hardiman, the Martin motto is *Auxilium meum a Domino* (*My help from the Lord*). It comes from Psalm 120:2 in the Latin Vulgate. Hardiman mentions the story that the crest and motto was granted during the reign of King Richard I, to Oliver Martyn, who supposedly accompanied the King to Palestine during the 3rd Crusade. Yet another Oliver. The original, as far as we're concerned.

Richard 'Humanity Dick ' Martin and his son Thomas Barnewall Martin linked the adoption of the motto to another later conflict, possibly in the latter 16th Century, a more or less Pyrrhic Good Friday victory over the ferocious O'Flaherties.

One should keep in mind a remark Queen Elizabeth I is said to have made about another matter: 'It's all Blarney!' I wouldn't say it's all blarney, but there is a lot of blarney, and, perhaps, a little Bohemian baloney (See Appendix III).

Burke's Landed Gentry gives the Martin motto (for all the branches) as: *Sic itur as Astra,* which can be translated as *In this way go forth to the Stars.* It seems less martial, but it is connected to battle. The motto comes from Virgil's Aeneid, Book IX, where, after a battle, Apollo addresses the young Ascanius, the son of Aeneas.

Burke's Landed Gentry appeared in various years, with varying content. The earliest I've found dates to 1833, while Hardiman dates to 1820. There are other references about the motto that are likely derivative of either Hardiman or Burke.

For the moment, my opinion is that the Martin motto is **Auxilium meum a Domino**, except for the **Martyns of Tullyra, Curraghmore, and Spiddall**, whose motto is *Sic itur as Astra.* This latter motto is on the Martin Chapel grave marker.

Timín Curran mentioned to me that when the Martin Chapel roof replacement occurred, he noticed about ten dirt mounds on the ground inside the chapel.

Let's consider a day, around 12 June 1862, spent in Spiddal by a newspaper correspondent, seemingly a member of the 'Established Church.' I'm reading between the lines.

He describes a Catholic burial service, along with a confrontation between the presiding priest and a young Protestant convert. By the end of the burial service, the parish priest collected about £7 10s. A nice haul. We pick-up where our correspondent described the Spiddal graveyard, adjacent to the RC church, as it was in June 1862:

A Day in Spiddal, County Galway
(FROM A CORRESPONDENT)

..........There is no wall enclosing the burial-ground; it may be said to be an open field. In this part the Roman Catholics are buried, but in the centre stand the ruins of a house, of small dimensions, and within it was the only place where Protestants were, until lately, allowed to be interred. Now they have a decent church-yard.......

The Daily Express
June 12, 1862

As far as I know, there was no local custom of placing residences within graveyards. In 1862, the Martin Chapel was 86 years old. Its builder, Stephen Martin, was dead decades, as were his three children. Thus the chapel likely had little or no maintenance in the decades preceding 1862.

Imagining the cemetery without the perimeter stone walls that now exist, and gazing at it while standing directly south of it (as I've done), near the Nimmo Pier, the Martin Chapel might have seemed to be in the centre of the graveyard. In 1862, were "the ruins of a house, of small dimensions" the Martin Chapel? I believe so. Thus, one wonders if the ca 10 mounds inside the chapel, that Timín Curran mentioned to me, represent Protestant burials.

When were they buried? Presumably the RC parish priest would have objected. If he was around. The oral history is that, for a time, Spiddal had no parish priest. A local person named Neachtain would come down River Rd to the chapel, and lead a rosary service. But the correspondent's account indicates there was a priest around. The parish register indicates that from 1842-1844, the Rev John O'Grady was administering both Knock (Spiddal-Tuam) and Spiddal Village (Spiddal-Galway). Court testimony about the O'Grady-Blake ruckus indicates this multitasking may have continued into 1845.

The correspondent noted that the Anglicans finally had their own churchyard, presumably to be used for burials. The GV shows the Anglican church lot was 0.19 statute acre. There would have been a small churchyard.

The St Joseph's birth registry and marriage registry survive in the *Representative Church Body* (RCB) Church of Ireland archives (referenced as *Killannin Parish*, not as St Joseph), in Dublin. There was no reference to a mortuary registry. Possibly it was lost. I'm not sure it ever existed. I have no evidence that any burials occurred in St Joseph's Churchyard. The correspondent references an early proselyting effort:

.....Before the working of the Irish Church Missions commenced, in this district, a Christian lady from Dublin made an effort to establish a school there, for the purpose of instructing the children in the religion of the Bible.

It is possible the "Christian lady from Dublin" is Ellen Smyly (née Franks). Another possibility, mentioned by James McCready (aka Mccredy etc) in his pamphlet, *The Reformation in Iar Chonnacht,* is a certain "Miss Bellingham," later known as Mrs Darcy. Returning to *The Daily Express* article, its author continues:

The schoolmistress she placed there was greatly persecuted, took sick, and died, and was buried in the enclosure above-mentioned. The priest persuaded the people that the whole of the burying-ground had lost its consecration on account of the Bible teacher being interred in it. The passions of the people were so worked up by the lecture from the altar that they went that evening, took up the coffin, and heaved it into the sea. At that time there was not a Protestant within a considerable distance. Now there is a church and a respectable congregation; and the Protestant clergyman, the Rev R Rudd, and his family, though carrying on a vigorous missionary work, are respected and beloved even by the Roman Catholics. And the people, who twelve years ago could not bear to have even a dead Protestant among them, are now satisfied to have a successful missionary work progressing in their midst...........

"Twelve years ago" would be 1850. It's stated the schoolmistress died without any co-religionists present. However, the Anglican Rev James Mccredy was in Spiddal in 1850. He wasn't in Spiddal in February 1847, but was there by November 1847, remaining into 1862 when he was succeeded by the Rev R Rudd.

Had any such disinterment occurred during Mccredy's tenure, he would have protested vigorously to the authorities, and would have been writing to the newspapers. A search of the newspaper archives, over a wide range of years, revealed nothing. Perhaps a red flag. If the disinterment occurred, it was prior to 1847.

The Anglican Rev John Garrett of Penzance noted that the Rev Cather was in the area in 1844. The *Limerick Chronicle* stated that, after completing church construction in Roundstone, the Anglican Rev John Cather (Cayther) was residing in Spiddal in July 1845. He was on the Spiddal Relief Committee in February 1847, along with the Anglican Rev Ferrock. Our knowledge of the local Anglican clergy suggests the much persecuted school-mistress died prior to 1844.

Who's to report the incident if no Anglicans were around? Certainly not the RC parish priest who allegedly incited the parishioners. And certainly not the parishioners.

What of the Royal Irish Constabulary (RIC)? Along Cois Fharraige, the RIC had a history of not logging every occurrence that merited reporting, such as a notorious 1847 eviction in Tully, and a WWI era Loughaunbeg naval mine explosion powerful enough to damage windows in Spiddal Village, four miles east. The authorities may have learned of the 1847 eviction from a newspaper article.

A check of the RIC service records reveals that RIC Officer Kerrigan, who testified in Spiddal in 1840, might have been a certain Peter Kerrigan. He is in the RIC records as Roman Catholic, 24 years old on 20 April 1837, when he joined the RIC in Co Mayo. It's not clear that the RIC archive shows his complete service record, and so it's not absolutely certain that he's our man. Peter Kerrigan left the RIC, one way or another, on 1 June 1853. If our Officer Kerrigan was still in Spiddal ca 1843, he was in the midst of an interesting situation.

Relations continued to be contentious. Seven years after the correspondent's visit, and contrary to his belief back then, the Protestant interment issue wasn't settled. From Inverin on 10 May 1869, Vicar Rudd of Killannin wrote to the Poor Law Commissioners in Dublin, protesting the Spiddal Village parish priest Martin Phew's refusal of a Protestant interment in the Spiddal Village graveyard. The Commissioners and the Guardians declared that they had no jurisdiction over the graveyard.

By the beginning of the 20th Century, the Cill Éinde graveyard was approaching capacity. Ca 1905, two new graveyards opened. One was out west of Spiddal by Knock, while the other opened in Coilleach, just east of Spiddal Village. Both are administered by the local (county) government. The Knock graveyard is more or less at capacity.

Cois Fharraige Prior To The Great Famine

Prior to the Great Famine (1845-1850), there was a long succession of crop failures of varying severity, with subsequent food shortages or famines. The mid-18th Century was an especially grim time.

In December [1739], there happened a most severe frost, which lasted nine weeks; it exceeded the great one of 1694, and by all accounts was worse than any that was ever remembered in this kingdom. This was afterwards called 'The Year of the Great Frost.'
Farrar's Limerick

A great frost rotted all the potatoes in Ireland in half an hour. The ice on the river [of Galway] from the west bridge to Ferryland [Terryland ?] – Galwoy, was so thick, that several hundreds of people played foot ball on it, from the Woodquay to Newcastle.
Dutton's Survey of the County of Galway

From late 1739 through 1742, 20% of the Irish population may have perished. The situation didn't improve much as time progressed. Hardiman's Galway history noted (page 225 therein):

The year 1745 was remarkable for a great fall of snow, by which vast numbers of sheep and black-cattle were destroyed. The farmers surrendered their holdings, and the best lands in the province were set for 5s an acre.

The above Farrer and Dutton notes come from the *Table of Cosmical Phenomena, Epizootics, Famines, and Pestilences, in Ireland* within the *CENSUS OF IRELAND FOR THE YEAR 1851.*
The nearly 300 page <u>table</u> (internal pages 41-333) starts in the pre-Christian era, and runs to 1851.
It is sobering reading.

Jumping forward to the early 19th Century, the Spiddal Relief Committee was writing;

To the High Sheriff of the County Galway
Committee-Room, Spiddle, June 17, 1822

Sir—Having this day seen your Requisition, we, the Committee appointed for this part of the county of the town of Galway, to Costello Bay, a distance of 15 miles, with a population of three thousand five hundred persons, more than one-half are in a starving condition, which daily increases, the people having no food to subsist on but the shell fish and dillisk found along the shores. The following persons have died from actual want of food: James Toole of Inverin Castle; Mary McDonough of same place; Patrick King of Loughaneberg, died on 16th June instant. Numbers are confined to their beds with bowel complaints, and total debility, occasioned by hunger, and very little hopes are entertained of their recovery.
We have the honour to remain,
Your very humble Servants,
JOHN BLAKE
A. WILLIAM. BLAKE
ANTHONY MARTIN
JAMES BLAKE
MICHAEL MORRIS
THOMAS L DUNDAS
PETER WARD, P. P. of Spiddle.

John Blake was the Blakes of Furbo incumbent, succeeded after 1836 by his son Andrew William Blake. Anthony Martin, if he was of Ross, would be *Humanity Dick* Martin's half-brother. Or he could be the son of the Stephen Martin who had the Martin Chapel built in July 1776. I suspect the former.

Earlier, in 1810, Anthony Crosby Martin took to Court: Richard Martin Esq, Thomas Martin Esq and others, and seemed to have prevailed. Richard and Thomas (Barnewall) Martin were father and son. Anthony and Richard Martin were half-brothers. I assume the dispute was over their late father's estate. Ca 1822, courtesy of King George IV, Richard Martin acquired the sobriquet *Humanity Dick*.

An 1810 Chancery Court Decree announced that Anthony Martin's agent would hold an auction of property situated from Athenry west across the Corrib. Hundreds of plots were listed, with sizes described as cartrons (30 acres) or quarters (four cartrons, 120 acres), possibly well over 10,000 acres. Some properties were recognizable. There were houses in Athenry and Galway, and four eel-weirs on the Corrib River. I like mine smoked. A quarter in Spiddal was included, and land in "Shanagarran."

The letter's signatory James Blake was the estate manager for his young nephew Patrick Blake of Gortnamona and Tully. Michael Morris of Spiddal *d.s.p.* in 1822. His brother Martin became the incumbent. Martin's son Michael eventually became Attorney General of Ireland, and later the first Lord Killanin. Thomas Laurance Dundas was born in Midleton Co Cork. His maternal grand-mother's maiden name was Bunbury, a gentry name prominent in Tipperary and Carlow, and well-known around Spiddal by the time of the Great Famine.

In 1822, relief money came from outside Ireland. The Dublin Evening Post reported that from May into August 1822, donations from the London Tavern Committee amounted to just under £12,000 (Irish). In early June 1822, a £50 tranche went to T. L. Dundas of the Spiddle Relief Committee, while two weeks later, the Committee received an additional £50. In late July, Dr Coffy received £10 for medicine etc for Spiddal and Barna, and more in August.

Saunder's News-Letter of 16 August 1822 reported that a quantity of "Oatmeal, Biscuit, and Rice, destined for the poor of Spiddle and its neighbourhood, was forcibly plundered from on board the vessel conveying it by these deluded wretches [the larcenous starving Claddagh fishermen].........."

A major jobs project of the time was the road from Spiddal to Moycullen. It was described as the road from the Spiddal Harbour to the Lough Corrib Ferry Pier. Alexander Nimmo provided oversight.

Anthony Martin of Ross was a pugnacious fellow. In 1823 he wrote Dublin Castle complaining about "outside labour" on the Spiddal-Moycullen Road project (NAI; CSO/RP/1824/615). That meant anyone not from his estate. He also alleged "fraud and extortion" involving to two supervisors, "Jones and Plunkett," especially in connection with some raffles. Alexander Nimmo dismissed the raffle organisers, and where the road proceeded through Anthony Martin's lands, employment was limited to Martin's tenants.

The other major jobs project was the "new line of road from Barna to the North Shore." According to the *Dublin Evening Post*, on 12 July 1824, the supervisor, Mr Jones, proceeded toward Spiddal at a very early hour, "where he engaged a great number of men," to work on the road.

In 1829, even the Spiddal parish priest Michael Lannon wasn't immune to the deprivation:

[Death] At Spiddle, on Sunday se'nnight [a week], of a tedious and lingering illness, brought on by an over-exertion in the cause of the poor, in the summer of 1822 [1829], the Rev. Michael Lannan, P.P., aged 30 years. This amiable and exemplary ecclesiastic discharged the duties of an ardent mission in a manner which gave every satisfaction to his superior, and which tended considerably to the inculcation of sound principles of religion and morality amongst his parishioners, by whom he was venerated and beloved.

The Pilot
September 14, 1829

Grim newspaper reporting, in the early 1830s, indicated that hunger and cholera were rampant. On 17 June 1831, the Rev Mr John Darcy was writing to the Mansion-house Relief Committee:

Gentleman—I am directed by the County of Galway central committee to request you will represent at the Mansion-house the great and growing distress of the district the Irish distress committee appointed them to superintend. It is impossible it can be anywhere exceeded........

.......Fourteen hundred families absolutely without food---the men prowling about in every quarter where there is a hope of finding anything that can be devoured, like wolves in search of prey---the women and children formed into groups about the doors, waiting the arrival of provisions, present a less alarming, but not less heart-rending picture. In a little village [Barna] within three miles of this town are 109 families, and among them but three pair of blankets. Everything that money could be raised on is already in the pawn-office...........

.......Doctor Kirwan came to us yesterday..........., and of the little we had to divide we gave him three tons of meal. This, he says, will scarcely afford a breakfast for them—still we could not do more. In the name of mercy I beseech you to send us some relief. Mr. Morris, of Spiddle, had been just now with me, and says, in distributing some meal yesterday, he saw several among those who were waiting to receive it weak, and two men actually fainted.

This distress originated with the failed 1830 harvest in the west of Ireland, ruined by an extended period of intense rain that started in mid-summer (around St Swithin's Day). A 15 June 1831 report, in the *Bury and Norwich Post,* claimed that upwards of 200,000 were in danger of perishing. The afflicted area ran from Clare to Sligo, and included Leitrim and part of Roscommon. On 30 June 1831, representatives of the various local relief committees gathered in Galway, to assess the overall situation in the district. There were 12,777 destitute (starving) families. Assuming an average of 5 individuals per family, one arrives at 63,885 destitute individuals. Excluded were an estimated 14,000 destitute in "Moyress." The relief committee compiled:

Summer 1831 --------------- Locality	Number of Destitute Families	Summer 1831 --------------- Locality	Number of Destitute Families
Clifden	2000	Cong	227
Gormna	900	Kilkerrin in Cunnamara	300
Ballinakill	1400	Barna N.E.	109
Roundstone	1500	Rahoon N.E.	400

Summer 1831 ---------------- Locality	Number of Destitute Families	Summer 1831 ---------------- Locality	Number of Destitute Families
Spiddle, Minna & Rahoon (part of)	1200	Arran	291
Moycullen	250	Ross	900
Rahoon West	200	Ballyovy	200
Oughterard	500	Carrobrowne	500
Killannann	300	Corrofin	400

There was all sorts of skulduggery associated with efforts to help the poor. In early July 1831, at the instigation of two Galway clergymen, P Hughes and W Feely, the *Galway Independent* procured some samples of the meal meant for the poor, and took them to Dr. Veitch for inspection. This would be *Dr James Andrew Veitch* (ca1770–1856?). He was Scottish born, Roman Catholic, and a military surgeon. He was the first superintendent of the Galway County Infirmary on Prospect Hill (1802–33). About the meal, Dr. Veitch reported "his opinion that one stone weight [14 lbs] did not contain a pound of nutritious food ! ! !" Apparently adulteration of meal was a common occurrence.

Around this time, the *Connaught Journal* reported: "Along the sea coast too, many families consider themselves most fortunate, if they can procure a sufficiency of sea-weed to subsist upon."

One of the Spiddal area committee representatives was the parish priest Thomas Loftus. In the National Archives of Ireland (CSO/RP/1831/2457) is his 15 July 1831 memorial from Spiddal:

Memorial of Thomas Loftus, parish priest, union of Spiddle [Spiddal] and Menna, [Minna], County Galway, to Henry William Paget, Lord Lieutenant, seeking the extension of medical aid in order to alleviate an outbreak of fever; lamenting that as many as 6000 people in the immediate vicinity are in 'utter distress' due to the lack of sustenance; observing that over the past few weeks serious fever has attacked the district with 37 cases of typhus and 23 of dysentery 'all occasioned by starvation'.

The National Archives (CSO/RP/1831/2113) have the 12-15 August 1831 expense records of Dr Thomas L Whistler who was attending the "fever-poor" in Connemara. After closing the temporary dispensary in Roundstone, he indicated that the remaining balance of £48 18s 1.5d would be applied to assist the sick poor in the Spiddal vicinity. His work (CSO/RP/1831/2528) in the Spiddal area covered the period 2 August 1831 through 12 October 1831.

He submitted a record of payment of 5 shillings he made to Michael Joyce for the transportation of medical supplies out to Spiddal. In one supply list I examined, the most useful item listed was opium. Palliative care? It's not clear there was a dispensary in 1831. Where were the supplies being delivered? To the Spiddal Coast Guard Station, I suspect.

How were the Cois Fharraige gentry amusing themselves? Let's consider one of the Comyn brothers, John S Comyn. "S" stands for Sarsfield or Stanislaus. One newspaper described him as "a young man of high spirits, and manifestly much inclined to dissipation." In 1831, Comyn reached his majority, and then established a London presence.

From the 21 Jan 1843 edition of the Limerick Chronicle:

At that time [ca 1831] he was an extremely handsome gentleman--- a young Irishman---fashionable, well dressed, a Milesian, a Galwayman, with excellent pretensions to appear in any society in which he moved in England or Ireland.

It was ca 1831 in London when a dashing John Comyn met Mrs Anna Maria Bennett (Burnett) Little. Anna Clements, who apprenticed as a milliner in Bath, eventually established her own successful business, and married a Bristol man named Bennett. Bennett turned out to be jealous (perhaps with some justification), with a violent temper, that eventually caused her to flee him. Then she took up with a man named Cooper, a principal in the Drury Lane Theatre, referring to herself as Mrs Cooper. Upon his passing he left provision for her, such that in 1831, she resided in one of the Alpha Cottages in the Regent's Park area (between Paddington and Regent's Park). Later, Dante Gabriel Rossetti resided in the same neighbourhood.

Newspaper accounts indicate her liaisons were more numerous and complicated than outlined here. But, we're not here to judge Anna Clements. John S Comyn, on the other hand, is another matter:

Having formed an acquaintance with her, he became devotedly attached to her, as a person with whom he would wish to be more intimately acquainted. She had reached that period of life which appeared to present great attractions to young men, being 'fat, fair, and forty.' Mr. Comyn became enamoured with her, and had the use not only of her house, but her carriages and horses.....

She followed to him to Dublin, moving her carriages etc to a respectable Upper Baggot-Street house. The two visited his family. She was well received. In the Spring of 1833, she moved back to London. The Limerick newspaper report continued:

The deceased returned to London, renewed his intimacy with Mrs Bennett, and being fond of sporting and amusements of all kinds, he went [on 30 May 1834] to the Epsom races, and, on returning in his cab, was hurled out of it upon the pavement in Piccadilly, and killed upon the spot.

Earlier I mentioned that seldom were various newspaper accounts of an event entirely consistent. The London *Morning Advertiser* edition of 2 June 1834 had a somewhat different report:

Coroner's Inquests

Dreadful Accident-- An inquisition was held on Saturday evening, before Mr Higgs, Coroner, and a respectable Jury, at the Gloucester Coffee-house, Piccadilly, on the body of Mr John Comyn, a private gentleman, aged 33 [incorrect], whose death was occasioned by the following accident:-

It appeared from the evidence, that on Friday night, about eleven o'clock, the deceased, who had been spending the evening at the Bath Hotel Piccadilly [later knocked and replaced with the Hotel Ritz London], got into a hackney cab. The cab-man drove at a very rapid rate, and proceeding down Bolton Street, Piccadilly, the horse slipped, and the deceased was precipitated to the ground. He was taken to the Gloucester Coffee-house, where he was attended by Dr Hyde, of George-street, Hanover-square. The deceased appeared to be sensible, and requested to be bled, during which operation he expired. The cab-man, on hearing the nature of the accident, made off, without applying for his fare.

The Jury expressed themselves dissatisfied, and agreed to adjourn, in order to give time for the cab-man to be brought forward.

A few days later the inquest resumed. The reckless cab-man was never identified.

Earlier that deadly Friday evening, the 24-year-old Comyn (his correct age) had been visiting his two sisters, Caroline and Harriet, who resided at Chester-place (by Regent's Park). In 1847, Charles Dickens briefly resided at #3 Chester-place. Not a low-rent neighbourhood. Where John Comyn was going, late that Friday evening, wasn't stated. But, we know where he was going.......

Mrs Bennett had a death mask made, and went into mourning. John S Comyn executed a will in 1832, another in 1834. John S Comyn left his lady-friend a £500 annuity. One sees where this is going. This is when the litigation started. Referred to as Mrs Little Bennett (I don't know how she acquired the name Little.), she went to Prerogative Court, and Judge Radcliffe ruled John Comyn's will proved.

Francis Comyn appealed the decision in the Court of Delegates. In testimony there Martin Morris identified himself as John S Comyn's agent, "and was on terms of the greatest intimacy with him." Morris testified that Comyn informed him that Mrs Little had become very accomplished at imitating Comyn's handwriting. Martin Morris had seen a document purportedly written by Comyn, that was actually written by Mrs Little. Morris testified that when the 1834 will was supposedly written in England, he knew that John S Comyn was in Galway for an extended period, covering the date the second will was supposedly executed.

Early in 1843, The Court of Delegates ruled that John S Comyn died intestate, reversing the decision of the Prerogative Court. He also *d.s.p.*. His siblings inherited his estate. But, Mrs Little persisted. Her appeal of an 1862 court decision was denied in 1863. Francis Comyn, and his sister Caroline, the Baroness von Stenz, litigated in 1865. This last action concerned a much earlier ca 1835 Lord Chancellor ruling important to the case. The case was still active in 1869. John S Comyn was dead 35 years, and litigation continued. Talk about beating a dead horse. By 1870, the litigants are probably starting to die off. It seems the British wheels of justice turned slowly.

In 1834, the year the playboy John S Comyn died, the Spiddal priest Thomas Loftus was worn out:

The Rev. Thomas Loftus, P. P. of Spiddle Galway, resigns from indisposition, and in doing so issues the following public notice, quite a novel thing among the Priesthood:---"The Rev Thomas Loftus, P. P. of Spiddle, feeling that the declining state of his health will not permit him longer in conscience to discharge his duties as a Spiritual Pastor, and having also acquired by his mission a full competency for the future support of his life, and hereby gives Notice that he resigns his duly in the parish of Spiddle, without accepting any pension or emolumont, although kindly proffered by the Right Rev. Dr, Browne.

Tipperary Free Press
February 8, 1834

In the early 1830s, while John S Comyn and his sisters Caroline and Harriet had a nice life in Galway, Dublin, and London, Cois Fharraige tenants, who helped finance the siblings' lifestyles, had cholera, typhus, and starvation. The parish priests who ministered to the tenants didn't fare much better.

Nor, sometimes, did the gentry. Oral history has it that Martin Morris's wife Julia contracted some contagion, possibly cholera, and died despite the best efforts of the doctors. A newspaper announcement stated that she died on 6 August 1833. Additional oral history, from Colm Pat Colm Keady, has it that a Spiddal "*Sick House*" was set up in 1834, by Martin Morris. Thus it seems the difficult circumstances of the early 1830s continued into that decade. Despite all that, in 1838 Spiddal was a summer holiday destination:

SALMON FISHERY AND SEA BATHING

TO BE LET, fully furnished, for the months of June, July, and August, the LODGE at SPIDDALL, near Galway. The House contains Seven best, and Six Servant's Beds, besides sitting Rooms Water Closet, and other offices. The use of a capital Cow, the Garden fully cropped, and other advantages will be granted. The Bathing, the Sea, River, and Lake Fisheries are of the first order.

Further particulars maybe known by an application, post paid, to M. M., Post Office, Galway

Dublin Evening Mail May 23, 1838

SALMON FISHING AND SEA BATHING

TO BE LET. From the 1st of May, for such term as may be agreed upon, SPIDDALL LODGE, near Galway, together with the River, which abounds with Salmon and Trout, and which, as well as the Sea is only a few yards from the Lodge. The House is most comfortably furnished, with every convenience for a respectable family, having 14 Beds; and Grass for a Cow, Sheep, and other advantages, will be given. Apply (pre-paid), to Mr. James Mooney, Rathdowney

Dublin Evening Mail April 29, 1840

Above is the earliest reference I have to the Lodge. M. M. would be Martin Morris. Nice to be known at the Post Office by your initials. The Anglican Rev John Moore of Rathdowney and his entourage summered at Bohoona Lodge, across several seasons. The Rev Moore was a sporting chap. The Press reported on the Galway Bay Regatta of August 1839:

GALWAY BAY REGATTA

The regatta commenced on Tuesday last, to all appearances under the most flattering auspices, the day being unusually fine. The quays on both sides of the river Corrib were densely crowded; never before have we witnessed such an assemblage, graced, too, so numerously by the rank and beauty of our town and county...................

SECOND DAY...

....................Yacht race for the Kearney Silver Box. Three yachts were started for this race, viz.:- The Daw, of Spiddle, Rev. Mr Moore Rathdowney owner; the Lousia, Mr. Wm. Evans of Galway owner; and the Jim Crow, of Galway, Messrs. James M'Donough and James Greham owners. The day was so calm that the Jim Crow was cast aground near Ardfry, and the two others so becalmed that by mutual consent the race was postponed to Thursday, the third day, when they came in as follows;

The Daw................	........1.......	........1.......
The Louise............	........1.......	........2.......
The Jim Crow.......	........3.......	........3.......

Saunders's News-Letter
August 27, 1839

The Rev. Mr Moore with his family and suite, who had been sojourning the summer months at Spiddal, whose unbounded charity, affibility, and humanity rendered him endeared to the poor during the last trying and distressing season, while every quality that could render the gentleman estimable and social, and the clergyman exemplary, made him a very great favourite with our aristocracy, took his departure yesterday morning from Nolan's Hotel, Eyre-square, for his seat, Rathdowney.
--Galway Advertiser

Saunders's News-Letter
November 19, 1839

The deprivation of the early 1830s, that prompted Martin Morris to open a sick house in 1834, persisted through the decade. We can borrow from a former resident of London's Chester-place. Along Cois Fharraige in the 1830s: "It was the best of times, it was the worst of times......"

It seems that Martin Morris's 1834 sick house was a private charitable effort. A centralised approach to deal with poverty and sickness resulted in the _Poor Relief (Ireland) Act, 1838,_ patterned after an 1834 English Act. Ireland was divided up into 130 so-called Poor Law Unions, whose number increased over time. The Poor Law Unions were overseen by the Poor Law Commission. Each Poor Law Union was directed by a 'Board of Guardians.' Most were elected, some were appointed (ex-officio).

A margin note in the original (Irish) Bill stated: "No Minister of Religion to be a Guardian", which stood in contrast to the 1834 English Act. The Irish Act also authorised emigration assistance.

The Poor Law Unions were empowered to build workhouses. Earlier, in a few urban areas, there were _Houses of Industry._ The Galway Workhouse, constructed during 1839-1841 on eight acres, was meant for 1000 paupers, and accepted its first inmates on 2 March 1842. About £9800 was spent on building and outfitting the structure(s). Later, a fever hospital was built just west of the workhouse. An 1841 Galway Workhouse, for 1000 people, demonstrates that the area was in significant distress well before the Great Famine. During the Great Famine, the workhouse population considerably exceeded the original intended capacity.

So we will encounter the "Guardians of the Poor of the Galway Union." In 1839, there were 37 elected Guardians and 10 ex-officio Guardians. The building block of the Poor Law Union was the Electoral Division (ED). An ED was comprised of townlands. EDs might be adjusted and even created after each decennial census (by removing townlands from existing EDs). In the 1841 Census, the Galway Union had twelve EDs. In the 1851 Census, the Union had twenty-six EDs. Within the 1841 Census, the Galway Poor Law Union ED populations were:

1841 Census---Galway Poor Law Union

Electoral Division	Population	Electoral Division	Population	Electoral Division	Population
Galway (15)	32,511	Annaghdown (1)	4,941	Oranmore (2)	4,480
Moycullen (3)	7,343	Lackagh (2)	3,753	Ballynacoortin (2)	3,407
Oughterard (3)	10,601	Athenry (1)	1,770	Stradbally (1)	1,264
Killanin (3)	11,501	Clare,Galway (2)	3,873	Arran (2)	3,521

The numbers in parentheses are the number of Guardians (as of 1839) each ED was entitled to elect.

The Arran ED is the Aran Islands, which had 3521 residents in 1841. The present population of the Arans is ca 1250 residents. The combined population of Moycullen, Oughterard, Killanin, and Arran rivals Galway. The total 1841 Galway Poor Law Union population was 88,965 individuals.

Given the remoteness of some of the western districts, likely this is a bit of an undercount. The combined population of Moycullen, Oughterard, Killanin, and Arran was 32,966 people, slightly more than Galway. Yet they elected 11 Guardians, while Galway had 15 positions.

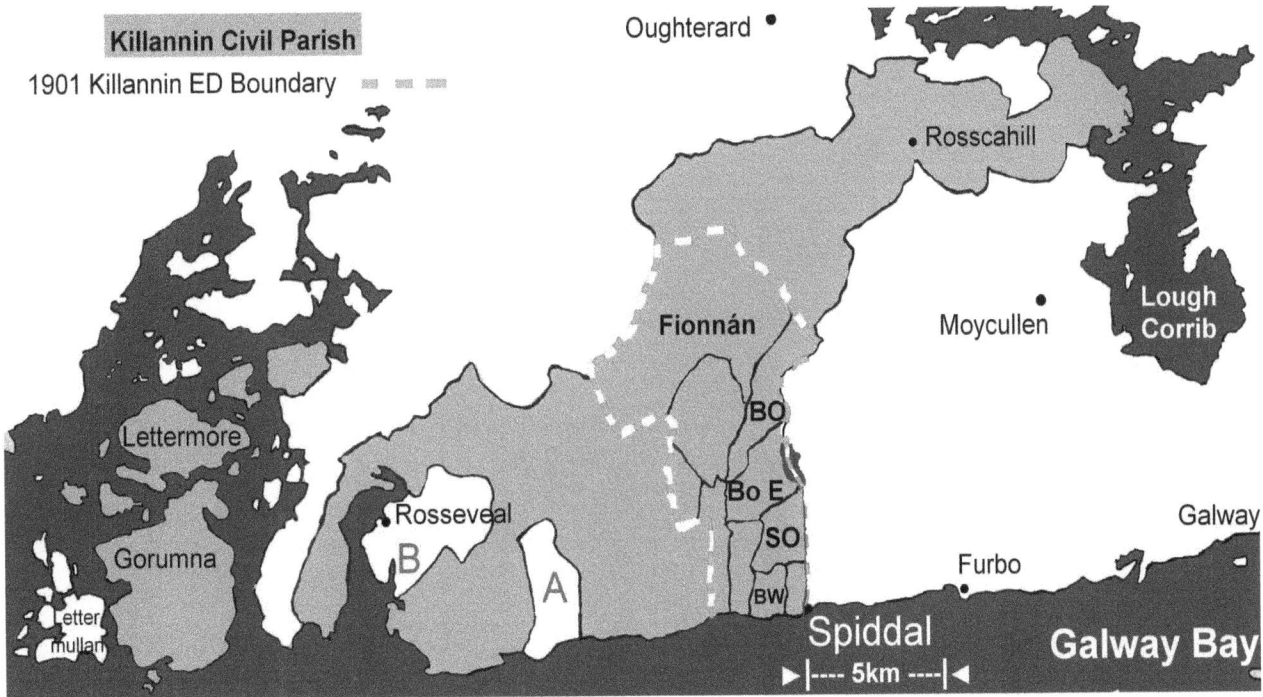

The Killannin Civil Parish and the 1901 Killannin ED

The Killannin Civil Parish is highlighted in the above map. One sees a convoluted situation. The domains labelled A and B (described on page 16), Lettermullan, and the western half of the Carraroe peninsula (west of Rosseveal), are not highlighted, as they are in the Kilcummin Civil Parish (as is Oughterard). Lettermore and Gorumna are part of the Killannin Civil Parish. In 1841, Region A contained 410 individuals, while Region B had 546 people. Regions A & B had 956 individuals in all.

What townlands made up the 1841 Killannin ED? I haven't found the 1841 legal definition of the Killannin ED, with its 11,501 people. In the 1841 Census, the population of the Killannin Civil Parish was 11,278 people.

I suspect that the 1841 Killannin ED was the Killannin Civil Parish, plus a bit. As far as famine relief is concerned, one wonders if Regions A & B may have been a de-facto part of Killannin.

After 1841, the Killannin ED was whittled down after each census, as new EDs were created. By 1901, the 1901 Killannin ED had ten townlands: Bohoona East & West, Kilroe East & West, Boliska Eighter & Oughter, Letterfir, Cloughernalowra, Shannawoneen, and Finnaun. The 1901 Killannin ED perimeter is highlighted in the map.

Anglican Clergy & The Irish Church-Missions

The Irish Church-Missions (ICM) was founded by the Church of England's Rev Alexander Dallas, who served under the Dublin-born Duke of Wellington before he found his true calling. Supported by the Church of Ireland, the ICM formally came into existence in 1849. Some mainline Anglicans might not have necessarily warmed up to the ICM.

Strictly speaking, the organization was *The Society For Irish Church-Missions to the Roman Catholics.* The reference to Roman Catholics was dropped from the name in 2002. They are still active, with their last stronghold being in Dublin, on Bachelors Walk.

Anglican proselytizing in Iar-Connacht predates the 1849 founding of the ICM. For Spiddal, there is missionary activity dating back at least to 1844, possibly to 1837. Activity that persisted, in the Spiddal area, into the first decade of the 1900s. The definitive account of the Connemara missions can be found in Miriam Moffitt's book: *Soupers and Jumpers: The Protestant Missions in Connemara.*

Apparently the Rev Dallas' and the ICM's belligerence toward the Catholic Church might have made them their own worst enemy. The belligerence was mutual. In 1862, the visiting Anglican Rev John Garrett of St Paul's (near Penzance), who had been ordained in Tuam ca 1845 by the Lord Bishop Plunket, described tension that existed between the RC Archbishop Dr MacHale and the local ICM missionaries. Two ICM scripture-readers, who in May 1855 attended a sermon of MacHale's, reported that he compared the local Anglican missionaries to 'droves of swine.' The gloves were off.

The ICM had many contributors among the who's who: The Duke of Norfolk, Arthur Guinness II etc, each pledging hundreds of pounds, with many more contributors of smaller amounts. While some donors might have thought themselves philanthropic, most wished to undermine the Church of Rome. The following table provides perspective on why the ICM was interested in Iar-Connacht.

| Parish or District | Diocese | Population | | | Extent |
		Established Church	Roman Catholic	Dissenters	
8. Ballinderry	Connor	4,000	1,200	300	11,000 acres
10. Belfast	Connor	30,000	30,000	40,000	19,000 acres
30. Lisburn	Connor	8,500	2,500	3,500	11,000 acres
34. Rathnew, Wicklow	Dublin	3,551	10,527	87	11 miles by 8 miles
35. Spiddal, Ballinakill	Tuam	523	41,755	12	40 miles by 20 miles
36. St. Nicholas, Cork	Cork	3,000	17,000	50	2 miles by 1½ miles

Population Table derived from the 1850 Thom's Irish Almanac

The original table is in the 1850 *Thom's Irish Almanac*, in the *Established Church* section of the *Statistics of Ireland.* I've extracted (above) a few entries from the much larger 1850 Thom's table to illustrate the sectarian population variations. I assume the data derive from the 1841 Census. The "Established Church" is the Church of Ireland.

For Ballinakill, we have 523 Anglicans, 41,755 Catholics, and 12 Dissenters. Belfast had more Dissenters than Anglicans or Catholics. Likely most of these Dissenters were Presbyterian. Other Dissenters belonged to the Wesleyan Methodist Connexion, or would be Congregationalists, Baptists, Quakers, etc. Some Methodists stayed with the Anglican Church until 1878, when they left and joined the Wesleyan Methodists.

The table shows the ICM missionaries in the west of Ireland had their work cut out for them! A significant criticism of the ICM was that their charity was offered judgmentally and conditionally, in contrast to other groups, such as the Quakers, whose charity had no strings attached.

Initially, the few Protestants in the Spiddal area were associated with some of the gentry, their staff to a certain extent, and the professional class: Constabulary, Coast Guard and Customs staff etc. In the west of Ireland, it would be a mistake to assume that these latter groups were uniformly Protestant.

In Spiddal in 1837, for occasional Anglican religious services, there was a 'licensed building," actually a room in a private house. It had no "permanent provision for a Minister." The mid-1840s on saw the first significant Anglican incursions into Iar-Connacht. Eventually (ca 1851), the ICM had a mission, school, a widows' refuge, and finally (ca 1854), an orphanage in Spiddal.

Volume II of an evangelical Anglican publication called *The Banner* describes some events out at Inverin/Knock from late 1851.

Inverin — The Lord is on our side: He has shown it. Last Christmas-day shows it. Only twelve months ago, and I had no congregation; I brought my agents to Caslah coast-guard station to get four Protestants there to join in prayer on Christmas day. On Christmas-day just past, I had 107 converts to unite with me in the praise of God. Others would have been there only the tide did not answer. And some of my converts being nearer to Spiddal went to hear Mr. Macredy. But at Inverin I had no wonder that the priests are opposed, as they are faithful to their master, and I endeavour to be faithful to Christ.

On Christmas-day the priest of Knock, before reading mass, asked the congregation ' are ye all ready with your money ? Go on, give out your money: if you do not, I will not read mass; and then the curse of God will be on ye, without Christmas mass.' The money was not forthcoming in a satisfactory manner; when the priest locked the chapel doors, barred them securely, and kept the congregation within, while he himself went to a remote part of the parish to read mass and collect more. The patience of the people could not wait his return, and so they broke open the doors of their prison, and went home without the mass.

The priest for a month before went about, commanding none to go to mass on Christmas-day without 'Silver' as no amount of the baser metal could render the Christmas mass valuable.

The above Anglican correspondent is unidentified, but is probably the Rev Coleman Conneely. The unidentified Knock parish priest doesn't come off so well, assuming the account is accurate. Remembering Father Fahy, perhaps one should take this account with a grain of salt. The "remote part of the parish" is likely Tully. My father's youngest brother Darby told me that, when my father was taken to the Knock Church to be baptised in 1925, his parents wanted him baptised as Darby. But the Knock parish priest refused, and baptised my father as Anthony instead. That priest saw no *Silver.*

A prominent Spiddal area Anglican clergyman was James McCready, possibly ordained in 1847. He wasn't in Spiddal in February 1847, but he was by November 1847, perhaps his first assignment.

In the 1851 Thom's Almanac, the Rev McCready is listed as a curate of the Ballinakill Union, posted to Spiddal. The four Ballinakill clerics listed immediately after him, posted to Clifden and Oughterard, have the designation "Missionary Curates" by their names. In the 1865 Cockford's Clerical Directory, there is at least one Connemara cleric I know to be ICM, whose listed patron is not the local bishop, but the "Trustees." Trustees of the ICM, I suspect. The Rev James McCready was evangelical, and cooperated with the ICM, but I hesitate to say that he was *of* the ICM. It seems that he got his marching orders from the Anglican Bishop of Tuam. We have a reference to the Rev James McCready's brothers being in Spiddal.

Henry Blacquire Lahiff, Esq, eldest son of Thomas Lahiff, Esq., of Cloone, perished on Thursday last, at Spiddal, Galway, while bathing with the Rev James McCready and his brothers. Mr. Lahiff, a most adventurous and expert swimmer, was struck by a heavy sea, which carried him a considerable distance from the shore. But assistance was out of the question. After some hours the body was found.

Ballina Chronicle
October 9, 1850

In the 1855 GV for Spiddal Village, there is a John McCready renting a property. He is one of James McCready's brothers. In the village valuation there is also a "Customs' watch-house." John McCready was a British Coastguard. From 1849-1851, he was assigned to Galway Town, while for 1853-1854 he was in Spiddal. He ended up in Kerry. Details can be found at the GENUKI website.

There was friction associated with the Anglican presence in Spiddal. In his ca 1854 pamphlet, *The Reformation in Iar Chonnacht,* the Rev McCready mentioned the ill-treatment of the local Anglicans.

The Rev McCready related that he had managed with difficulty to rent a village house for £4 a year. According to the Rev McCready, upon learning of this, the outraged parish priest Columb McGragh pressured the landlord Morgan Darcy, who clumsily attempted an unsuccessful Sunday eviction. Now everyone was angry at Darcy. Darcy made his peace with McCready, and resolved his dilemma with the parish priest by immigrating to Australia, abandoning an unspecified £40/year position, all according to the Rev McCready. Morgan Darcy was the Barna District relieving officer (see page 11).

At an 1852 Guardians' meeting, P S Comyn complained that the Rev McCready erected some "*sheds*" in Spiddal, for proselytzing, and was enticing Oughterard persons with offers of food and clothing. James Blake of Tully objected, saying the paupers weren't from Oughterard. Comyn retorted what mattered was they weren't from Spiddal. Comyn was Catholic. With a middle name of *Sarsfield,* one has good reason to suspect he was Catholic. Blake was Protestant. Proselytizing might have been the unspoken issue. However, the 1861 Spiddal West Auction Prospectus (Appendix II) shows that, in 1853, Comyn was willing to rent to the Anglican Rev McCready. The chairman stated that individuals had freedom of movement, so there was no issue. In June 1854, there was a letter to the *Tablet* newspaper from the RC Rev Lyons, referencing "a list of fifty-four persons who left the Jumper camp at Spiddal...." Earlier, there may have been at least seventy persons in the "camp."

Unsurprisingly, the ICM trumpeted its proselytizing success. However, it's not just about how many converted, but also about how long they stayed converted.

At the 1851 Census was probably too soon to evaluate their proselytizing success, as the ICM was only getting established in the area in 1850. The Thom's Almanacs, published after the 1861 Census, don't seem to have a parish breakout analogous to the 1850 table (page 48), complicating comparisons. Claims about ICM success likely were exaggerated, which over the long term might have hurt their fund-raising prowess.

There was a Smithills Bolton (Greater Manchester) gentleman John Horrocks Ainsworth (JHA), who in the 1850s contributed towards a Spiddal area school, flax mill and "House of Refuge." Responding to pleas from the Rev Mccredy, in March 1853 he sent £25 to support the "House of Refuge." It's also stated that he sent an additional £25 in July 1853, to "help them over a difficult time." JHA interacted with the Bunbury family (see Appendix IX), who had an estate on the east side of Spiddal.

The Summer 2015 Newsletter of the Friends of Smithills Hall, has an article: *John Horrocks Ainsworth and the Irish Connection,* by Margaret Koppens, inspired by a letter from Tim Curran of Spiddal. The patron of the *Friends of Smithills Hall* is the Duke of Norfolk.

In 1852, the Duke of Norfolk pledged £250 to the *Society for the Irish Church-Missions to the Roman Catholics.* Not too surprising, except that the Duke, Henry Charles Howard (1791-1856), was baptised Catholic. He wasn't a practicing Catholic, but apparently was considered to be Catholic anyway. After the *Catholic Emancipation Act of 1829,* the future duke took the oath of allegiance, campaigned for a parliamentary seat, and was elected to the House of Commons, the first Roman Catholic in the House since Emancipation. Yet he's helping finance the ICM. He ascended to the House of Lords in 1841.

The *Great Exhibition* of 1853 was held on the grounds of Leinster House, likely inspired by the 1851 *Great Exhibition* of London, held in Hyde Park. The catalog of the *Irish Industrial Exhibition of 1853* survives, and includes a listing (page 277): "Mecredy J., Spiddall, Co. Galway, Proprietor. Tweeds manufactured at the Spiddal Industrial School." Does the word "Proprietor" mean he was profiting from the endeavor? The attendance was international and amounted to many thousands of people a day. The 21 June 1853 issue of the Freeman's Journal had an extensive report:

THE GREAT EXHIBITION

.......The visitors included large numbers from England, Scotland, and Wales, who were easily distinguished by the peculiarities of dress and accent; and we were also glad to see mingling in the crowd some of the honest frieze-coated peasantry from the rural districts of our own country....

...It appears that less than a year ago, a Protestant clergyman in the west, seeing a number of weavers and other humble industrious hands in his district in great distress, bethought himself of setting them to work, by way of experiment, at the manufacture of tweeds. The articles in question are the result, and the good man who-irrespective of sect or party, and looking only to the benefit of his brother men and his country- contrived to accomplish this much, is the Rev J. Mecredy, of Spiddal, in the country of Galway.

The tweeds thus contributed from the Spiddal Industrial School are of a great variety of patterns, most of them being very pretty; the quality is good—indeed, considering the circumstances, and especially the very recent origin of the manufacture, not merely good, but wonderfully so, they are retailed at moderate, or rather let us say, the excessively low price of half-a-crown per yard, and are not merely to the eye fair value for the price, but possess the additional recommendation of being even better than they look; in fact, in point of durability there is nothing to surpass them. One of the Spiddal weavers attends in charge of the goods. We understand that he has already received no small number of orders........

The Evening Freeman, on December 15, 1859, reported on prizes awarded by the Royal Dublin Society, at their agricultural show earlier in the week. In the "Best Flax Seed Sample" category, Thomas Bunbury won second prize, a small silver medal.

On 14 October 1853, a *New York Times* (NYT) article described a public lecture given by the Rev Dr Tyng, a New York Episcopalian clergyman, on missionary progress in the west of Ireland. On 6 August 1853, Dr Tyng left Dublin for Galway, and was invited by the Anglican Bishop of Tuam to join him on his tour of the west. Dr Tyng described arriving in Spiddal, about a year after St Joseph's Anglican church was consecrated.

Dr Tyng notes that ".... four years before there were but fifteen Protestants in the parish........ ," and that the church had somewhat more than 200 parishioners. There were 18 clergyman "actively engaged in the work of reformation." I suspect he was referring to the Anglican Union of Parishes of Ballinakill.

The Rev Tyng mentions the mission school-house had about 75 children in attendance, and that there was accommodation for teachers and widows. There were three other schools in the parish, having 225 children, for a total of 300 children. He stated: "There were 187 converts from Romanism."

For the Bishop's 1853 summer visit, Dr Tyng related that converts who walked to Spiddal from 10-12 miles out were attacked by crowds. There was an accusation of connivance involving the parish priest. These Anglican parishioners returned home with a constabulary escort.

The Rev Colman Connelly (Conneely) is listed in the 1855 GV. Patrick Blake is making a few quid off Connelly, renting him five acres within the Cartronlahan townland, along with a house on a separate smaller plot. The 1857 Thom's Directory lists Coleman Connelly as an Anglican missionary cleric. He was active at least as far west as Lettermore.

On 21 Dec 1853, in the Spiddal Petty Sessions, the Rev Connelly was convicted and fined "for keeping a ferocious dog near the highway without log or muzzle." Possibly a mastiff, as we're about to see.

The fine was three shillings plus court costs (typically one shilling six pence). Colman Connolly was probably subject to harassment, and would have felt more secure having a menacing dog about.

In April of 1854, Patrick Lyons and James Mecredy (as the newspaper spelled his name) were lobbing salvos at each other in the pages of *The Galway Mercury.* At one point, the newspaper's editors intervened, characterizing some of the Rev Mecredy's rhetoric as a "very shrill and squeaking cadence", and as "empty bravado." Some of the exchange seems silly.

The Rev Connelly had an earlier 1851 appearance in the Petty Sessions. A special correspondent's report appeared in *The Galway Mercury* on Saturday 29 November 1851. The report described one case before the Spiddal Petty Sessions on Thursday 27 November 1851:

SPIDDAL PETTY SESSIONS-THURSDAY
(FROM OUR SPECIAL REPORTER)
Magistrate presiding---John Scully, Esq., R. M.
ASSAULT BY JUMPERS
The Queen, at the prosecution of James Kyne v. the Rev
Coleman Connelly, Robert Barry, and Bartley Conneely.

The complainant James Kyne had a solicitor, Mr Rochefort. The Rev Connelly represented the defendants. The assault allegedly occurred on Sunday evening 16 November at 'Loughanebeg.' Kyne related that he, Thomas Walsh, and John Beatty were returning home on the road from a 'Holy Well.'

According to Kyne, they were passing Barry's house when Barry came out and started beating Kyne. Then the Rev Connelly came out to the road, and gave Kyne a fist in the face and some kicks. Bartley Conneely allegedly appears with the clergyman's pistol, handing it to the Rev Connelly, who then menacingly points it at Kyne.

Mr Beatty testified that the Rev Connelly struck him on the back of the neck with the pistol. Kyne also mentions that Connelly's dog, a mastiff, obeyed Barry's commands, and sank its teeth into Kyne's thigh.

Thomas Walsh testified that Robert Barry's wife called out to her brother, the Rev Connelly, "to shoot the rascal [Kyne]." On cross examination, James Kyne admitted he had a bit to drink, but wasn't drunk. Then the other shoe dropped, as he also admitted that while passing Barry's door, he did yell out "Jumper!" One story is that the term 'Jumper' may have originated during an early 1760s Welsh Methodist revival, where worshipers were described as jumping for joy.

The defence witnesses saw no pistol, nor did they see the admittedly vicious dog bite anyone.

Rochefort protested Connelly's improper *as Gaeilge* conversation with a witness, under the nose of Magistrate Scully, who according to the Rev Connelly had no Irish. A conversation that, according to Mr Rochefort, suborned perjury. It was a remarkable situation: witnesses with little or no English, testifying in front of a magistrate who had no Irish. There was no mention of an interpreter. The assizes and quarter sessions could have salaried interpreters, but not the petty sessions. Presumably there was some informal consensus about the translating that day.

The parish priests Colm McGragh and Patrick Lyons were in the courtroom, along with the Anglican Rev James Mecredy. Connelly hurled invective at the priests. The session became so raucous that Magistrate Scully threatened to eject Connelly. Eventually, the defence rested. What did the Court do?

> ...his Worship stated that he considered there were grounds for informations against the defendants, and that accordingly he would return them to the Quarter Sessions. He would therefore require Connelly to find bail, himself in £50, and two suritie for £25 each, and for the others in half that sum.
>
> *Mr Connelly*---You must put me in gaol then, for I have no person to find me bail, but many who would shoot me by direction the Priests.
>
> *Mr Rochefort*----That's a falsehood.
>
> *Mr Connelly*---You are a liar,
>
> The *Court* then interposed,
>
> *Mr Connelly* asked if his Worship if he would take the Rev Mr Mecredy, who was present, as bail for the entire sum of £50, and the money, if necessary, would be lodged in a few days.
>
> *Court*---I have made my decision and I can't deviate from it.

If the Rev Connelly thought his fellow Anglican, the Rev James Mccredy, was 'in his corner,' he was about to get disabused of that:

> The Rev Mecredy to Connelly—It is better perhaps that you should go to gaol.
>
> *Mr Connelly* (meekly) I will go to gaol then, many better than me have gone there.
>
> *Mr Rochefort*---To show that we are not actuated by any bitter personal feelings in this matter, I will ask your Worship to accept Mr Mecredy's offer of bail for the whole sum.
>
> *Court*—I don't see how I can depart from the order I have made.
>
> *Mr Rochefort*---Unless our consenting would assist your Worship.
>
> *Mr Connelly*—I thank you for your sympathy for me, but I do not want it. I will go to gaol; but I advise the Court to consider the consequences of sending me there....

Later, Magistrate Scully changed his mind, and allowed the Rev Mccredy to post bail and surety for the three men. I'm not sure the case went to the Quarter Sessions.

To be an evangelical Anglican preacher out west of Spiddal, apparently one needed a King James Bible, a ferocious dog, and a gun. The Wild West. I suspect that the Irish-speaking Rev Coleman Connelly was a local fella. If so, then I'm probably related to him.

From the 8 November 1855 Spiddal Petty Sessions, as reported in the *Galway Vindicator*:

SPIDDAL PETTY SESSIONS-Thursday

Magistrates presiding—Andrew Blake, and _____Morris, Esqrs Millett and McDonough v. Griffiths and others.---This was a case and cross case of assault. The prosecutors, 'scripture readers', swore that Griffiths, a Coast Guard, with other Coast Guards met them at Lettermore, after leaving a shebeen-house, where they had been taking refreshment, and assaulted them.

On cross-examination, it appeared that they had partaken of such a quantity of spirits that they could not swear to any fact with certainty.

Griffiths was examined and proved that he only acted for the protection of the prosecutors who were Bible-readers, and incapable of taking care of themselves.

The Bench, after some consideration, decided there was no charge against the defendants, at the same time, pronouncing a very strong opinion on the disgraceful conduct of the prosecutors in the case.

AWFUL DEATH.---The body of a man named Gibbons was found dead on Wednesday morning on the beach near the Coast Guard Station, in the same locality, Gibbons was a teacher in one of the proselytising schools, at Lettermore, and had crossed over in company with the Rev. Mr. Connolly to give evidence in the above case. In the evening he continued drinking ardent spirits to an excessive amount, and was crossing the river in a small punt, he landed, and though within a few yards of his own house, he sunk and died. An inquest was held on the body by Mr. George Cottingham, and a highly intelligent jury. The medical evidence of Dr. Morgan was that he had examined the body and found no marks of violence.

The jury returned a verdict that deceased had died from the excessive use of ardent spirits, and subsequent fatigue and exhaustion.

A week later, the editors of the *Galway Mercury* inserted a disclaimer in the 17 Nov 1855 edition:

We are authorised to state the Rev Mr Mecredy had no connection whatever with the Jumper case which was tried on Thursday, the 8th instant at Spiddal.

Ouch. The Rev Mecredy didn't want to be associated with the Rev Connelly. A loose canon?

In the GV enumeration, the Rev McCready is occupying a £7 house in Inverin. For comparison, in the GV, Martin Morris's substantial Bohoona Lodge was valued at £8. In the OS, this £7 house would be "Cashel House," known to most people as "Inverin Lodge." We have a number of references to 'James Blake of Inverin Lodge.'

James Blake was dead before the end of May 1853, while the GV surveyors were present in the summer/fall of 1853. Thus, it's no surprise that James Blake isn't listed in the 1855 GV for Inverin.

A birth announcement appeared in the 2 May 1855 edition of the Freeman's Journal: "April 22, at Inverin Lodge, county Galway, the wife of the Rev. James Mccredy, of a daughter."

The Rev James McCready was a witness in a 28 Jan 1858 Petty Sessions Court case brought by RIC Sub-Constable James Costello. John Curran and Pat Conneely of Bohoona East were charged with "willfully and maliciously throwing stones at the Church and disturbing the Congregation" on Christmas Day 1857. Peace on Earth, good will to men. Relations didn't improve as 1858 progressed.

Back in the summer of 1850, a few days after the Rev Alexander Dallas was in Spiddal, he met the Rev Abraham Jagoe in Roundstone. By the summer of 1858, the Rev Jagoe and his family were in Spiddal.

On 26 August 1858, the Rev Jagoe was writing to the *Dublin Warder and Weekly Mail* documenting the Protestants' horrible treatment in Spiddal. He described how, on 23 August 1858, Mrs Jagoe, her two children, and her servant, were bathing at the spot used by the ladies (possibly at a spot later known as the "Nun's Strand," by Cnócan Glas), when four young men and boys, aged from twenty to twelve, came down, dropped their clothes, and cavorted nearby "exhibiting their persons in the most outrageous manner," requiring Mrs Jagoe to have the RIC summoned.

The Rev John Darley and his family, renting Bohoona Lodge, likely had similar experiences. About this time, there is a reference to a "Jubilee" celebrated in Spiddal. What or whose Jubilee I know not. This might have inspired/incited the Rev Jagoe to preach about the defects of Romanism, likely elevating the overall tension, as possibly evidenced by the above incident.

There were other insults. There is an old trad song, *Rosin the Bow* (aka *Rosin the Beau*). Seemingly it (or some variation of it) was a drinking song in early 1800s America. The Clancy brothers recorded it in 1959. Ca 1858, someone wrote a special set of lyrics for it. I call it *The Labours of Abram Jago:*

The Labours of Abram Jago
Air---" Rosin the Bow. "

I've rambl'd all missions in Ireland,
and now to curs'd Spiddal must go,
Where insults and hunger's awaiting
The labours of Abram Jago

Chorus
The labours of Abram Jago, oh ! ho !
The labours of Abram Jago;
Where insults and hunger's awaiting
The labours of Abram Jago

Since I first doffed my *white apron*,
Tis now fifteen full summers ago,
When at Holmes'* I met with Lord Roden,
Who caused me a souping to go.
Chorus—Who caused me, etc

He told me " cry down with the Pope,"
But Peelers take always in tow,
And at the end three winters' reading,
I'll promote you to a choker, Jago
Chorus--I'll promote you, etc

I have seen some missions, surree,
When reader in Tuam long ago,
When women sold apples and cherries
To the tune of to hell with Jago
Chorus—To the tune, etc

Now that I'm all but exhausted,
And beyond a white choker can't go,
And this damnable word, COCKAMALA,
Prostrating my spirits so low,
Chorus—Prostrating, etc

I'm as pale and as thin as a specter,
From expounding the *word* to and fro,
And thro' the *Lord* I hoped to be Recter,
But alas ! To my grief, 'tis no go.
Chorus, But alas ! Etc

Now that I feel I'm departing,
From reading thro' weal and thro' woe,
I give my sweet curse to Lord Roden,
Who caused me from Holmes to go.
Chorus, Who caused me, Etc

Get now a couple of tomb-stones,
Place one my head and my toe,
And don't forget to scratch on them
" Here lies *Cockamala go dho.* "
Chorus, Here lies, Etc

*"was Butler at Holmes' when, to my misfortune, Lord
Roden gave me my mission."

Lord Roden was Robert Jocelyn (1788 - 1870), the 3rd Earl of Roden, an eventual grand master of the Orange Order. For his conduct connected to a murderous sectarian riot at Dolly's Brae in Co Down on 12 July 1849, he was stripped of his position on the commission of the peace. A rather militant fellow.

According to Thom's Almanac, in 1860, the Rev Jagoe was in Castlekirke. In 1861, he was in Cong, and may have achieved his goal (as stated in the song) of being appointed *Recter*. I can believe he was happy to leave *curs'd Spiddal* behind, and that he could have rued the day he met Lord Roden.

In 1860 came the end of the Rev McCready's Inverin Lodge residency. From the *Dublin Evening Mail* for 14 November 1860.

FIRE AT INVERN LODGE---A fire which caused the entire destruction of Invern Lodge, the residence of the Rev. Mr. McCready, incumbent of Spiddal, broke out Wednesday morning last. It was discovered about two o'clock on that morning; and the inmates having received timely warning no loss of life ensued, and many were enabled to secure a large portion of the household effects. The dwelling was however, burned to the ground. The fire appears to have originated in that fruitful cause of similar occurrences namely, the woodwork allowed to communicate with or run into, the flues. We have not heard whether the premise were insured.---*Galway Press*.

It wasn't arson. I have no references indicating that Inverin Lodge was rebuilt.

In November 1862, after acknowledging McCready's 15 years of excellent service in Spiddal, the Anglican Bishop of Tuam announced the Reverend Mecredy's transfer to Kilkerrin (probably the place south of Glenamaddy in East Galway), to be succeeded in Spiddal by the Rev Richard Rudd of Clifden.

In August 1863, advertisements appear for the rental of "Inverin House." Two sitting-rooms, four furnished bedrooms, kitchen etc, with excellent walled gardens, near Galway Bay. Advertised by the Rev R Rudd of Inverin House, Galway. In 1864, it was being advertised by the Rev Richard Rudd as "The Vicarage." I suspect this was constructed, somewhere in Inverin, after the destruction of Inverin Lodge. Perhaps completed in 1862. In 1861, the Rev Rudd was posting letters from 'Bohona Lodge.'

The Rev Mccredy appears in the GV, as the Blakes of Tully were renting him a half-dozen or so parcels of land out west of Spiddal. Ca 500 acres in all, with an annualised valuation of nearly £90. One might wonder what the Rev McCready was doing with nearly 500 acres of land out west of Spiddal. In the GV, some of the land the Rev Mccredy (McCready) was renting was described as mountainous.

Eventually it seems he leased seaweed collection rights. On 12 Nov 1863 the Rev Mccredy was very busy in the Spiddal Petty Sessions, as the complainant in four separate court cases. His place of residence was listed as Ballinasloe. It seems he didn't stay in Kilkerrin too long.

For two court cases, it seems he had delivered seaweed (a fertiliser) to individuals at Clynagh, for some agreed upon price. Apparently he wasn't paid, and so he went to court to get paid.

On Sunday, the Rev Mccredy was ministering to people's spiritual needs. The rest of the week he was profiting from their agricultural needs. In the other two court cases, he sued John Flaherty of Rosseveal, over two six-month periods of unpaid house rent.

About this time, a 'position wanted' advertisement appeared in the *Dublin Evening Mail*. A 32-year-old Protestant man, diligent, good at accounting, previously successful in managing a 200 acre farm with stock and tillage, is looking to manage a gentleman's demense or farm: "Salary expected, with board, £20 per annum. From Protestant gentlemen only.—Address C., Steward, Inverin Galway." A man of discriminating taste.

On 8 May 1863, the British Museum received the publication, _Good News from Ireland_ by the Rev John Garrett MA, the Vicar of St Paul (Penzance). It is his journal of a late summer 1862 tour of Irish Anglican facilities. He starts in Dublin and works his way west to Tuam, and then farther west across the Corrib into Connemara. He is no stranger to Connemara. Prior to his ca 1845 Tuam ordination, he had been "engaged for two years as an Inspector of Schools in various parts of Ireland." He covers the period from 1837 to 1862, although his first-hand experience probably dates from ca 1842 on.

Garrett was also the *Hon. Secretary in England to the West Connaught Church Endowment Society,* created in 1859. From June 1859 to 31 December 1861, the Society collected £6,460. £250 came from "B L Guinness Esq." This is Benjamin Lee Guinness, Lord Mayor of Dublin in 1851, a son of Arthur Guinness II. About £6,000 of the above total was held in interest-bearing government stock. £5,000 of that stock was committed to the "Churches of Moyrus and Sellerna." Ca 1860, the Rev McCready contributed £2 to the *West Connaught Church Endowment Society.*

Arriving in Spiddal in 1862, the Rev John Garrett comments on how much the village has improved since his Spiddal visit in October 1846. That's hardly surprising. A map in the Rev Garrett's 1863 document references an 1837 Spiddal licensed building, mentioned earlier (page 49), suggesting an occasional ca 1837 Anglican clerical presence in Spiddal. Garrett stated:

"But I know, that eighteen years ago, in 1844, there was a missionary curate (Rev. John Cather, now Rector of Westport) who had charge of about one-half of the district, including all the territory from Roundstone, near Clifden, to Spiddal and the Arran Islands; and I found him in that charge in October, 1846, when I visited Spiddal, where he was accustomed to hold occasional services in a room on the coast."

"A room on the coast" was a room in the Spiddal Coast Guard Station. In 1845, through the Great Famine era, the Rev John Cather was residing in the Spiddal area. The ICM didn't come into existence until 1849, so "missionary curate," above, doesn't refer to the ICM.

A table within *Good News From Ireland* categorises the Anglican houses of worship in "Western Connaught," for 1862. There were four categories:

Churches where there is a permanent provision for a Minister.
Most of these cluster up around Clifden into Mayo, along with churches in Arran (Inishmore), Oughterard, and Ross.

Licensed Buildings where there is a permanent provision for a Minister.
Among those were buildings at Cashel, Costello, and Inverin.

Churches where there is no permanent provision for a Minister.
Interestingly, this includes churches in Spiddal and Tully.

Licensed Buildings where there is no permanent provision for a Minister.
Among those listed are Barna, Clynagh, Inishmaan, Letterfrack, Lettermore, and Moycullen.

In 1862, Inverin had no proper Anglican church but had provision for a permanent minister. Spiddal had a proper Anglican church but no provision for a permanent minister. By the end of 1862, the Rector of Killannin Parish, the Rev Rudd, lived in Inverin, while the most expansive parish church was in Spiddal Village. Curious.

The Rev Rudd continued the ICM collaboration with Mrs Bunbury. From the 26 Sept 1864 edition of the *Dublin Evening Mail*:

THE FLAX MOVEMENT

We believe there are now five scutch mills in operation in the county of Galway, and in a few weeks two more will be at work. At Spiddal Mrs Bunbury has labored indefatigably for years for the promotion of the growth and manufacture of flax in one of the wildest districts of the West, and we are glad to find that she has been successful.

We found there a few days ago a scutch mill, ingeniously constructed, at work under the superintendence of a North of Ireland man. A number of girls employed in the mill showed they had been trained by skilled hands. Mrs. Bunbury has this year grown three, and the [Anglican] Rev. Richard Rudd, rector of Spiddal, eight acres of flax. The samples of both already scutched are very superior...

Not everyone took kindly to the Bunbury presence along Cois Fharraige. The *Cork Constitution* for Feb 28, 1866 reported on the mutilation and slaughter of his sheep out by Inverin. It was the fifth such malicious occurrence directed at Mr Bunbury over the preceding seven months.

Incidents like the above destruction and mutilation of livestock, along with arson, and even gunfire directed at habitations, were not rare occurrences. Periodic parliamentary reports summarised these incidents in tabular form, providing nature of the crime, the victim, the supposed justification, and whether or not the crime was solved. The reports show that a low-level war of retribution was occurring.

Seldom were perpetrators caught. There were a variety of justifications for the offenses. One person was victimised for being the landlord's agent. The above victim, Thomas Bunbury, was a landlord. One victim had assumed the holding of a recently evicted tenant. Another victim refused to participate in a rent strike. Of course, a rent striker would have been victimised (in a different way) by being evicted. Simple apolitical personal grudges were probably lurking in the tables as well.

Lochlainn Ó Tuairisg kindly provided me with transcripts of some Comyn and Blake communications to Dublin Castle for the early to mid-19th Century, about strife out west of Spiddal Village.

A December 1819 memorial by Laurence Comyn about the "tenantry of the lower designation," complained that widespread poitín (moonshine) production had made the tenants surly, aggressive, and most importantly, delinquent with their rent. In late August 1819, his tenants torched a house of his, and lopped off the tails of some of his cattle, among other acts of defiance. The Land War of the latter Nineteenth Century is well known, but we see that the local resistance goes way back.

St Joseph's Anglican Church

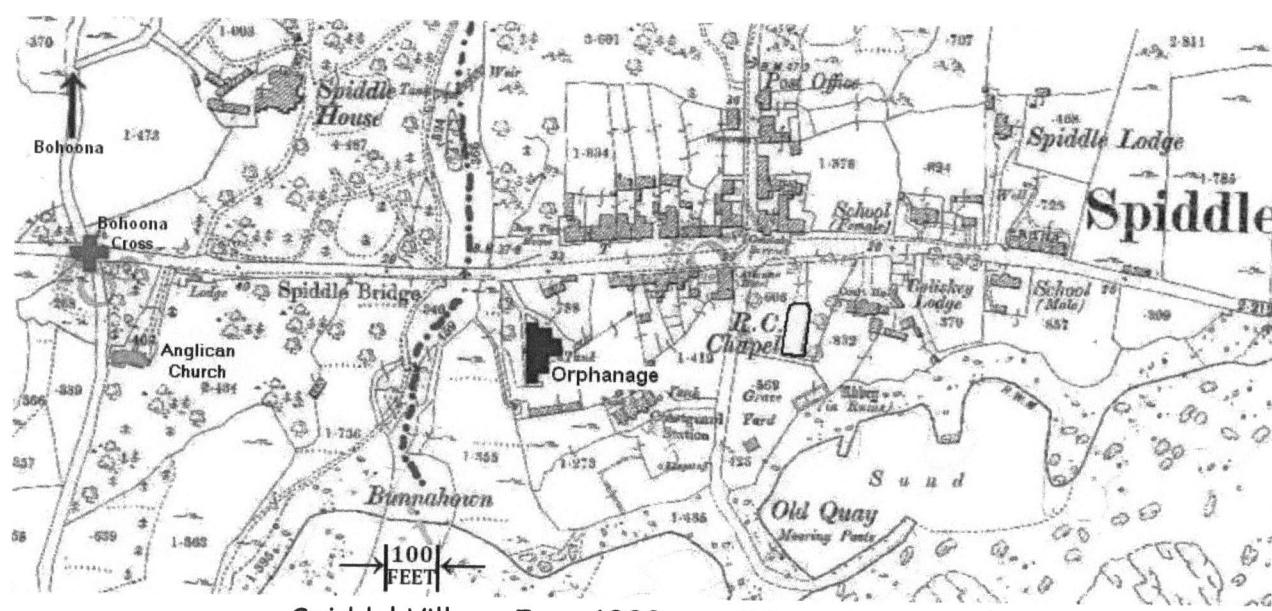

Spiddal Village June 1893 --- OS --- Annotated

On the Ordnance Survey Map above, I've indicated the Spiddal Orphanage, St Joseph's Anglican Church, and Bohoona Cross and the Spiddal (Boluisce) River (dot-dash line). The RC Chapel noted above is the Rev Colm McGragh's 1857 achievement.

A call for church construction proposals referenced the Anglican Rev Macready. The church building site was obtained from Martin Morris. A later narrative about Margaret Lappin (née Kain/Kane /Keane), born in Shop Street Galway in 1842, refers to this church as St. Joseph's.

NOTICE TO CONTRACTORS.

SPIDDAL CHURCH.

PROPOSALS will be received on or before MONDAY, 23rd June, for the COMPLE-TION of the WORKS required to Finish the above Church, agreeably to the Plans and Specifications lodged with the Resident Clergyman at Spiddal, who will give all further instructions.
Separate Proposals for the TIMBER WORK, SLATING AND PLASTERING, and PAINTING, will be
received by the Rev. James Macready, Spiddal.

Galway Vindicator and Connaught Advertiser,
June 11 1851

This church was to be the centrepiece of the Anglican Killannin Vicarage. A table in the Rev Garret's 1863 article stated that the Killannin Vicarage was eighteen by nine Irish miles in extent. (One statute mile = 1.27 Irish miles.)

The following article, by Dr Michael O'Neill, is about the surviving architectural plans for churches in the Anglican Diocese of Tuam: <u>Architectural Drawings Project</u>

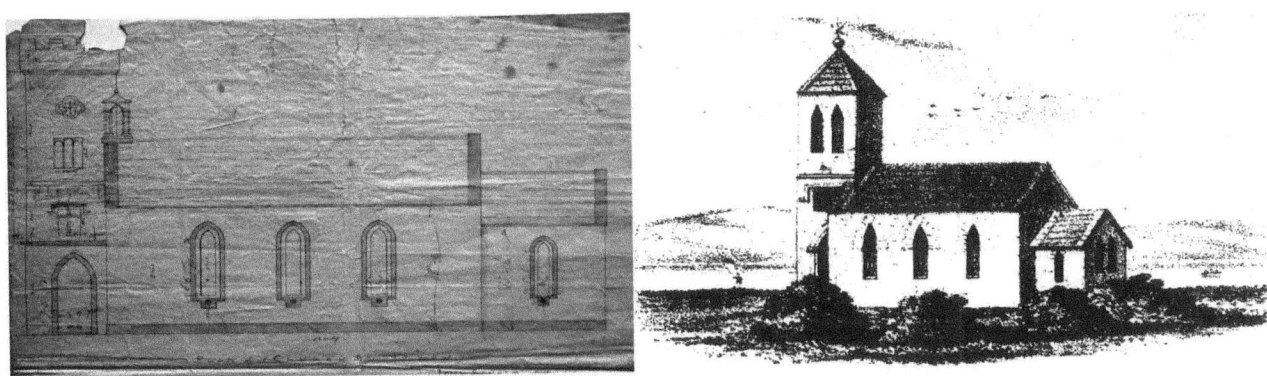

St Joseph's Anglican Church, Spiddal

From Dr O'Neill: "Spiddal church was designed by John Semple in 1845, either the Dublin architect or a member of the Semple family of building contractors in Galway." The left panel above, is courtesy of Dr Susan Hood, of the Church of Ireland's Representative Church Body (RCB) Library (PF/26). The drawing, above right, comes from Tim Curran.

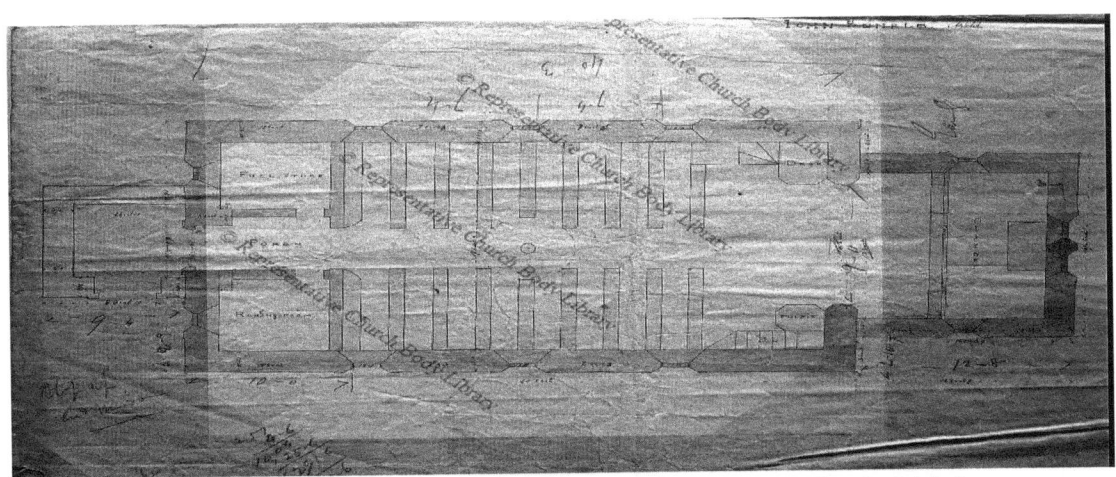

Interior Plan for St Joseph's Anglican Church, Spiddal

The architect provided two options, displayed in the left panel at the top of this page. The first option was for a church with a small bellcote at a gable end. The second option was for a tower with a crenelated parapet (modified with a pitched roof in the actual construction). Dimensions are penciled in on some portfolio drawings. For the main rectangular body of the church (see above), the exterior dimensions are 40 feet by 22 feet. The plans show nine rows of (ca eight foot long) pews on each side of the centre aisle, within that main rectangular body, allowing about 100 skinny people to sit.

Volume II of the ICM's *The Banner Of The Truth In Ireland* chronicles 1852. Starting on 29 July 1852, the Anglican Bishop of Tuam (*Thomas Span Plunket, 2nd Baron Plunket, 1792–1866*) made a grand inspection tour of the western part of his diocese. The schedule is fascinating because it shows the extent of the missionary activity.

The Bishop came down into Connemara from Co Mayo. Contrary to his published schedule, the Anglican Bishop of Tuam was a day late, and consecrated the church on Friday 20 August 1852:

> This Church affords accommodation for 160 persons.
> Immediately after the consecration, 140 persons were confirmed.
> 23 being original Protestants, and 117 converts. They came
> from Spiddal, Inverin, Casla, and Lettermore.

There is other interesting information in the Bishop's tour schedule. Generally he would inspect all the facilities in a location: churches, schools, orphanages etc. The two "Connemara Orphan Nurseries" are listed for inspection. Schools would be inspected as they were "finished and licensed." The Spiddal Orphanage wasn't open in August 1852, as it isn't listed for inspection.

The narrative about Margaret Lappin references the 10 Oct 1878 marriage, in St Joseph's Church Spiddal, of Caroline Matilda MacNeice (born in 1852 on Omey Island, but a Spiddal area resident in 1878) and John Frizelle (a Sligo-born RIC man, stationed at Inverin).

Caroline and John had a son Frederick (b 1881), who as a RIC Sergeant was assigned to Derry. On 3 May 1922, near the western shore of Lough Neagh, he was killed by three men with revolvers.

Caroline MacNeice had a brother John MacNeice (1866-1942), father of the poet Louis MacNeice. For a time, John MacNeice was a Ballyconree teacher. Later, ca 1895, John MacNeice left Ballyconree, became a cleric, and then the Rector of Carrickfergus (1908-1931). He favored Home Rule, opposed sectarianism, and thus opposed the 1912 Ulster League and Covenant.

John's and Caroline's father, the Rev William MacNeice (1826-1901), was a teacher on Omey Island for 27 years. The narrative about Margaret Lappin continues that, on 27 Feb 1879, the Claddaghduff RC Curate William Rhatigan assaulted the 53-year-old MacNeice in the Omey mission-school. The school's windows were smashed in the melee. A mob assault nearly a month later at Claddaghduff injured MacNeice's daughter. Now we leave the narrative associated with Margaret Lappin.

In Spiddal, on Saturday evening 10 July 1880, the south facing windows of St Joseph's Church: wooden frames, glass and all, were thoroughly smashed by a number of rather strong individuals, as the stones found inside the church were said to weigh nearly a cwt (112 lbs) each. Fortunately, the stones missed the church's organ.

On 12 July 1880, the Anglican Rector of Killannin, George Shea, wrote to the *Dublin Daily Express*, stating that he received a letter from the villagers of Spiddal, in which they stated their "......abhorrence of the gross outrage and sacrilegious violation of the Protestant church......" Canon Shea stated he had no doubt about their sincerity.

Continuing on with conflict.... According an account in the *Galway Advertiser*, on 9 Sept 1920, Edward Krumm was at the Galway Train Station platform, behaving as you'd expect of an armed drunk Black & Tan. Seán Mulvoy and a boy, Seán Turke, confronted Krumm. Krumm was shot (dying later). Mulvoy was killed, and the young Turke escaped unharmed. A retaliatory Black & Tan rampage led to the death of Séamus Quirke.

During the platform confrontation, Mícheál Ó Droighneáin and Tom Redington were at the rear of the train, offloading rifles intended for an attack on the Spiddal RIC barracks. On 14 May 1921, Ó Droighneáin and his men did attack the Spiddal RIC.

This was a Saturday, traditionally when Spiddal farmers would stack their horse-carts tall with turf, and would proceed, very early in the morning, to the Galway market. Local people wouldn't sell turf to the RIC. So the RIC contingent, along the main road near the RIC barracks, intercepted the carts, confiscating what turf they needed. Thus, it was morning attack, that wounded two RIC officers before the IRA withdrew.

My maternal grandfather Seán Joe Caulfield drove a turf cart into Galway on many a Saturday. My mother would follow him on foot, from Boluisce Lake into Galway, with a basket of eggs on her arm.

Oral history has it that Seán Joe had a run-in with the Black & Tans. It's unclear if he was on the road to Galway on this particular Saturday.

Later that May 1921 day, lorries of Crown reinforcements (Tans) arrived, took hostages, conducted at gunpoint interrogations, beatings, and in the evening carried out the usual retribution.

Seán Joe Caulfield & His Turf Cart

Concerning that violent Saturday evening, Mícheál Ó Droighneáin noted:

They burned four houses – Eamonn Breathnach's in Sheeaun; Pádraic Costello's in Ballydonnellan, Pádraic Folan's in Salahoona, and my father's house, in which nobody had slept for some weeks. A few weeks before that, the Tans had come to the house by night, forced my father and mother, and sister, up to an upper room, and then threw a grenade into the kitchen, which smashed two windows and peppered walls and ceiling.

Mícheál Ó Droighneáin was an East Connemara IRA Brigade Commander for 1917-1921. He also describes a 12 June 1921 IRA operation at St. Joseph's Anglican Church.

There were about eight Protestant Tans in the Spiddal Barracks, and they came to Service on Sunday in the Protestant church there. This church is now a dwelling house belonging to Lord Killanin. It was remodelled. I collected most of the group I had on the 14th May. I selected a Sunday, four weeks after the first attack - 12th June [1921] I think it would be. The church was situated about three hundred yards west of Spiddal, about thirty yards in from the public road.

There was a little gate- lodge (and is still) beside the gate leading to the church. This lodge was occupied by Paddy Thornton, his mother and sister. We occupied this lodge, and had the Thornton's removed to another lodge at Lord Killanin's. Paddy was working for Killanin. We occupied the church itself, and had six men in it, under the command of Morgan Davoren. I had half a dozen others in the wood between the road and Lord Killanin's house - they were spread out at regular intervals.

I had three men west of the river, and covering the barracks. Pádraic Folan and myself were at Bohoona Cross [marked with a cross on the map, page 60], inside a loop-holed wall, which had a view of the road from the Spiddal direction. This cross was within thirty yards of the church. In this case, we were to let the Tans march on towards the church, in the gate, and close up to the church itself, before making any attack. The boys in the lodge had a couple of Mills bombs on this occasion, which they were to use. Masses in Spiddal at that time were at 8.30 and 11 o'clock. We arrived and took up our positions long before anybody came to the 8:30 Mass, so as not to be seen by anybody. The Tans came to Service usually at ten o'clock the minister coming out from Galway for the service.

To our dismay this Sunday morning, nobody turned up to the church. We stayed on. The people were arriving for the eleven o'clock Mass. We let them pass. We waited until a quarter to twelve. Then, the thought struck me that they would come, mixed up with our own congregation coining from Mass. So, to avoid this, I came out, and gave the order to withdraw. It was at four o'clock p.m. that Sunday, the Minister came out from Galway for his service, and he didn't stop at Spiddal, but went on to Tully first, and afterwards came back to Spiddal to conduct the service. When the Protestant members of the barracks opened the church, they noticed the sign of occupation, and there was consternation among them, to see how near they went to being trapped. They examined the place all around, saw the loopholes in the wall at Bohoona Cross, but never found out anything about the occupation of the lodge.

Eventually, St Joseph's closed, and the Morrises converted it into a 2-story residence. When Martin Morris provided the land, a possible stipulation was that the property would revert to the Morris family if it ceased to be used for religious purposes.

RCB records for Killannin Parish reference a "Preacher's Book" (1902-1922), and some "Miscellanous Loose Papers" for 1917-1927, but not later.

In the 1901 Census, there were several National School teachers in Spiddal, including Peter Greany. The oral history is that Peter Greany and the parish priest were maneuvered into conflict. But the parish priest had dictatorial control over the teachers and the school. There was no way for Peter Greany to win. It's said that Greany moved a bit west, and rented the recently converted house from the Morrises. When this happened is unclear. It seems he felt a deep attachment to St Colmcille of Iona, and referred to the property as Iona House. Peter Greany died in March 1932, at Ard na Gréine, up Baile Eamonn. There may be another place with that name, over by Furbo.

Taking the stories at face value, all this suggests the Morris family converted the church into a residence sometime after 1922, but before 1932, possibly ca 1928.

Redmond Morris kindly provided records that reveal what actually happened. In April 1928, the Church of Ireland (CoI) sold the property to Peter Greaney for £80, stipulating that he demolish the church within six months of purchase. Instead it seems he converted the church into a residence ca 1928. Perhaps just demolishing the belfry was enough to placate or mislead the Church of Ireland. Peter Greaney's spouse, Elizabeth, died in March 1934 in Iona House. In late October 1949, two Greaney daughters sold the property to the third Lord Kilannin for £1250. Thus, just about a century after Martin Morris provided land for a church, the property ended up back in Morris hands.

The Great Famine Era Along Cois Fharraige

Farming, raising livestock, and fishing were well known activities along Cois Fharraige. Another source of unsteady income would come from salvage and plunder. Over the years, ships were always getting into distress around Spiddal. There is an 1821 report of tobacco bales washing ashore from Spiddal to Costello, from a distressed smuggling vessel.

Stealing seaweed was profitable, as long as you weren't caught. The Spiddal Petty Sessions of 29 May 1843 reported, during a three-week absence of Andrew Blake, the organised plunder by boat, of seaweed belonging to him and his Furbo tenants. Blake and his tenants appeared to prosecute sixteen individuals, "travellers," for the theft. The "travellers" were too busy to attend the session. But they did send their solicitor, Michael Nevin, Esq., to represent them. The Court was unanimous, fining each offender 6s plus 20s costs, or alternatively, one month's imprisonment with hard labor.

Creatures with salvage value got into distress:

Provincial Intelligence

An enormous dead whale, 157 feet in length, was stranded at the
Spiddal coast, Galway, calculated to be worth £1,000, but before
Mr [Peter] Comyn, on whose property if floated in, had been aware of it,
the country people had it nearly cut up and taken away.

Statesman and Dublin Christian Record
8 Dec 1843

The Galway Vindicator reported the whale was worth £1200, was in 14 feet of water, and was pretty much stripped by the local people before Peter Comyn caught on. When was the last time a 157 foot (48 meter) long whale was gliding around Galway Bay?

Cois Fharraige residents had a liberal concept of salvage, that differed from that of 'The Admiralty.' One person's salvage was plunder to the Admiralty. On 12 December 1844, the Swedish vessel *Svea* wrecked off Spiddal. It seemed to be carrying casks and cotton. John Thornton, Michael Conneely, Michael Feeny, Patrick Faherty, and Mathias Donoghoe were charged with plundering the ship and its cargo. There was a Patrick Concannon involved who was prosecuted in absentia, in the Spiddal Petty Sessions, in early March 1845. The rest were tried in the Galway Assizes in late March 1845. Constable Jamison provided eyewitness testimony.

There was an interesting complication. It seems the ship's agents hired a Galway person as their local agent, who, in turn, hired the above men. For some of the time the men were onboard, they were working on behalf of the ship's agent. On other occasions when they were onboard, they might have been working on behalf of themselves. What's not to like?

When the witness Constable Jamison was cross-examined, the reporter wrote: "...Witness never was a dancing-master; did not come here to teach the prisoners the polka, but to prosecute them."

I don't know about the polka, but the jig was up when Martin Morris Esq testified to the excellent character of some of the men, whom he knew for forty years. It took the jury a few minutes to acquit.

A book, *An Irishman And His Family; Lord Morris and Killanin,* by Maud Anna Morris Wynne, published in 1937, has some anecdotes about Martin Morris. It was said "he could lift the kitchen table with his teeth." According to Wynne, a ram was being delivered, in the usual Irish fashion, by tossing it out of a boat near the Spiddal shore. However, the ram got confused and headed in the general direction of the Aran Islands. Martin Morris swam out into Galway Bay to retrieve it. I hope he didn't use his teeth. Sounds like a man who wasn't easily intimidated.

About £1800 worth of cargo was salvaged and auctioned off on 7 January 1845. Including 120 barrels of rosin, 60 barrels of turpentine, ca 2300 oak staves, 2.5 tons of undressed damp whalebone, and 250 damaged cotton bales. I wondered why local people were carving out hunks of cotton from the bales rather than just hauling them away. It turns out a bale weighted about 428 lbs. Presumably when dry. The Galway merchants seem to have prevailed over some Englishmen who also attended the auction.

On 26 Sept 1846, the schooner Lyra was stranded at Spiddal while transporting wheat, shipped by Henry Comerford Esq, of Galway. The salvage claims section of the Admiralty Court met on 27 Sept 1846, to consider several salvage claims:

ADMIRALTY COURT, GALWAY
Salvage Claims
........Amongst several others, the following claims were read over;----

Peter S. Comyn, P.P. [??]	£ 167
Rev. Francis Kenny, P.P.	300
Sylvanus Jones, R.M.	8

On the claim of Peter S. Comyn, Esq., being called. Mr. Comyn came forward and stated he wished it to be particularly understood that he did not make any claim upon his own part of the services rendered, but upon the part of his tenants, whose services he believed would not be disputed. His dog, "Jack" had performed some good, and the insurance company recognised it by giving him an embossed silver collar, and his tenants freely gave up their claim for a sum 30l, 10l. of which he paid to one of them, Mr. MacDonagh, and the remaining 20l, amongst the men generally..........

About the time of the GV, Henry Comerford owned five townlands in Kilcummin Civil Parish, covering Lettermullan, Furnace Island, and a number of other isles, and two townlands in Killannin, part of hundreds if not thousands of acres he held in Galway and Clare. In 1857, Sir William Gregory (second wife, in 1880, Isabella Augusta Persse; Lady Gregory) sold his indebted Kinvara estate to Henry Comerford. This is the Gregory of the infamous quarter-acre 'Gregory Clause.' Briefly put, no workhouse admittance for you if you rented more than a quarter-acre. Over time, Comerford doubled and tripled the rents, impoverishing many.

A blurb appeared in the Galway Vindicator, called "*A SHIP IN DANGER—CANINE SAGACITY.*" It explained that Peter Sarsfield Comyn's dog 'Jack' swam out to the Lyra wreck. The Captain somehow attached to Jack a letter detailing the ship's precarious situation. Jack then swam back through the raging surf to his master. Jack deserved more than a dog collar.

The Court ruled that the Resident Magistrate (R.M.), Sylvanus Jones, in two visits to the site, was acting in an official capacity, and was entitled to nothing.

A representative of the Lyra's owners claimed that, in keeping his parishioners in line, the Rev Kenny was merely doing his job as parish priest, and therefore wasn't entitled to £300. It was admitted that some token remuneration would be appropriate, and was left for the Court to ascertain. The justices awarded the Rev Francis Kenny £20.

Now we'll come ashore. The 21 Nov 1845 edition of the Freeman's Journal contained agricultural reports from all over Ireland. For Spiddal we have:

THE POTATO CROP ---LATEST INTELLIGENCE
(FROM THE CORRESPONDENTS OF THE FREEMAN.)

Spiddal, county Galway, Nov 1845

I walk daily some villages to have personal information. I examine with my own hands the potatoes. Some villages are as yet free from the rot, as far as the cup potatoes are concerned; but one-half of the lumper potatoes, which are, alas ! Too generally sown, I much fear is lost already, and such as are pitted are also rotting in the pits.----I was not very uneasy until I heard this, thinking that from the immense quantity of potatoes set this year that it would be impossible for the poor not to have a reasonable supply; but when I find them rotting to the pits after digging them,

I am not without serious apprehension for the future, particularly so when the oats is all going to the rents, which are more *cruelly exacted* in this part of the world, by an *excoriating agent*, than in any part of the country.

This last sentence is a swipe at James Blake of Tully, agent for his nephew Patrick Blake of Gortnamona and Tully.

Hely Dutton, in his 1824 *Statistical and Agricultural Survey of Co Galway*, noted:

Lumpers are much used, as they are more productive from a little manure than any other kind, but they are a wretched kind for any human creature; even pigs, I am informed, will not eat them if they can get any other kind. Cups are in great estimation, as they stay long in the stomach, of course require strong powers of digestion, especially as they are usually dressed by the country people 'with a bone in them'...

By 1846, the Rev John O'Grady had mounted his public campaign on behalf of his parishioners:

DEATHS FROM STARVATION

The Rev John O'Grady, P. P., Spiddal co. Galway gives the following state of his parish in a letter to his Excellency and Lord Lieutenant:--

I must confine myself to facts, and assure you that starvation, the consequence of untimely legislative interference, has set in, by consigning already two of my parishioners to a premature grave. One has left a widower and four helpless children in extreme necessity, and the other is equally circumstanced, both of whom would have been alive this day, had they the mere necessities of life to support them in their distress.

I have this moment three hundred families without any means of subsistence, and unless the kind landlords who have given their tenants some meal for the past month, continue their charitable course the two ensuing months, I can, alas I without fear of contradiction, assure your Excellency, that tens and twenties of my poor people will suffer the penalty of starvation.

I have received this week £30 from the kind dispensers of the Indian Relief Fund, which has enabled me to give employment to one hundred persons three days of this week, and to an equal number the other three days----leaving the third hundred unemployed, to the mercy of God.

The very best efforts of landlords will not be able, without the powerful and immediate assistance of government, to relieve us. I can assure your Excellency, that not one of the above had any means of subsistence either for themselves or families this week, and Providence alone, under such painful circumstances, is the best judge of how they could eke out a miserable existence, were it not for the timely supply I got from the charitable Indian Fund dispensers, to whom individually and collectively, I return my best thanks. * * * No words can adequately express the distress of my poor people, who are pledging [to the pawn shop] their blankets, their clothes, and every portable article they have, to enable them to live a few days!

Drogheda Argus and Leinster Journal
13 June 1846

Although addressed to the Lord Chancellor and the Lord Lieutenant, O'Grady had a wider audience in mind. Letters and articles in the newspapers influenced public opinion, and thus could be used to pressure the authorities, and raise money. Eventually the pawn shops had so many blankets that they stopped accepting them. Blankets that might have harboured disease carrying vermin, and smallpox.

A dispatch from "Costello Bridge," in the *Galway Mercury and Connaught Weekly Advertiser* on August 22, 1846, described the sudden death of Thomas Folan of the village of "Bontragh, near Tully," attributed to malnourishment. A subscription was started to defray his burial expenses. He was one of the public works laborers who had just been informed by the Board of Works that their 10d a day wages were being reduced to 8d a day. Some went on strike. But they had little leverage.

The correspondent continued: "As in other parts of the country, the rot in the potato crop had destroyed almost every field between this and Spiddal, so that you need expect no supplies from the west of Galway. Heaven only knows where this will end." By the end of August, the public works programs across Ireland were suspended, only to be reinstated later as conditions worsened.

There was a June 1846 newspaper advertisement: "A Medical Superintendent is advertised for the Dispensary at Spiddal, Galway. Salary £80 per annum." Thus Spiddal had a dispensary during the Great Famine. In January 1922, the advertised salary was "£220 per annum."

As the Great Famine progressed, the opinion, across the Irish Sea in London, was that famine relief expenses should be borne, to the greatest extent possible, by the Irish themselves. Initially relief was financed via the poor-rate, which proved insufficient, requiring the imposition of an additional levy on Irish tenants and landlords, via the Labour-Rate Act (1846), to support infrastructure projects. A jobs program. See *A History of the Irish Poor Law* by Sir George Nicholls. He wrote about this act, which

made a local charge, to be defrayed by a rate levied and assessed in a manner similar to the poor-rate, which makes the landlord liable for the whole on tenements under 4ʟ, yearly value, and for half the rate on tenements valued above that amount.

For 1842, Nicholls noted that 630,272 Irish tenements were rated under £5, a further 504,301 holdings were valued between £5 and £50, while 46,565 tenements were valued above £50. The £4 liability threshold in the 1846 Act shifted a significant new tax burden onto landlords. This must have started them thinking about how to rid themselves of these tenants, if they weren't already thinking about that.

On Monday 12 October 1846, the Moycullen Presentation Session occurred, under the auspices of the "Labour Rate Act", and was reported on by the Galway Mercury on 17 Oct 1846: "…...the Magistrates and Cess-payers assembled in large numbers to determine on what Public Works of a reproductive nature could be approved of, for the purpose of affording employment to the poor people......"

A who's who of the gentry was present, including Martin Morris, Francis and Peter S Comyn, and the various Blakes. A large contingent of clergy was also present, including John O'Grady and Francis Kenny, along with several thousand "peasants" gathered outside. The meeting was chaired by Robert Martin Esq of Ross. £40,000 was to be apportioned across the EDs of the Moycullen Barony. At the end of the day, the Killannin ED was to receive £12,271 17s 6d. A unanimously passed resolution, to be forwarded to the Lord Lieutenant, pleaded for food depots for "Outerard, Spiddal, and Lettermore."

Townland populations were plunging. The Spiddal West population decline (see page 7) was stunning, nearly a factor of three decline. There were exceptions. The census data shows a 54% Spiddal East population increase from 1841 to 1851. Presumably as those nearby evicted or afflicted sought refuge with extended family? This exacerbated the deprivation in Spiddal East. A few weeks after the Presentation Session, from Spiddal House on 30 October 1846, Thomas Bunbury was writing to the British Prime Minister, Lord John Russell, pleading in vain for additional famine relief for Spiddal East. A Bunbury letter to the Prime Minister, via the Dublin press and especially the London press, to the extent it aroused public indignation, might have been more effective. Wishful thinking on my part, likely.

Collecting the various rates, used by the Poor Law Unions to finance famine relief, was a challenge. The 1847 *Thirteenth Annual Report of the Poor Law Commissioners* (see Appendix XIV) has a table summarizing the all-Ireland monthly returns of the poor-rate collection, from March 1846 through March 1847. Over that period, the Poor Law Unions' net balance went from a positive £52,115 to a negative £4619.

The worst year of the Great Famine is said to be 1847, "the Black '47", and the Poor Law Union financial situation would only get worse. For March 1847, across Ireland, the tax collectors were collecting 17% of what was actually due. In months to come the shortfall would be even worse. In the third week of March 1848, the Galway tax collector Pat Martin collected £40, and left £3476 uncollected. Pat collected one per cent of what was due, and the Dublin authorities were not happy. As we'll see shortly, this was the least of Pat's troubles.

On 28 September 1847, the *Dublin Evening Packet* published a letter from Thomas Bunbury, where he advocated for the establishment of a fishermen's organization and fishery pier somewhere along the coast. He alluded to the local gentry indifference to supporting a new Cois Fharraige harbour.

Alexander Nimmo stated, in his account of the Spiddal pier construction in 1822, that some gentry reneged on their promises of financial support. Perhaps Bunbury's appeal would have been more effective had he pledged a nominal sum. To be fair, he and his wife were involved with flax production and the weaving efforts in Spiddal. Their main estate (Lisbryan House) was in Tipperary, and they seemed to summer in Spiddal.

Much tension existed between the Catholic and Anglican clerics. But, they could cooperate, as indicated by an account of a 3 February 1847 meeting of the Spiddal Relief Committee, and the November 1847 Killannin Fever Hospital Committee letter (upcoming).

For the 3 Feb 1847 Spiddal Relief Committe meeting, the RC parish priests John O'Grady and Francis Kenny were present, along with Anglican clerics John Cather and Mr. Ferrock. I'd assumed the Capt Hutcheson mentioned was the Spiddal RIC man, although now I wonder if he is actually Dr Hutchinson, an area physician during the Great Famine, a military doctor perhaps.

The issue of the Blakes (of Tully) interfering with the Relief Committee efforts out in Tully provoked "warm words" between John O'Grady and James Blake, that resulted in the raucous meeting being abruptly adjourned. Andrew Blake of Furbo, a member of the Committee, was unable to attend that day. It might have been all the more exciting had he been present. Part of the Blake interference included the son of Mr James Blake, assaulting people out by Tully. I have no evidence that the son was prosecuted.

Father John O'Grady was indefatigable on behalf of the Spiddal area famine victims. O'Grady's Spiddal assignment was nearly over. In late Feb 1847, a few weeks after the boisterous Spiddal Relief Committee meeting, Archbishop MacHale announced the Rev John O'Grady's transfer to the "united parishes of Moinvea and Abbeyknockmoy." Curious timing. Andrew Blake was Catholic gentry, and rather disliked O'Grady. One wonders to what extent Andew Blake, or someone else, was whispering in the Archbishop's ear about getting John O'Grady transferred, to pastures elsewhere.

O'Grady's replacement was to be the Rev John McCullagh, the past curate of Carnacon, Co Mayo. The Rev Francis Kenny overlapped the Rev John O'Grady in 1846, and remained in Spiddal Village into 1848. He continued O'Grady's efforts to publicise the Spiddal area residents' plight. This involved letter writing campaigns as well as testifying at government hearings.

Surprisingly, in his history of Irish Poor Law, Sir George Nicholls stated (page 340): "The harvest of 1847 proved to be a good one. Contrary to expectation the potato crop was free from disease...." But, so few seed potatoes went in the ground that, at harvest, potato prices were exorbitant, beyond the reach of the peasants, especially those in the west of Ireland.

Those along Cois Fharraige in late 1847 might have objected to Sir George's harvest assessment. Documentation exists about conditions in the Spiddal area for the autumn of 1847. On 18 Nov 1847, the Committee of the Killanin Board of Health wrote to the Poor Law Inspector Capt Hellard:

I am directed by the Committee of the Killanin Board of Health, to forward to you for your consideration and assistance, the following resolution passed by them this day :--- Resolved that, we behold with the utmost sorrow and dismay, the fearful return of famine and disease to this destitute district, visiting in their destructive career, not only their former surviving victims, but hundreds besides, who had hitherto escaped their dreadful influence.

......No language can express, and the mind can scarce conceive, the awful privations which more than half our population are now calmly and patiently enduring; one well-known but melancholy fact will sufficiently describe their sad condition; that is, that we are fully assured, that many families are at this moment endeavouring to prolong a miserable existence, on one meal a-day of turnips alone, plundered sometimes at the risk of their lives, from the gardens of their more fortunate neighbours. Human life cannot be long sustained by such precarious and deplorable subsistence...............

A. W. Blake, Esq., Chairman.
Rev. James Macready.
Rev. Francis Kennelly, P.P [Spiddal]
Rev. John M'Cullogh, P.P. [Knock]

The Committee of the Killannin Board of Health consisted of the Spiddal area Anglican and Catholic clergy, chaired by Andrew W Blake of Furbo. Francis Kennelly is Francis Kenny.

This letter prompted Capt Hellard to travel to Spiddal and points west to see the situation for himself. He described what he found to "Count" Strzelecki, a British humanitarian aid official.

Captain Hellard to Count Strzelecki :--November 30, 1847.

Having been directed by letter of the 23rd instant, to report upon the accompanying resolution of the Killanur Board of Health, I acquaint you, that upon inquiry along that line of coast, more particularly in the neighbourhood of Spiddal, I found a great deal of distress, there being, I may say, little or no work for the peasantry in that locality, consequently poverty must exist. On the estate of Tully, nine miles west of Spiddal, I was informed by James Blake, Esq., J. P., that he had employment for the tenantry, at which they could earn from 8d. to 9d. per day, but that they positively refused to work, " stating that they were waiting for the public roads to be commenced," which was fully corroborated by Patrick M'Nalty, steward on the estate, who also stated that the men were then idle at home, and would not hear of coming to work, although frequently requested by him to do so;..............

Shortly, an Inverin man, John Costello, will testify that James Blake was actually paying much less.

The 11 Dec 1847 edition of the Galway Vindicator reported on a meeting on the Galway Workhouse conditions, held earlier in the week. Dr Browne reported that 106 people were in hospital. Seventeen had "Fever," seventy-two had "dysentry," and seventeen had other diseases. There were no deaths from fever that week, but four from "dysentry," and six children died from other causes. On 15 Dec 1847, Capt Hellard, the Poor Law Officer, stated there were 160 people in hospital that day.

A 2 June 1847 Central Board of Health certificate authorised 40 beds, 2 nurses, and one ward-maid for a Spiddal Fever Hospital. It opened on 25 Aug 1847. Andew Blake was requesting additional beds in early December 1847.

A letter from the Poor Law Commissioners was read. It contained a reference from the Board of Health of the Killannin district about the "erection of several additional beds for the hospital." This is the Spiddal hospital. The Commissioners wanted additional information before approving the request. At this point, Mr Martin (of Ross) said that

..........although he held a considerable portion of property in the district, he should confess that was the first intimation he got of such being in existence.

He was not alone singular in this respect as there was a great portion of the district to which he belonged ignorant of it. He wished to know where it was situated?

The Chairman said it was located in Spiddal.

Mr A. W. Blake (Furbo) expressed his surprise at Mr Martin who had a considerable property in that district being ignorant of the existence of a fever hospital in it. It was established on the 25th of August last, and had afforded a great supply of relief as was well known to the gentlemen connected with it. It was situate a little beyond Spiddal, and was doing an immense service in that district. After some conversation between Mr. Martin and Mr. Blake the subject then dropped.

A week later, on 15 Dec 1847, was the weekly meeting of the Galway Board of Guardians:

Mr A. W. Blake submitted an account of the number of persons relieved at the Killanin temporary fever hospital, and after some observations on the subject concluding by moving the extra beds, to the number of 70, be supplied to the western district—that is 10 for Spiddal and the remaining 60 for other temporary fever hospitals of the district.

Mr Blake's report after a short conversation was agreed to.

The Spiddal Fever Hospital required about £75 for the month of December 1847. The facility didn't stay open all that long, closing I suspect by the end of 1848.

There is also oral history that Bohoona Lodge had a sort of annex, roughly a kilometer west of the Lodge. I'm tempted to say that if you found yourself out there, you probably weren't on the Morris A-list. One story has it that a Morris guest there, observing the local boats out on Galway Bay (the location is elevated), made an unkind remark, and promptly choked on a morsel of food.

It's logical to suspect that this building, between Salahoona and Creduff Villages, was Martin Morris's sick house. The boundary between Creduff and Salahoona Villages qualifies as being "a little beyond Spiddal." I believe the "Killanin temporary fever hospital" occupied Martin Morris's old sick house.

We have James Kelly's August 1853 data for the buildings at the Salahoona-Creduff boundary. These seem to be the only suitable structures "situate a little beyond Spiddal."

Former Spiddal Fever Hospital -- August 1853

Structure	Quality	Length (ft)	Breadth (ft)	Height (ft)	Valuation		
					£	s	d
(Vacant) House	1C+	42	23.6	15.6	5	4	2
Kitchen	2C+	17.6	32	7.6	1	5	8

He referred to the first structure as a vacant house, and to the second structure as a kitchen. It was a large kitchen. For "Quality", "C" is okay, but...not the best. "1" means a slate roof, "2" is thatch.

James Kelley made no reference to a hospital. I'm convinced the vacant house was the hospital, and so I've indicated that in titling the previous table. When the GV assessors subdivided the Bohoona West townland, for their accounting convenience (Version 1 of their maps), they singled out this area.

There is oral history of a 'soup kitchen' in Salahoona, with the assumption being it was in the village, where the brothers Patrick and Eamonn Keady had their holdings.

But we know that possibly hundreds of people could show up, and so you want the soup boiler to be away from your residence. James Kelly's "kitchen" was large enough to be functioning as a 'soup kitchen', and was located in between the concentrations of houses in Salahoona and Creduff Villages. The possible proximity of a soup kitchen to a fever hospital would have been its own (possibly unrecognised) public health issue.

The oral history also has it that, south of the buildings in the previous table, and south of the Coast Road, was a doctor's office. Not too close to the fever hospital. The Spiddal physician was a Dr Hutchinson, who attended the Spiddal patients and compounded medicines for both the Spiddal and Moycullen hospitals. On 24 February 1848, Major M'Kie wrote to the Commissioners stating that for part of February, Dr Hutchinson was ill. Dr Hutchinson would also visit the Moycullen Hospital. It seems that, for a time, the Moycullen facility lacked a full time doctor.

There is a reference to a Dr Thomas L Whistler in the area during the Great Famine, and there is the Dr Thomas Whistler who served the Spiddal area in 1831 (page 42). A newspaper remark has convinced me that they are son and father, respectively. In late 1849, an esteemed Dr Whistler was in Oranmore, about to transfer to Bray. I don't believe the father was alive when the Great Famine arrived.

A significant number of the afflicted who entered the sick house, and later the fever hospital, never walked out. The surrounding land is a de-facto graveyard. The oral history is grim. Having closed sometime in 1848, it is no surprise the buildings were vacant in 1853. I'm not sure they were ever occupied again. As memory faded, I suspect the stone was nicked to build other structures. Little of the sick house remains, with nothing to indicate what it once was. Some local lore has this building as older than Bohoona Lodge (ca 1800).

Sick House / Fever Hospital

There is a cillín nearby, west of the fever hospital, in a sandy strand on Galway Bay. One wonders if, in desperate times, fever victims might have been interred in the sandy soil there.

A mid-December 1847 meeting of the Galway Guardians had an accounting of the Galway Workhouse situation.

There were 1277 paupers resident, each costing the Poor Law Union 1s 6d per week. In the previous week, 46 paupers had been discharged and 9 died. There were 300 people awaiting admission, most evicted from Lettermore the previous week. They arrived on 11 boats that sailed from Lettermore.

For the upcoming week, the Galway Workhouse management was expecting to need:

5000lbs of bread; 26lbs of cocoa; 200lbs of meat; 3360 lbs of Indian meal; 2000 quarts of buttermilk; 900 hundred quarts of sweetmilk; 4lbs of tobacco; 5 boats of turf; 3 tons of coal; 56 lbs of candles; 112lbs of soap; 7lbs of tea; 170 lbs of sugar; 168lbs of rice.

One of the Guardians, Martin Morris, objected to giving the paupers tobacco. Dr Browne said that it was absolutely necessary, for the medicinal needs of the asthmatic patients! Some other Guardians also objected, but then another Guardian, Mr Ireland, observed; "what use had they in a doctor if they were not to be guided by his advice." Assuming it was good advice. Martin Morris withdrew his motion, and so the asthmatics got their medicinal tobacco.

From the provision list, we see the importance of bread. Henry Comerford's wheat on the Lyra, grown in East Galway and also (likely) in Clare, was destined for the Liverpool market. In the midst of the Great Famine, Galway was exporting wheat and other grains to Britain. Tables in the *Statistics of Ireland* section of the 1850 Thom's Irish Almanac (pages 159 & 161) indicate that, for 1845, tens of million bushels of grain crossed the Irish Sea from Ireland to England, while tens of million pounds of butter were imported into just Liverpool from Ireland.

The British government export data in the Thom's tables likely understated the actual amount of Irish exports to Britain. Irish livestock and meat exports to Britain were also significant. Much grain that remained in Ireland didn't make it into the food markets, for it was brewed/distilled into alcoholic drinks, consumed in Ireland and exported to Britain. Any potential Exchequer intervention, to retain some would-be Irish agricultural exports meant for Britain, represented a potential disruption of the British food supply chain. Ireland was Britain's granary, dairy, brewery, and distillery. Proposals existed to import grain; perhaps wheat from Odesa, that required special milling, or possibly Egyptian wheat, after the inferior mud-laced grain was cleaned and milled in Malta. It's all rather incongruous.

The potato blight afflicted continental Europe too. Consequently, unprocessed corn (maize) was imported from the USA by a number of European countries. As the Great Famine progressed, eventually the European demand for American corn exceeded the available export supply. Early on, the British authorities complained that the imported corn had to to be twice ground in the stone mills to be palatable. The limited milling capability in Ireland was largely committed to private enterprise. Thus much imported corn was ground in British government facilities. Transporting corn to Britain, to be milled around Britain and at Malta, and then transported to Ireland, was a tremendous logistical problem. Early in 1848, there were discussions about French hand-operated corn-mills for Galway.

It was decided that it wasn't absolutely necessary to mill the corn. The suggestion was to boil the corn (uncrushed was okay) for an hour or so. However corn treated this way was still hard, sharp, and minimally digestible. Consuming it caused painful gastro-intestinal distress and intestinal damage.

Nixtamalizing corn, by soaking the kernels in a warm calcium hydroxide solution, softens the kernels, and makes them much more palatable. Lye will work too. This processing dramatically increases the corn's nutritional (niacin) value, while it dramatically reduces mycotoxin levels. Corn on the stalk is attacked by molds (Aspergillus for example), that produce mycotoxins (eg aflatoxin), some of which are carcinogenic. Flour (Masa Harina) and dough (Masa) can be made from nixtamalized corn.

European explorers (including Columbus) were aware of nixtamalization, but spurned it. Extreme niacin deficiency, called pellagra, was oftentimes fatal. The over-reliance on unprocessed corn was a scourge in 18th Century Spain and 19th Century Italy (especially in Lombardy and Veneto) and in 20th Century America. At various times in these places, corn became a near mono-culture. The Italian peasants called pellagra *mal del padrone* (the boss's disease). In the American South, from 1900 to 1950, 87,000 individuals died from pellagra. Indigenous Central Americans relied heavily on nixtamalized corn, and largely avoided niacin deficiency, pellagra, and gastric issues.

It's not clear that pellagra was a significant issue in Ireland.

By 4 July 1848, Americans had donated in excess of 9900 tons of food to Ireland. Some fraction of that included barrels of hominy; nixtamalized corn.

That this simple extraordinarily beneficial procedure wasn't more widely appreciated was a tragedy.

Initially, bread, baked under contract to the workhouse by Galway bakers, was distributed. Following the example of other <u>Unions</u>, by early 1848 it was decided that it was more economical to bake the bread in a (to be) newly installed <u>workhouse oven</u>, once the Galway Workhouse's contract with the bakers expired in late March 1848. The bread's composition changed as well, presumably due to the high cost of wheat.

Some <u>directives</u> specified 'breads' of just rye, or rye with maize or barley etc. By April 1848, the Galway Vice-Guardians seemed to have settled on a bread composed of Indian corn meal, rye meal, and barley meal. Across Ireland, innovative <u>bread baking</u> occurred. There was a bread made of oatmeal and parsnips. A Viennese recipe, using wheat and beet-root, "was successfully tried in Dublin, and is excellent." It sounds somewhat more appealing than oatmeal and parsnips.

The Guardians and the Poor Law Commissioners sparred over the latter's insistence that the paupers be given "cooked" food. The implication for remote sites (Spiddal) was that supplies would be ferried out to sites where the food would be prepared. For Spiddal, likely the Coast Guard Station. Of course, one already prepared (baked) food item transported out to the remote areas was bread.

About the soup, during the 3 February 1847 Spiddal Relief Committee meeting, there was mention of (soup) boilers without much detail. The standard boiler used by British troops was eight gallons, much too small to be useful. After <u>discussions</u> between Dublin Castle and the Exchequer, the chosen standard boiler was to be cast iron with a one hundred gallon capacity. There seemed to be intermediate sized boilers around.

The Spiddal-Galway parish priest testified at the 15 Dec 1847 Guardians meeting:

The Rev Mr Kenny addressed the Board at some length on the state of the district with which he was connected.

He represented its poverty in glowing terms, and concluded by imploring of the Guardians in the name of charity, in the name of humanity and justice, to provide some extra accommodation for the famine stricken poor is his, as well as every other pauperised district in the Union.

Mr. A. W. Blake bore testimony to Mr. Kenny's statement, and said that no man had a better opportunity of knowing the distress and poverty that prevailed in the Spiddal district, than what the Rev. Mr. Kenny had.

The Rev. Mr. Kenny's observation made a deep impression on the minds of the Board, and a committee was therefore appointed to provide the most suitable accommodation, as an auxiliary workhouse for the purpose. Captain Hillard and Doctor Browne were requested to accompany the committee in the selection of a house.

The Rev Kenny got on with Andrew W Blake Esq much better than John O'Grady did. Three months later, on 15 March 1848, the Rev Kenny was back before the Vice-Guardians. The previous week, 33 workhouse occupants died, a significant increase over Dec 1847.

The workhouse master's provision request for the coming week was similar to the previous December. There were some changes. He wanted not five boats of turf, but twenty boats, and two bottles of wine. And a bottle of Malaga too. I don't think Capt Hellard had a high opinion of the Master and Matron of the Galway Workhouse. Before judging them too harshly, ask if you would want the job.

The Rev Kenny was lamenting the dire situation in Spiddal. He mentioned that many entire families had contracted fever, and that the day before, he administered last rites to an entire family. He was requesting that a week's worth at a time of dry food, meat, and bread be sent out to Spiddal.

Capt S Hellard (aka Hilliard or Hillard) was <u>writing</u> to the Poor Law Commissioners on 19 Dec 1847:

WITH reference to a former report, I beg leave to acquaint you that the resident magistrate yesterday committed 92 persons to gaol for a month each for begging, the majority of whom are from Connemara, and in the greatest possible distress, it appearing that these unfortunate people committed the offence in order to be sent to prison, after being refused admission to the Union workhouse for want of room.

This of itself should induce the Guardians (if anything will) to immediately carry into effect the 1st section of the Extension Act, and thus make room for the able-bodied within the walls of the workhouse.

That admissions refusal left Capt Hellard vexed at the Galway Poor Law Guardians, whom he considered to be defying the law. The workhouse would reach capacity daily, and hundreds could be turned away. By late December 1847, things were coming to a head with some of the Galway Guardians, versus the Poor Law Commisioners and Capt Hellard. In their 22 December 1847 resolution, Lord Wallscourt stated to Capt Hellard:

........-- Sir,--"Take notice that, at the request of several of the Poor Law Guardians,........, I shall feel bound to move on Wednesday the 5th day of January next--"That we withdraw ourselves from the duties of this Board, and call on the Commissioners to appoint paid Guardians.

Wallscourt

One suspects Lord Wallscourt and the above "several of the Poor Law Guardians" had enough of the criticism. On 28 December 1847, at Capt Hellard's urging, the Poor Law Commissioners issued a decree dissolving the Galway Board of Guardians. So Lord Wallscourt, you can't resign, because you're dismissed.

Joseph Henry Blake (1797-1849), was the third Baron Wallscourt of Ardfry (near Oranmore). The late genealogist _Leo van de Pas_ noted the third Baron had great physical strength, and was a boxer, now and then prone to somewhat demented and violent behavior. I wonder if the third Baron ever sparred with the bully Arthur Blake, the pugilist son of James Blake of Tully. I'd have paid to see that.

The third Baron liked to roam naked about his manor house, carrying a cowbell that alerted the servants of his approach. Who better to help oversee the Galway Workhouse?

Sympathetic to socialism and the French Revolution of 1848, the third Baron died in Paris in May 1849, of cholera. The National Galleries of Scotland have a mezzotint <u>portrait</u> of the third Baron's wife Elizabeth (Locke), Lady Wallscourt. She is radiant, seated and extravagantly clothed, plucking the strings of a guitar. No cowbell for her. Apparently, she made the naked Baron carry the cowbell around the manor house. The story goes that she divorced the third Baron.

The third Baron was succeeded by his son, _Erroll Augustus Joseph Henry Blake_ (1841-1918), the fourth Baron Wallscourt, who died in Monte Carlo. The fourth Baron's second wife hocked the manor house's roofing lead to finance her gambling addiction.

The fifth Baron was Charles William Joseph Henry Blake (1875-1920). He lamented that, while born with a title, he lacked the income required to maintain proper appearances. He was a broke alcoholic gambler when he went *d.s.p.* in 1920. The peerage went extinct. In 1921 in Brighton, his widow poisoned herself. Factoring in the Blakes of Gortnamona and Tully, it seems that some of Caddell's descendants were in decline. In 1950, three of the fourth Baron's granddaughters, known locally as "the three gay mice," legally reclaimed the manor house and 33 acres of the estate. Later, the house figured in the movie; *The Mackintosh Man.*

Let's return to the relative sanity of the Galway Workhouse. In 1847 the category of outdoor relief was created, to be provided outside the walls of the workhouse. A number of criteria had to be satisfied to obtain aid. Relief was provided to widows with two or more legitimate children.

One of Capt Hellard's objections to how the Guardians ran the Galway Workhouse was the presence within of the aged, orphans, and a number of widows each with one child. Their presence meant that the "able-bodied" men were turned away. He asked the Commissioners in Dublin for authority to move the orphans and these widows and their children onto outdoor relief. The Commissioners wrote:

The Commissioners to Captain Hellard :--January 7, 1848.
In accordance with your recommendation, the Commissioners have issued an order authorising the Vice-Guardians of Galway Union to give out door relief under the second section of the Irish Poor Relief Extension Act to widows with one child, dependent on them; also to children, both of whose parents are dead.

Now Capt Hellard could move the orphans and widows out of the workhouse. Enlisting in the Royal Navy, one can imagine Samuel (I think) Hellard musing about the high-seas career ahead of him. Little could he know that, in late November 1847, he wouldn't be at sea, but would be on land, riding out west of Spiddal observing the sick, starving, and dying. Two months later, in late January 1848, Capt S Hellard of the Royal Navy wasn't writing to the Dublin Commissioners as usual, for he was on his death bed, succumbing to a "fever of very malignant character." Little could he know.

In 1847, and in 1849, other Poor Law Unions, like Galway, had their boards dissolved. But the fundamental problem remained. These unions, especially in the west, were in essence insolvent. In 1849, aid was approved for the worst off Unions, mostly in the west of Ireland. Aid that was recouped by taxing the better off Irish Unions. London was bound and determined that the Great Famine was an Irish problem, to be suffered only by the Irish.

On 29 Jan 1848, the Galway Vice-Guardians, who replaced the Galway Guardians, wrote to Dublin:

"We have to state that three of our relieving officers could not leave Galway, up to a late hour on yesterday evening, with bread for the out-door paupers in the Killannin, South Outerard, and Moycullen divisions, in consequence of their not being able to procure an escort during the day, there having been a bread cart plundered on the road leading in the same direction during the last week, and within a short distance of Galway."

How many Killannin residents received outdoor relief? For the week ending 12 February 1848, in the Galway Union, there were 8395 individuals receiving this relief, with about 20% being from Killannin. For the Galway Union, by early April, this increased to nearly 25,000 individuals. The number peaked on 1 July 1848, at 32,191 people, nearly one third of the total pre-famine Galway Poor Law Union population, declining into the autumn.

If the Killannin ED figures tracked the Galway Union behavior, then in April at least 5000 individuals across Killannin, a huge geographical area, would have received aid. At the summer peak, it's possible ca 6,500 people were receiving aid within Killannin, when the surviving civil parish population was 8,000-9,000 individuals.

In the 1841 Census, that part of the Killannin Civil Parish in the Barony of Moycullen amounted to 67,155 acres, whose few improved roads were mostly at the district's periphery. Luckily, most of the civil parish's population was at the periphery. One road is now the modern N59; from Galway to Moycullen, Rosscahill and Oughterard. There is the modern R336, running west along the coast from Galway through Spiddal, until it turns north, just southeast of Rosseveal. It's a huge area.

The Killannin ED's great extent and rough terrain necessitated further action. At the Guardians _meeting_ of 24 February 1848, the Killannin ED was split into three relief districts, each with its own relief officer (in parenthesis); Killannin South (Patrick Turke), Killannin North (Martin Griffin), and Killannin West (Francis O'Connor). I don't know the shared boundaries of these sub-divisions. Aid would be delivered to places having a RIC barracks and/or a Coast Guard Station.

In 1841, the populations of Finnaun, Letterfir, and Boliska Oughter (east of Letterfir) townlands were 3, 8, and 20 people respectively, 31 individuals in all, on 11,500 acres. It's probably safe to say that nobody was coming to help them. A swath of the Killannin Civil Parish extends northeast from Finnaun all the way to Rosscahill and Lough Corrib (see page 47). From Finnaun, the swatch remains thinly populated until it approaches Rosscahill and Lough Corrrib. Thus the "North" relief sub-division would seem to be up around Rosscahill. If "Killannin South" encompassed a good deal of Cois Fharraige, then the Lettermore/Gorumna area likely was in "Killannin West."

Delivering aid in the Lettermore vicinity was challenging, as the causeways presently out there didn't exist back then. The Gorumna to Lettermullen causeway dates to 1886, the mainland to Lettermore causeway dates to 1891, while Lettermore to Gorumna dates to 1897.

Aid for "Killannin South" might have been delivered to Loughaunbeg/Inverin and Spiddal.

Remembering the October 1846 Moycullen Presentation Session resolution (page 69) to the Lord Lieutenant, "Killannin West" likely had Lettermore as the main relief depot. From there, much aid would have been dispatched by boat.

In the last days of January 1848, the former Guardian Lord Wallscourt appeared before the Vice-Guardians, complaining about a certain Pat Martin, for a supposedly improper assessment of his estate. Poor Pat can't catch a break.

As the nonpayment of the poor-rate was a huge issue, the authorities engaged the courts. On 14 March 1848, a list was published of those to whom "professional applications" had been made. There were some familiar names on the arrears list. Peter S Comyn was down for owing £17 14s, Martin Morris £15 1s, and Patrick Blake £36 1s 11d. Lord Wallscourt was not on the list.

The tax collector Pat Martin's travails continued. In late March 1848, Major M'Kie, Capt Hellard's replacement, attended the weekly Guardian's meeting, and noticed that Pat Martin was absent. The Major would have been very interested in how much tax Pat was collecting. Pat was missing because, two days prior, he and his assistant were collecting taxes when they were severely beaten on Quay St. That may not have been the first time Pat was clobbered. Eventually Pat was authorised a constabulary escort. Pat finally caught a break. It was also publicized that the military could be summoned. Eventually they were summoned, and they did march on Spiddal.

On 13 August 1848, Major M'Kie reported to the Poor Law Commissioners on the state of the Galway Poor Law Union. From the section about crops:

Moycullen--Wheat is only grown on the southern side; small quantity; very light crop. Oats: breadth short; average crop. Barley: very little; average crop. Potatoes: great breadth; totally gone.

Killanin--Not a wheat country; but to tho north, same remark as Moycullen. Oats: small breadth; crop average. Barley: small breadth; crop average. Potatoes: considerable breadth; all blighted.

Oughticonel [Oughterard]--The same as Killanin. I may assert that this division depended entirely on the potatoes.......

All the small holders, and indeed many of the largo holders, had been impressed with the belief, that the potato disease would disappear, and speculating on that idea, they could not be persuaded to sow turnips. Another reason for rejecting this crop was, its liability to degradation, from which cause they suffered great loss last year.

Major M'Kie mentions that, in Claregalway, despite being sown three times, the green crops failed, with the turnips being destroyed by attacks of "the fly."

While all this was occurring, there were evictions. Large scale tenant evictions often caught the newspapers' notice. Isolated evictions and other landlord actions often escaped the notice of the newspapers.

Dublin Castle records contain interesting things. Lochlainn Ó Tuairisg's transcript of a 5 September 1848 letter (NAI OP 11/726), shows that Francis Comyn wrote to Dublin Castle, describing a "distress for rent" (seizure of a tenant's personal property as rent; possibly crops, likely livestock), in Loughaunbeg, that turned violent. Comyn had two men detained, and then released, after his bailiff refused to cooperate in charging the men. Comyn then dismissed his bailiff.

At Dublin Castle, Galway-born Thomas Redington, the under-secretary of state for Ireland, acknowledged the Lord Lieutenant's receipt of Comyn's September letter. Then Redington rebuked Comyn for, in essence, taking the law into his own hands. Redington wrote: "I am advised to inform you that his Excellency [the Lord Lieutenant] would have deemed it necessary to bring your conduct under the consideration of the Lord Chancellor." Comyn must have been surprised. Occasionally a gentry gentleman's comeuppance occurred.

In a much earlier 7 December 1819 letter to Dublin Castle, Laurence Comyn, Francis Comyn's father, referenced his Cois Fharraige *tenantry of the lower designation*. One wonders if Dublin Castle might have thought of the Comyns as *gentry of the lower designation.*

In mid-November 1848, a poor-rate collector and his assistant seized a group of cattle from a Spiddal townland, to satisfy an arrears. They were then set-upon by a group of Spiddal area residents who reclaimed the cattle. By the time the Spiddal RIC arrived, the men and cattle were long gone. By the end of 1848, the authorities' patience with the gentry and others in poor-rate arrears was exhausted.

On 12 December 1848, the *Southern Reporter and Cork Commercial Courier* reprinted an article:

POOR RATE COLLECTION
CRUSADE OF 1848

"Fie don't! O fie: 'tis an unweeded garden
That grows to seed, things rank and gross in nature.
Process it merely. That it should come to this ! "

Hamlet

The good work goes bravely on. In our last publication we announced,
'That Colonel Sir Michael Creagh, Bart., had arrived in town [Galway]
to superintend the collection of the Poor Rate. ' So be it.

Horse, Foot, and Artillery, Steamers, and Marines, have commenced
the crusade of 1848, by making their first 'Sortie' upon Spiddal....

Galway Vindicator
December 1848

On Thursday 7 December 1848, a force of about 112 men of the 68th (Durham) Regiment of Foot, some sailors and marines ("Gunners and Powder Monkies") from the "St Albans", about ten Dragoons, ten Constables, and a trumpeter, assembled after a 3:00 am reveille.

Under the command of Col Sir Michael Creagh, Bart., the force seemed to be organized into two columns. Along with some Galway officialdom, "twelve carts with bread, " and the Poor-Rate Collector George R M'Donnell, this "harlequin force" proceeded to Spiddal and deployed. It seems troops "escaladed" the walls surrounding the Morris estate: "The seizures for arrear of poor rate were made upon the property of Mr Martin Morris, first High Sheriff for the Town of Galway under the Corporate Reform Act....."

For the trip out to Spiddal, there is reference to a "harassing march." I take this to mean it was a very brisk pace that, along with the 3:00 am reveille, ensured the element of surprise.

It seems that the twelve carts with bread represented charity, a diversion, and the authorities' unrealistic expectation about how much they'd confiscate. Concerning what the authorities hoped to collect, there was no need for twelve carts.

The final report was that on 12 December 1848, a grand total of £6 15s 6d was realized from the auction of "three carts of barley, one of oats, and three of hay, with a few fat sheep." This from a Spiddal area raid conducted by a force exceeding 100 individuals, a disappointing result given the manpower involved.

On the gentry arrears list, the champion deadbeat was Arthur Bell Martin of Ballynahinch.
He owed £255 17s 6d. He wrote to the Guardians, stating that his tenants were in arrears, not mentioning that he was heavily mortgaged. He proposed a £30 weekly payment plan, intimating if that was unacceptable, the workhouse would be flooded with paupers (after the evictions started).

It seems the authorities felt there was still more treasure to be found in the Spiddal area. In early January 1849, Capt Hawker, Ensign Trant, and 40 men of the 68th (Durham) Regiment of Foot bivouacked in Spiddal, to assist in the collection of the "poor-rate." One newspaper lamented that such brave men were reduced to confiscating pigs and asses. At least pigs and asses (the four-legged kind) don't shoot at you.

I don't know how long they stayed in Spiddal, but I do know the 68th was enjoying the weather in Malta in February 1851, as a prelude to their later involvement in the Crimean War, during which they might have longed for Spiddal.

The injustice and resistance continued. In early January 1849, the *Galway Mercury* was reporting:

WORKING OF THE POOR LAW

A few days ago, Mr Cross, Poor-rate collector proceeded to Barna, near this town, accompanied by four bailiffs, where he succeeded in seizing some cattle for the rate.

On removing them off the land, he was attacked by a large number of men, by whom he and his men were beaten, but notwithstanding, he succeeded in removing the distress. The matter was to have come before the Petty Sessions on yesterday, but the Court was adjourned on account the County Sessions being going on.

As a poor woman who never had any land, but was in the habit of keeping heifers at grass on hire, was proceeding to this town, from near Spiddal, on Friday last, the heifers strayed into a townland that owed poor rate, and were at once seized by the collector's bailiff, and sent into Galway, where they were sold, together with two car-loads of hay, and some sheep, seized from James Blake, of Invern Lodge, Esq, and some others.

At about the same time there was a newspaper announcement: "Informations are taken at Spiddal Sessions, Galway, against Michael McDonald, poor rate collector, for trespass and illegal distress." Apparently Michael McDonald and his men were breaking into houses and stealing.

James Blake of "Invern Lodge" was the agent for his nephew, Patrick Blake of Tully and Gortnamona, who was on the poor-rate arrears list for £36 1s 11d. Thus there's a good chance the hay and sheep, seized from James Blake, actually belonged to Patrick Blake, who did owe back tax.

On 23 January 1849, the Galway Vice-Guardians, Messrs. Lucas and Fitzmaurice, filed a report with the Poor Law Commissioners. Their report led with:

> Great destitution exists in the union, especially in the western district,
> comprising the electoral divisions of Killannin, Moycullen, and Oughterard.

For the week ending on 13 January 1849, 10,898 persons received some form of workhouse relief, either indoor or outdoor (remote) relief, one-eighth of the total 1841 population. The number on relief was a much larger fraction of the surviving 1849 population. There was no regional data breakdown, but much of the relief would have been aimed at the above mentioned EDs. Their report concludes:

> The stock of potatoes in the union is very small. The later sown crop was totally destroyed.
> That portion of the early sown crop saved has not rotted to any extent; and we are led to believe that the stock of potatoes required for seed is very limited indeed.

The 5 May 1849 issue of the *Galway Mercury* discusses the Spiddal agricultural situation:

ROYAL AGRICULTURAL IMPROVEMENT SOCIETY OF IRELAND
MATHEW BOLE - GALWAY WEST
March 31, 1849

Sir...Since my arrival here I have gone over the greater part of the extensive barony of Moycullen (remaining only a day or two in each locality, in order to make known the object of my visit to the working farmers with the least possible delay), and I am glad to state that I have been everywhere well received by all classes................

Next day I proceeded to Furbough, and called on A. W. Blake, Esq, honorary secretary to the local committee,....................I was introduced by him to Martin Morris, Esq., Leneboy, and his son Michael Morris, Esq., high sheriff...

I then proceeded toward Spiddal, and found the farmers along the coast making great efforts to plant the potato; I asked many of them what they would do if the potato crop should fail this season, and the universal reply was, "If the potatoes fail this year, we have nothing to do but lie down and die."

I explained to them how they might have plenty of food, even in the absence of the potato, by cultivating peas, beans, parsnips, carrots, Swedish turnips [aka 'Swedes'], and cabbages, which would be fully as abundant and as good as their old favourite.

They were quite ignorant of any of these crops, except turnips and cabbages, which they said were very good; and one of them described his turnips to have grown as big as his fist and as thick as potatoes on the ridge last year.

I explained to him how he might have them as big as his head instead of his fist, by sowing them in drills instead of broadcast on the ridge...................

They appeared thankful for my advice, and many of them eagerly asked of they would get the seeds for nothing, as they had no money to buy them; but if they got them for nothing, they would not spare their own labor, and would do as I directed.

I told them I had no seeds at present at my disposal, but urged them to prepare their land and manure, and that, in a short time, some charitable persons might send them seeds. I have transcribed the above remarks at full length from my journal, as it is a fair description of the general state of things in this barony.

Mathew Bole,
Practical instructor

Mr Bole's geographical domain could have covered 200 plus square miles, that it seems he was initially covering on foot. In a later communication to Dublin, it almost seems like he was rationalizing his purchase of a horse to aid in getting around. Without faulting Mr Bole, telling the farmers in 1849 that someone might send seeds later doesn't sound promising.

There were efforts to acquire seed, and at least one member of the gentry (O'Flaherty) in the Oughterard/Moycullen area is said to have purchased seed for his tenants. In the *Farmer's Gazette and Journal of Practical Horticulture* edition of May 11, 1850, is a section called *Green-Crop Seeds*. It contains a letter Matthew Bole posted from Spiddal, dated May 5 1850: "Sir-Herewith I send you half-notes for £10, which I received from the members of the local committee in the Oughterard Union, for the sale of Swedish turnips and other seeds at half-cost price, and they beg you will send down 10 cwt....." He mentions that, for his isolated district: "there is not an ounce of any kind of seed to be otherwise obtained in it."

It seems someone was subsidizing the cost of the seed. If £10 got Mr Bole 10 cwt of turnip and other seeds (1 cwt = 112lbs), then restated, a shilling got him nearly 6 lbs of seed. Thus, it seems the market rate was a shilling obtaining almost 3 lbs of seed. For parsnips and carrots, the 1857 Thom's Almanac recommended sowing 5lbs of seed per statute acre.

For Swedish turnips, Thom's recommended 2 ½ pounds of seed per statute acre. Thus 1- 2 shillings or so obtained enough seed to sow an acre. About this time, the Galway Workhouse was spending 1s 6d a week on an inmate. In November 1849, a report appeared in the press about a Spiddal tenant farmer, John O'Connor, on P S Comyn's estate. He had a turnip crop with some fine specimens reaching seventeen pounds.

At the Great Famine's height, 1846-1848, Spiddal wasn't being advertised as a summer resort area. By 1850, even though conditions in the area were still grim, the recreational situation changed.

SEA-BATHING LODGE.

TO BE LET for the Season (Furnished or Unfurnished),
GOODVILLE,
situate at Spiddal, 9 [Irish] miles from Galway, commanding a
Splendid view of the Bay, Clare Mountains, and Isles of Arran.
There is a beautiful Strand and Bathing Place within two
minutes' walk of the house. There is also every facility of
accommodation from Galway, the post passing twice each day.
For particulars, apply to Mr. E. Good, Abbeygate-street,
Galway. A Coach House and Four-horse Stable attached.

►The Interest in the Lease will be Sold.

Galway Mercury and Connaught Weekly Advertiser
May 25, 1850

When the assessors were in Spiddal in 1853, Goodville was vacant. I suspect this property was just west of the present-day Spiddal Public Library. By 1893, "Goodville" might have been known as "Boliskey Lodge." From some public references to his charitable donations, I suspect that Mr Good was Roman Catholic.

For May 1850, Mr Bole makes no mention of the green-crop situation in Spiddal. Mr Bole's "Agricultural Report" of 3 March 1851 was published in the 8 March 1851 issue of the *Galway Vindicator*, and discussed the green-crop situation.

Agricultural Report
Outerard, Galway
March 3, 1851

......Went on to Spiddal, and observed similar operations [the diligent collection of seaweed] performing in the intermediate villages. Called on the Rev James Macready, who received me with his usual kindness, and would continue to afford me every assistance in his power to promote the prosperity of the struggling farmers in this neighbourhood.

Having gone over the properties of Mr Comyn, Mr Morris, and Mr Blake, in the neighbourhood of Spiddal, I called on the Mr McCullagh, P. P., Knock; he complained very much of the swede turnip seed, he got for distribution in his parish---said that the plants ran up to stems like rape without bulbing; and requested that I would mention in my report to the Council, that in future, they may have seeds collected with greater care---. Such complaints are chiefly confined to the seaside, where the plants were forced by seaweed, on rich muddy soil.

On the clay lands they succeeded much better, and the market of Outerard is abundantly supplied with turnips of excellent quality---growing from the same lot of seed.

Yet, I must state that in all parts of the district there was evidence of a mixture of spurious seeds---the hybrids of some extraneous species of the brassica tribe, which considerably lessened the value of the crop.......

Thus there were green-crop diversification efforts along Cois Fharraige. Among the more esteemed members of the "brassica tribe" are cabbage, broccoli, and cauliflower.

On Thursday 4 June 1851, the weekly meeting of the Galway Guardians occurred. Among the gentry in attendance were Peter Sarsfield Comyn, James Blake, and Martin Morris. The primary topic was the Galway Poor Law Union's massive debt, and the rate-payers' penury. There was no ready solution.

A claim was that in the Killannin ED by Lough Corrib, there was enough cultivation occurring to put the squeeze on those people to pay. There was another problem up there. The tax collector there, a Mr O'Flaherty, was caught confiscating two pigs from a person who owed no tax. He sold them for what seemed a pittance, and then pocketed the money. There was a lot of frustration at this meeting. James Blake (of Tully) chimed in:

....Mr Blake said he had paid as much rates as most persons in the Union, and he only wanted fair play. A vast extent of land was waste, and the tenants were gone away from their holdings; so that the difficulty was not to find the landlords, but the tenants......

For just the June quarter of 1850, the report was that James Blake evicted 26 families consisting of 147 individuals. Evicted legally this time, apparently. Yet in 1851, James Blake, who drove his tenants away with his relentless exploitation and extreme cruelty, is complaining that his tenants can't be found. Martin Morris was frustrated:

Mr Martin Morris said, if the potatoes failed this year, he would give up the property he held in Spiddal to the Guardians to do what they liked with it....

How did the potato crop turn out? A few months later, a report cited a Connemara parish priest:

POTATO CROP IN CONNEMARA—EVICTIONS

A respectable Catholic clergyman from Connemara, with whom we have spoken this day, states as the result of his experience, that fully one half of the potato crop is diseased, along the coast from Clifden to Spiddal.

We regret to be obliged to state on the same well-informed authority that a wholesale system of eviction is being carried on, on the property of the late Mr Martin of Ballinahinch. Upwards of 150 houses have been levelled in the districts of Rusmuck and Lettercalla.

The angel of extermination is is expected in Killeen in a few days.
Roscommon Journal
11 October 1851

Neither Blake nor Morris abandoned their land. Although, for the Blakes of Tully, this was a sort of beginning of the end, as they were physically gone from Tully by the end of the decade, when the heir to the estate was residing in the Ballinasloe lunatic asylum. The Blake lands were in the Encumbered Estates Court by early in the 20th Century.

Martin Morris's descendant held Cois Fharraige lands into the second decade of the 20th Century, and then sold most of the estate to the Congested Districts Board (CDB).

AB Martin of Ballynahinch kept up the pace, evicting 48 families (279 individuals) in the June quarter of 1852.

We saw that, during the mid-December 1847 Guardian's meeting, a committee was formed to find an appropriate Spiddal building to be an auxiliary workhouse, since the Galway Union's poor finances would have precluded the construction of an appropriate structure. I had thought nothing came of this. But an interesting exchange occurred toward the end of the 8 July 1852 meeting of the Guardians:

..........A letter was read from John Davern, Spiddal, requesting payment for the use of his house which contained the boiler for the auxiliary workhouse. The *Chairman* remarked that it was a most extravagant charge.

Davern replied that the *'Jumpers'* would give him double the sum for it, and that he was the confidential steward of the Rev. J. M'Cready for several years, and would have continued so until he asked him [Davern] to *'Jump'*. He told him [Davern] that St. Patrick was a Protestant, but he could not believe it.

Chairman---I hope you did not wish him farther than Purgatory.......
       ---(This dialogue occasioned great merriment.)
Galway Vindicator and Connaught Advertiser,
July 10 1852

A "confidential steward" might have been Davern protecting himself from his neighbours' wrath. In a small village like Spiddal, I'm not sure how one could be a "confidential" anything. The basic claim, that there was a boiler and a workhouse (of some sort), was uncontested. Thus it seems there was an auxiliary workhouse in Spiddal. It also seems the matter wasn't settled at this meeting. There is another reference, presumably from the 4 August 1852 Guardian's meeting:

The Chairman [John Redington Esq] read a letter from Gavin [Davern], of Spiddal, requesting payment for the use of his house, it being occupied by the boiler. His account was for 111 weeks at 1s. per week. The boiler and appendages were offered to him in lie of his debt which he accepted.

Galway Vindicator and Connaught Advertiser
August 7 1852

It appears that Davern's house and the boiler within were in service for over two years. Ca 1853, both John Davern and Edward Good have significant properties in Spiddal Village. One wonders if Edward Good's "Goodville" might have been an auxiliary workhouse prior to 1851.

In the Barony of Moycullen 1851 Census summary section is the population for Spiddal Village: 111 people: 55 males and 56 females in 17 houses, along with 6 uninhabited houses. Listed next is an "Auxiliary Workhouse," having 235 occupants: 80 males and 155 females. This was the Moycullen Auxiliary Workhouse, which started out as a fever hospital.

The workhouse, referenced by Davern in July 1852, presumably close to his Spiddal house, is not listed in the 1851 Census summary. Seemingly, it closed by the time of the census, which occurred on 30 March 1851.

Remember that, in March 1848, it was publicized that Peter S Comyn was in poor-rate arrears to the tune of nearly £18. Which must have been embarrassing. For the period 1845-1850, I doubt the Comyns were collecting anything like £1200 per annum in rents. It's not clear that Laurence Comyn's government securities were yielding a 3.5% a year dividend. Land is not a liquid asset. It seems the Comyns may have ended up in difficult circumstances, a liquidity trap perhaps, along with other gentry. Otherwise, as gentry, why would you let your name appear in the newspapers over a ca £20 debt?

On August 11 1855, Peter Sarsfield Comyn advertised land for lease in the *Weekly Chronicle (London)*. On offer was: 87 prime acres at Killeen Farm, 292 acres at Athyshonock (in the Barna vicinity), 1225 acres of "Superior Mountain Pasture" at "Shanegerane," and the entire townland of "Middle Spiddal" (said to be ca 500 acres, but actually 340 acres). Nearly 2,000 acres were on offer.

Leasing that acreage out would raise a lot of money. I don't know about the Athyshonock and Killeen lands, but it seems there were no takers for the Spiddal area properties. Early in the 20th Century, Spiddal Middle and Shannagurran were in the possession of Francis Laurenzo Comyn, who inherited from his father Francis, who inherited from his brother Peter Sarsfield Comyn, who *d.s.p.*.

Referring back to the Chancery Court case (page 13) earlier in April 1861, Justice Mountifort Longfield stated; "...The petitioner [Peter Sarsfield Comyn] is now the absolute owner of one portion, and has obtained an order for sale...." That "one portion" was (or included) Spiddal West.

Peter S Comyn advertised the 727 acre Spiddal West townland lease for sale, at an auction to be held on 3 December 1861 (Appendix II). On 10 December 1861, the *Dublin Evening Post* announced that

Michael Morris, Esq, Recorder of Galway, has become the owner by purchase of the Spiddal property, lately in the hands of P Sarsfield Comyn, Esq. There was an enthusiastic demonstration in Spiddal on Thursday last [5 Dec 1861], when it became known that Mr Morris had become purchaser of the property.

Michael Morris paid £2500.

One of Peter Sarsfield Comyn's legal representatives in the April 1861 Chancery Court case was Michael Morris; helping ensure that Comyn could sell the Spiddal West townland eventually. By Christmas 1861, Morris owned the townland. One wonders if this wasn't the plan all along.

Spiddal Village Ca 1853

The *Medical Charities (Ireland) Act of 1851* granted the Poor Law Commission control over Irish medical relief. This brought the dispensary system under control of the Poor Law Commission, to be locally administered by the Guardians. Consequently, the 3438 EDs that existed in 1851 were organized into 718 Dispensary Districts. Spiddal Village was the seat of a Dispensary District. Moycullen was near its edge.

In the 1855 GV for Galway, there is a Spiddal Dispensary, associated with Denis McIntyre, representing the Guardians of the Poor of the Galway Union. In the VOB, for ca November 1853, it's stated that the dispensary was a room in Denis McIntyre's house. A dispensary had no beds. One had to present oneself to obtain medication (such as it was), or perhaps have someone travel to the dispensary on ones behalf. I've been told that a descendant of McIntyre's was the Spiddal Postmistress in the 1880s. Eventually, a Spiddal Dispensary District doctor decided that he preferred to live in Moycullen. There was a subsequent unsuccessful attempt, by Cois Fharraige gentry, to require him to live in Spiddal.

The table below characterizes of a number of Spiddal Village buildings that are referenced in this narrative. The Valuation Office assessors were in the Spiddal area during the summer and autumn of 1853.

Spiddal Village — Selected Buildings of Interest -- 1853

Structure	Quality (see pg 25)	Length (ft)	Breadth (ft)	Height (ft)	Valuation		
					£	s	d
RC Rectory	1A-	36	16	9.6	4	9	7
Stable (Roofless)		30	16	7			
RC Chapel	2C	63	22	7	4	7	5
Mecredy #1	1A-	31	22	16	5	11	11
Mecredy #2	1A-	23	13	14	2	2	10
Mecredy Office #1	1B-	10	13	6	0	4	4
Mecredy Office #2	1B-	31	22	8.0	1	5	6
Mecredy #3	1A-	107	22	18	20	18	9
John Davern -- House	2B	36	20	8	2	6	6
John Davern -- Office	3C	28	12	5	0	3	6
Edward Good -- House	2B+	56	22	8	4	7	1
Edward Good --Shop as House	2B+	18	22	8	1	7	7
Edward Good -- Stable-Office	3B	25	19	7	0	12	8
Anglican Church (Main Body)	1A	40.6	22	17.6	9	5	6

The valuations, that subsequently appeared in the 1855 Griffth Valuation for Galway, are substantially lower than these 1853 numbers.

In the assessments, under "Quality," the designation of, "1," a slate roof, is almost always a gentry or clergy associated building. One notices that the RC rectory is in excellent condition, while, from preceding list, we see that the RC chapel is in poor shape.

The testimony of a Roman Catholic RIC man Officer Kerrigan, in 1840, confirmed that the Spiddal Village RC chapel was more or less a wreck.

Edward Good's house was advertised as a summer holiday home: *Goodville*.

Appendix II, the *Spiddal West Townland Prospectus 1861* has the comprehensive list of Spiddal Village properties, including the terms on which the individual leases were held.

The VOB provide some insight into what Bohoona Lodge was like, as measured by the assessor James Kelly, on 6 August 1853:

Bohoona Lodge -- Specifications -- 6 August 1853

Structure	Quality (pg 25)	Length (ft)	Breadth (ft)	Height (ft)	Valuation £	s	d
House	1B	62.6	21.6	18.0	10	1	0
Projection in front	1B	13.6	5.6	18.0	0	10	6
Same	2B	21.6	5.6	18.0	0	16	6
Addition behind Kitchen	2B-	23.6	47	10.6	0	16	6
Coach House	2B-	39.6	18.6	10.6	1	1	3
Laundry Office	2B	11.6	18.6	8.0	0	6	1
Office Store	1B	15.0	7.6	6.0	0	3	5
Dairy Shed	2B	15.0	7.6	6.0	0	2	9

Referring to the "Quality" table on page 22, we see that the main building had a slate roof, and was of better than average quality. In the VOB, for many significant Spiddal structures, a breadth of 22 feet often occurs.

In 1854, our boiler-man John Davern was in the newspapers again:

> John Davern appeared [in the Spiddal Petty Sessions] to answer a charge......
> for having, during moments of postprandial enjoyment, hiccuped
> 'to hell with the Queen.'
>
> *Galway Mercury, and Connaught Weekly Advertiser*
> May 27, 1854

John Scully RM, of the Spiddal Petty Sessions, shipped Davern off to the county prison, for trial at the next Assizes. Trial for what, wasn't specified. Davern probably shouldn't have wished the Queen "farther than Purgatory." The accuser was a dismissed (possibly disgraced) Coast Guard Officer, Capt Richardson. Perhaps not the most trustworthy witness. The Galway Summer Assizes commenced on 31 July 1854. The published accounts of the session that I've found don't reference John Davern.

Boluisce Lough

'Superior Mountain Pasture' in 'Shanegerane'

Up Above Bohoona

The Clancy Crypt And The Martin Chapel

Boluisce Waterfall
Courtesy of Seán Ó Neachtain

Cois Fharraige Looking Toward Galway Bay And Clare

"NEAD LE FARRIGE"

THE NEST BY THE SEA SPIDDAL JUNE,1882.

The Spiddal Orphanage

Good Times Along Cois Fharraige

Tully

My paternal grandmother, Bridget Faherty, came from Banraghbaun South (*Banrach Bán Theas, Bontragh*) near Tully. Her parents, Michael and Mary Faherty (née Conneely) paid rent to the Blakes of Tully.

The Blakes of Tully had two habitations near but not actually in Tully. In the OS maps they are referred to Cashel House in the "Inveran" townland, and Blake's Lodge in the Cartron townland. The Lodge may be the older of the two. The boundary between Tully and Cartron runs down the middle of boreen (more or less) leading to the Lodge, which was just inside Cartron townland. One could easily but incorrectly think the Lodge was in Tully. Perhaps, ca 1838, there was a boundary shift. Before that boundary adjustment, the Lodge was in Tully. Hence the *Blakes of Tully.* That's my theory.

Blake's Lodge was about a mile northwest of Cashel House. Oddly, the 1841 Census shows no structures and no tenants, while the 1851 Census shows one structure with four occupants. The GV assessors and surveyors were at the Lodge in the summer/fall of 1853. They valued 111 acres of land, listed no structures, and no tenants. Some structures came after 1853. The GV assessors did misplace things out there. Me too. The OS maps shows an RC chapel in Tully, while the GV assessors listed it under Inverin. In 1838, the Blake Lodge had an extensive orchard, most of which was gone by 1893.

In the 1838 OS, directly south of Cashel House on Galway Bay (the locality is *Travore Bay*) was a vaguely fish hook shaped pier, that is not in the 1893 OS. Likely the pier wasn't more than a jetty of roughly piled rocks, incapable of surviving the unrelenting storm surges without constant maintenance.

Over the decades, without much scrutiny, the Blakes of Tully were likely dislocating people based on various whims. The oral history is that the construction of Cashel House (as the OS calls it), on prime land, first required the eviction of the tenants occupying the land. We'll call this the first Tully eviction. It might have occurred in 1824, when Patrick Blake became the incumbent of Gortnamona and Tully.

Lochlainn Ó Tuairisg kindly provided a transcript, revealing that, on 11 June 1816, Valentine Blake JP (the first Blake into Tully) was writing to Dublin Castle from Tully, about unrest at an event that occurred in Tully: "........The animal custom prevails here among the lower orders to meet on the 9th June, which instantly ends in a row, the effect always of drunkenness......."

Two of the unrest ringleaders he arrested escaped overnight, partially because of a lack of police reinforcements. He reassured Dublin Castle about his "efforts to protect this place." Valentine Blake died ca 1819, when his heir Patrick (b. ca 1803) was still a minor, so the estate was supervised by Valentine's brother James Blake. James remained as the Tully agent, once Patrick reached majority in 1824. In 1816, when Valentine Blake wrote to Dublin, he might have been writing from the Lodge.

Patrick Blake seems to have been a true absentee landlord, seemingly exerting little on-site oversight. James Blake imbued his children with his character. Their abusive treatment of the tenants, which included sexual assault, also figures in the Tully area oral history.

In 1840, James Blake imposed on the tenants an agreement by which, in addition to the rent, they would give him one day a week of free labour. James Blake had the public road construction contracts, and forced the tenants to work on the roads gratis.

To further intimidate the tenants, Blake filed dozens processes (court actions, as many as 63 by one account) against the tenants in the Courts, confiscating their livestock and impounding them in Moycullen (16 English miles distant).

Blake's 1840 agreement formally codified practices that extended back much further in time. A statement from James Blake appearing the 20 March 1846 edition of the (Dublin) *Pilot* confirms this. Concerning the issue of the labor, James Blake stated:

.........Labor is very difficult to be got in that country, and I collected the tenants, about twenty-five years ago, and promised them sixpence a day for any work I might require myself. Their answer to that was, that they would not agree to work for sixpence, or for any wages; but that they would sow my oats and potatoes, and any little work I had about my house, without any charge. They never objected to the labour, and never grumbled till this clergyman put them up to it-----till this repeal question was put afloat................................

"About twenty-five years ago", ca 1820, was when Valentine Blake died. Likely the tenants were too afraid to object to the labour requirement. As we'll see, James Blake's promises were not worth much.

"This clergyman", mentioned by James Blake in 1846, is of course John O'Grady. John O'Grady stated his belief that Patrick Blake knew exactly how the tenants were being mistreated by James Blake.

"This repeal question" was Daniel O'Connell's effort, via the Repeal Association, to repeal the 1800 Acts of Union between Great Britain and Ireland. The (Dublin) *Pilot* was a favored newspaper of the Repeal Association.

A few years prior to the 2nd Tully Eviction, an interesting court case was heard in the Galway Quarter Sessions on 21 Oct 1844. As reported in the 26 October 1844 edition of the Tuam Herald, and other outlets, the case was Barnacle vs Blake. The Plaintiff James Barnacle's attorney was James Donelan against James Blake Esq of Tully. Mr Barnacle, the first of a number of plaintiffs, was demanding £3 14s 8d, for his pre-1840 uncompensated labor at a place called *Iveragh* (Inverin, likely).

The Galway Vindicator characterized James Blake as "anxious to convert his nephew's generosity to his own profit, enforced in the most odious manner from the cottiers, work and labor without the least remuneration to them."

Patrick Blake claimed that, when assuming control of the estate in 1824 after reaching his majority, he wiped off nearly £2000 of rent arrears, reducing the rents by a quarter as well, in return for the tenants reclaiming some waste land. Blake wiped off arrears that he could never hope to pocket. Arrears that could be taken as evidence the rents were way more than 25% too high. Strictly speaking, the arrears weren't forgiven, as there was a quid pro quo, which itself ended up in dispute. According to the tenants, "some waste land" reclaimed amounted to 80 acres.

On a technicality, the judge ruled that the 1840 agreement precluded the tenants from seeking pre-1840 labor compensation. Mr Donelan stated he would appeal. But I found nothing more.

The second Tully eviction came in late December 1847 into early January 1848, during the worst of Great Famine. James Blake had a son Arthur, the bully boxer. Arthur had a brother Richard, cut from the same cloth. They had a much younger brother, Henry, about ten-years-old at the time, who also figures in the testimony.

Capt Hellard may have learned of the evictions via a newspaper article. The other obvious place to check was the RIC logs. The RIC was aware of the eviction activities, but logged nothing about them. Possibly out of connivance with, or deference to, or fear of, the Blakes? As no process server or other official was involved, it was clear the evictions were illegal. After becoming aware of the events, Capt Hellard arranged with Magistrate Kernan to have a hearing at the workhouse on 27 January 1848.

There exist communications about workhouse staff mortality statistics across Ireland. The workhouse was perhaps the most <u>dangerous place</u> in Ireland not just to work, but to frequent. Capt Hellard often frequented the Galway Workhouse. On the originally scheduled hearing date, 27 January 1848, Capt Hellard was on his deathbed with a malignant fever, and was gone by 30 January 1848. His temporary replacement as Poor Law Inspector was Major P M'Kie.

The rescheduled testimony of thirteen Tully area evictees can be found in:

<u>Papers</u> Relating to Proceedings for Relief of Distress, and State of Unions and Workhouses in Ireland, 1848

Witnesses

"Tully" Evictions Dec 1847 – Jan 1848

Tenant	Village	Tenant	Village
John Costello	Inverin	Mary Feeny	Tullymore
Bridget Faherty	Tullymore	James Folan	Ballinahown
Mary Faherty	Tullymore	Thomas O'Malley	Inverin
Daniel Conneely	Tullymore	James Donohoe	Inverin
John Donohoe	Tullymore	John Donohoe	
Mark Conneely	Tullymore	Bridget Donohoe	Bunraghbawn
John Toole	Inverin	Thomas M'Donagh	Garomna*
John Magan	Tully	Michael M'Donagh	Garomna*

*Estate of Mr Christopher St George, MP

John Donohoe was mute, and could not provide testimony. Chistropher St George MP also carried out additional evictions up near Oughterard. In the March 25 1848 list of those gentry in arrears for non-payment of the Poor-rates, he was the number two deadbeat, behind Arthur Bell Martin. About the evictions, from the 1848 Proceedings, we have the testimony of the first witness John Costello:

Notes of Examinations taken on oath before Major P. M'Kie, Poor Law Inspector for the Union of Galway, at Derrynea Lodge, on the 14th and 15th days of February, 1848, relative to matter which appeared under the head of Relief Applications," in the annexed extract taken from the " Galway Mercury " of 29th January, 1848.

Many of the witnesses being unable to speak English, Mr. Thomas J. Read is sworn Interpreter.

First Witness, John Costello, being duly sworn, states.

I live at Invern; I applied at the workhouse in Galway for relief after New Year's day, I stated to the Board of Guardians that my house was thrown down by Pat M'Nalty, Arthur Blake, David Costello, Edmund Walsh, John Conneely, a man named Faherty, driver to Mr. Blake; all those persons were present: Pat M'Nalty is steward to Mr. Blake, Arthur Blake is son to James Blake, Mr. James Blake is agent to Mr. Patrick Blake of Gortnamona. I only know that David Costello was with Mr. Arthur Blake; Edmund Walsh and Faherty are both drivers or stewards to Mr. James Blake; I don't know in what capacity John Conneely was; Pat M'Nalty had a crowbar with which he was throwing down the house, Arthur Blake had also a crowbar and was throwing down the house, when one of them got tired he gave the crowbar to another; David Costello was throwing down the house; Edmund Walsh was present when the house was down, and along with the persons who were throwing it down; he threw three of my children out on the street; one of them was sick at the time; her name was Anne; she died last week; was near four years old; Coleman my son died on Friday last, aged ten years, from cold and hardship. My house was completely destroyed, and it was near dusk when it was thrown down; myself and my family had to sleep in the open air; it was raining and snowing that night, and it blew very hard; my wife and remaining child are now lying sick, and have a bad chance of recovery; my wife says that if she dies, she will attribute her death to the cold she got that night for want of a house; it was on the 31st December my house was thrown down; I asked Arthur Blake for God's sake to leave the house over me until that night would be over, to which he replied, that he would if I gave him a pound; Faherty and Edmund Walsh, who are both drivers or stewards to Mr. Blake, were also throwing down the house; I built the house myself about eleven years ago on a mountain garden; I had no rent to pay for that, but I had to pay three pounds and a half a crown in the year, besides a day's work every week for sea-weed and some land I held near the sea-shore; Mr. Patrick Blake was the landlord, and Mr. James Blake the agent. The land and sea-weed was taken from me about six years ago; I lived in the house ever since, and was served with no notice of ejectment to give it up until it was thrown down; my wife and child are now lying sick in a hovel I made against the ruins of the house; when my child Coleman died there was over six inches of water about him; Pat M'Nalty and Arthur Blake had the appearance of having taken drink; I knew by them that they had drank whiskey; Edmund Walsh came to my house first, and told me to take my children out of it; I said I would not, if they were killed in it; the others came up and threw down the house shortly after; Arthur Blake and Samuel Mullowney came to my house and searched it some nights before; they found nothing improper in it; the late and present priests of the parish can give me a good character, and so can every person on the estate; my wife nursed the last child (named Henry) that Mr. James Blake had, about nine or nine and a half years ago; I don't know why the land was taken from me; Mr. Blake said, " I would rather feed goats than ye;" I owed half a year's rent; Mr. Blake seized my corn in about a year afterwards; I paid him the half year's rent; I supported myself ever since by having a boat between myself and two others in which we fished, and I tried to earn a little; the boat and all I had were sold before I applied at the workhouse; we got 2l. 10s. for the boat; I believe I would not be alive now, but for the charity of John Hernan; I was employed with others in building a wall for Mr. James Blake; Pat M'Nalty is the man that hired me; I worked for a fortnight at that wall, and all I got for it was two shillings and six-pence.

Not so long after John Costello's wife nursed James Blake's infant son Henry, James Blake would rather feed goats than help John Costello.

There is a tale of the seven nested envelopes, with the innermost seventh envelope containing the parish priest's potent curse on the Blakes. The priest reasoned that it would take Blake some time to open seven envelopes, providing the young lad who delivered them time to ride away fast and far. The Blakes are vividly remembered, and are well-cursed.

Intermarriage meant that some of the Ballynahown gang knocking often occupied houses must of had relations around Tully and Inverin, adding another dimension to the tragedy.

The 18 November 1847 letter of the Committee of the Killannin Board of Health (page 70) to Galway prompted Capt Hellard to travel to Spiddal and points west, to assess the situation for himself. There James Blake informed Capt Hellard that he was offering local men 8d-9d a day wages, to no avail, stating that the men preferred to work on the local road works (when these projects were operational).

The Inverin evictee John Costello described his efforts to earn a living. He was no idler. At the end of his testimony, John Costello states that he earned 2s 6d for a fortnight's work on the Blake estate. That's 2d to 3d a day.

What happened to the "8d to 9d per day" James Blake told Capt Hellard he was offering?
No wonder the Tully area men didn't want to work for James Blake. They understood him perfectly.

Major M'Kie, who visited the area after the evictions, included his own observations:

I have visited the ruins of these huts (not any great distance from Mr. Blake's residence); I found that many of these unfortunate people were still living within the ruins of these huts, endeavouring to shelter themselves under a few sticks and sods, all in the most wretched state of destitution; many were so weak that they could scarcely stand when giving their evidence. The site of these ruins is a rocky wild spot, fit for nothing but a sheep-walk.

It appears from the information I have been able to obtain, that these people had many of them been living in these huts for years; renting patches of land on the rocky shore, and earning a precarious and scanty subsistence by the culture of the potato, paying even for the sea-weed to manure the land. The total failure of the potato crop left them without any means of subsistence, and being unable to cultivate the land, they had given up their holdings, but continued to occupy the huts, paying no rent.

It has been stated, and I believe with truth, that Mr Blake and many of his tenants had lost sheep, and suffered from depredations on their turnip crops. These people having no means of subsistence, suspicion fell on them, and it was resolved to root them out.

Mr. Blake, sen., was present on the 15th [Feb], and had the perusal of the whole of the depositions, of which he took notes. He denied any knowledge of the proceedings, he being absent at the time they occurred. I asked, if, as a magistrate, he had not on his return from Dublin made any inquiry as to the acts of violence committed during his absence. Mr. Blake said he inquired of the police, who had made no report of the matter, although fully aware of it. I have made inquiry, and find this to be true; they were well aware that the people's houses were thrown down, but made no report to the Inspector.

I pointed out to Mr. Blake that the depositions implicated himself, as it had been asserted to be by his orders, and that his sons and servants were the leaders; that the depositions were on oath. Mr. Blake assured me he had not in any way sanctioned those proceedings, which he admitted to be illegal; and promised to send me an affidavit to that effect on the following day. I have not heard from him since.

In November 1847, only a month before the Tully events, the Committee of the Killannin Board of Health's warning of the potential for tragedy was prescient: *...that many families are...... endeavouring to prolong a miserable existence, on one meal a-day of turnips alone, plundered sometimes at the risk of their lives, from the gardens of their more fortunate neighbours....*

James Blake conveniently managed to be in Dublin for the evictions. Patrick Blake is supposedly unaware of the situation until early April 1848, and went unchallenged about how that could be. From the *Galway Vindicator:*

BLAKE OF TULLY EVICTIONS.

With considerable gratification we give publication to the following letter from Patrick Blake Esq., of Gortnamona, proprietor of Tully, the scene of so many horrors which were recorded in out publication of Wednesday last. The high character and position in society held by Mr. P. Blake, strengthened us in our belief, that the atrocities so revolting to humanity perpetrated upon his estate were without his knowledge privacy or consent. The letter of Mr. Blake is candid frank, and dictated with a spirit we shall ever regard from a man of honor. There is but one duty Mr. Blake has now to perform to outraged public opinion. The Government have removed Mr. James Blake from the commission of the peace, let him now be removed from the agency of the estate.-- A man capable of acting as he is charged with, and, that, too, upon the sworn testimony of fifteen witnesses is unworthy of holding any office or any situation:--

TO THE EDITOR OF THE GALWAY VINDICATOR
Gortnamona, April 7, 1848

Sir--- I was yesterday favoured by the receipt of a copy of your paper of the 5th instant, in which, for the first time, I have seen a detailed account of the illegal and unjustifiable evictions, which took place on my property at Tully in this county, in the month of December last, and I have now distinctly to state, that I have not directly or indirectly authorised or sanctioned such disgraceful conduct, and to no person can it be a source of more sincere regret than to your

Obedient humble servant,
PATRICK BLAKE

I request that you will have the goodness to insert this letter in your next publication.

The *Vindicator's* fawning editors were certainly laying it on thick. They were willing to take on James Blake, Patrick Blake's uncle and agent. But confronting Patrick Blake was a different story.

The House of Commons Hansard transcript of 28 March 1848 details James Blake's fate:

.....Directly the report of that inquiry [of Major M'Kie] was brought under the notice of the Lord Lieutenant, he submitted the whole case to the law officers of the Crown, who gave it as their opinion that Government could not legally undertake a criminal prosecution. Lord Clarendon's next step was to intimate to the Lord Chancellor that Mr. Blake's name should be removed from the commission of the peace. The Lord Chancellor did not immediately act upon that suggestion; but he transmitted a statement of the case to Mr. Blake, and, according to the practice, afforded him an opportunity of making what explanation he chose. He regretted to state that for a length of time no explanation was received from Mr. Blake; and when at last it did arrive, it was considered so unsatisfactory, that his name was struck off the list of magistrates.

Although James Blake took the fall for his nephew, it was deemed impossible to legally mount a criminal prosecution of James Blake.

Apart from being dropped from the magistrate list, not much else seemed to have happened to him, except he did get around to dying. He seems to have been alive and kicking early in 1851, while the wedding announcement for his second daughter Jane indicates that he was dead prior to May 1853.

Cashel House of the OS maps seems to be referenced in the newspapers as the "Inverin Lodge," after the townland it was located in. In the November 1853 VOB, it was associated with (the late) James Blake, with his name crossed out, replaced by Eleanor Blake, wife of Patrick Blake. The initial £33 valuation was reduced to £19 "for dilapidation." By March of 1855, Inverin Lodge was devalued about another factor of two. Over the decades, seemingly little expenditure was made to maintain the place.

John Wallace is in the 1855 GV for Tully. Tim Robinson mentioned that he was the Blakes of Tully agent sometime after the 2nd Tully eviction, likely replacing the late James Blake. John Wallace was in Tully in 1844, as he was involved in an 1845 court case. Early in 1845, his wife got into an argument with a certain Blake. Not James Blake Esq JP of Tully, but Jemmy Blake (diminutive of James or perhaps Jeremiah).

This disagreement jogged Jemmy's memory about a supposed event of the preceding June (1844). Jemmy alleged that John Wallace was laying in wait, with a pistol, for Tully RIC Sergeant Heeran. Why would Wallace want to shoot Heeran? According to Jemmy, Wallace was afraid the RIC man Heeran would lead the Revenue Officers to Wallace's malt stash. This hints at bootlegging.

Jemmy had severely fallen off the wagon some years earlier, which damaged his credibility. He would bring whiskey to the Revenue Officers, and help them consume it while they all played cards.

Jemmy and his associates, who supposedly had knowledge of Wallace's alleged behavior, were all highly inebriated around that time. Jemmy's witnesses offered no corroboration. Jemmy made an additional accusation against a man named Glynn, who supposedly planned an armed attack on the Blake's Inverin residence. Enough whiskey had flowed that Glynn was said to "scarcely know a cow from a horse." In sorting through the various accounts, it seems whiskey tainted everything.

At the Petty Sessions hearing, the magistrate James Blake Esq came off the Bench to be a character witness for John Wallace, saying he had known him for eighteen or nineteen years. Blake also mentioned that John Wallace helped defend the Blake Gortnamona residence from attack, and that other gentlemen thought highly of him. It would seem that, in Gortnamona, the Blakes were about as popular as they were in Tully.

The Petty Sessions magistrates dismissed Jemmy Blake's cases against Wallace and Glynn. A remark from the Bench insinuated that perhaps Jemmy was being manipulated by another party. Just another day at the Spiddal Petty Sessions.

In July 1857 Patrick Blake died, and his son Patrick Minor inherited. Tim Robinson relates that rents were paid to the son even though he resided in the lunatic asylum in Ballinasloe. Eventually, the Wallace family, the Blake's bailiffs and rent collectors, occupied Cashel House. The last occupant was an Anglican missionary. The Rev James McCready, it would seem (see page 56).

Wallace is buried in the St Colmcille graveyard at Cloghmore (Cloghmore South, An Chloch Mór Theas), as are my paternal Great Grandparents Michael Faherty and Mary Faherty (née Conneely). I can't find my great grandparents' grave, but I know where the senior Wallace is buried, in an area off from most everyone else. There is a simple low above ground crypt. The inscription on top of the crypt says "Wallis."

A paternal 2nd cousin of mine related the following story. When the senior Wallace was to be buried, a big hunk of Connemara granite was found in his plot. Apparently the gravediggers dug and dug, but could put him in the ground only if they turned him sideways. Perhaps the existence of the crypt provides some credence to the story. This oldest part of St Colmcille is severely overgrown.

My cousin mentioned that the treasure hunters, with their metal detectors, have thoroughly scoured the Inverin Lodge property (now owned by my cousin) for the Blake family silver. When the Blakes abandoned Tully, the easy silver was long gone, if there was any silver there to begin with.

I'll mention in passing that, in 1851 and 1852, there are newspaper reports of promising lead/silver deposits discovered in Tully (*An Tulaigh*) and Derrynea (*Doire an Fhéich*). I suspect they turned out to be lead deposits with a trace of silver. The ca 1838 Ordnance Survey does show, in Kilroe West (*An Choill Rua Thiar*), on the north-side of the Coast Road, a lead mine. This is the hard way to obtain silver. In the 1838 & 1893 Ordnance Surveys for Tully and Derrynea, there are no mines marked on the maps.

In the Spiddal Petty Sessions for Nov 1897, are five complaints for trespass against Derrynea residents Mary McDonagh (a widow), Tom Ridge, and Bartley Feeney. It is the complainant that is of interest.

The complainant was "Valentine Blake, Committee of the Person and Estate of Patrick Jas Blake, a Lunatic." The inclusion of the phrase "of the Person" leads me to suspect that the lunatic Patrick Blake was alive in 1897. He would have been about 73 years old.

In the 1901 Irish Census, for the Ballinasloe and Dublin lunatic asylums, the guests are not listed by name, but by initials. However, their occupations are given. So one looks for "P. B.", having occupation "Gentleman", or "Son of Gentleman." The lunatic Patrick Blake seems not to have been alive in 1901. The complainant is not Patrick (Senior) Blake's son Valentine Fitzpatrick, who died in Bray in 1870, but is Valentine's son Valentine Alexander Blake, Patrick (Minor) Blake's nephew.

Patrick (Minor) Blake is absent from the Blake genealogy (Appendix VII). The Blake genealogy states that Patrick Blake had only one son, Valentine Blake, named after his grandfather, as was the custom in naming the first born male child. The grandfather was the first Blake into Tully. It seems that Patrick (Minor) was white-washed from the family tree. I found no civil death registration for him. I looked under P. B., Blake, Black, Caddell, and Caddle.

There is another Blake of Tully genealogy consistent with Burke, but also having some additional detail, assembled by Francis Skeet and published in 1906. Just prior that time, a Skeet woman married into the Blake family. Patrick Minor makes no appearance in this genealogy.

Relations might have improved, up to a point, with Patrick Blake Senior's death, and succession by his son Valentine Fitzpatrick Blake. 'Up to a point', because a January 1887 eviction was conducted on behalf of the late Valentine's minor son, Valentine Alexander Blake.

On 11 July 1870, the Rev Patrick Lyons wrote to the Freeman's Journal acknowledging donations for building a chapel at Tully, "a remote and very poor district in the west end of the Parish of Spiddal, where the inhabitants are too poor to build one by their own account...."

Nearly £77 was raised. Archbishop MacHale of Tuam contributed £10, while Valentine Blake Esq of Gortnamona donated one acre of land and £10. Patrick Blake Minor's brother Valentine died in Bray later that year, in November 1870. George Morris Esq JP, of Wellpark, contributed £10 and a full complement of roofing timber.

John Wallace of Inverin was down for £2. Other records of that time indicate there was an Inverin shopkeeper of that name. The Rev John O'Grady of Athenry was down for £2. Four members of the Tully RIC barracks contributed a total of £2, while several Sub-Constables, Constables, and Coast Guards from Galway to Mayo together contributed nearly £5.

One can put the evictions and the famine in perspective by returning to Cois Fharraige Landowner table on pages 7 & 8. In 1841, for Tully there were 137 people in 25 habitations. In 1851 we have 38 inhabitants in 6 houses. Nearly a factor of four decline. For Inverin, the population declined by a factor of two. For Ballynahown South, Derrynea, and Banraghbaun South, we note similar devastation.

As we saw earlier, Spiddal West was hard hit, with the number of occupied houses and the population each dropping by nearly a factor of 3.

For the townlands making up the western part of the Spiddal-Galway RC parish (marked 'A' and 'B' in the map on page 16), the combination of starvation, disease, eviction, and emigration caused the population to decline by nearly a third, between 1841 and 1851. In the 1841 Census, the Killannin Civil Parish population was 11,278, declining to 7,976 for the 1851 Census, a 29% decrease.

In addition to Spiddal East, Loughaunbeg also showed a significant 54% population increase between 1841 and 1851.

The Spiddal Orphanage

Rummaging about in the 1901 Irish Census for Spiddal Village, I found a building complex with over seventy residents within. The original census forms revealed the building(s) to be an orphanage. As best we can, let's ascertain when it came into existence. By 1911, it had disappeared from Spiddal.

The Anglican Rev James McCready documented the challenges of proselytizing in *The Reformation in Iar Chonnacht,* published by Hardy and Sons in Dublin. An orphanage depiction was included (below).

Spiddall New School House and Refuge for Widows and Orphans
(from *The Reformation in Iar Chonnacht*)

In the Manuscripts and Research Archive Library of Trinity College Dublin (TCD) is a scrapbook (*Irish Scraps to Amuse my dear Admiral from LCB May 27, 1857*), containing a <u>watercolour</u> sketch of a *famine Orphan Refuge at Spiddall, County of Galway*, by Louisa Catherine Beaufort. Louisa Catherine Beaufort (1781-1863) was born in Wales, where her Huguenot-descended father fled, for a time, to escape his Irish creditors. Apparently she never married. She was an author, antiquarian, and an artist, who wrote, sketched, and painted, to support herself and her parents. She was the first woman to have a paper presented at the Royal Irish Academy, in 1827. *My dear Admiral* is her brother, Admiral Francis Beaufort, who developed the Beaufort wind-force scale.

At first glance, the Beaufort watercolour (which I can't show you) and the above sketch seem to be very similar, perhaps because they were both executed from more or less the same vantage point, near Bohoona Lodge. A careful inspection reveals differences. Once I was convinced that Beaufort executed the above sketch. I no longer believe that. Other illustrations in her scrapbook are associated with a <u>manuscript</u> (in the Huntington Library of California) describing an 1842-1843 tour of Leinster and part of Munster. Of great interest is whether or not she penned any commentary to accompany her Spiddal orphanage image. An open question, it seems.

The Rev McCready didn't identify the artist who rendered above illustration. Perhaps it's his sketch, perhaps along with most of the other sketches in the pamphlet.

Louisa Beaufort's "refuge" never was really a "famine" facility, for as we'll see, the large building, depicted on the previous page, was erected after the Great Famine ended, and the children who populated it didn't come from the severely famine-afflicted areas.

In his polemic, the Rev McCready stated "the whole population of the village is 170, of whom 120 are Protestants. There was no church, no school-house, no school." That 70% of the Spiddal Villagers were Protestant, would have been news to some of those villagers I suspect. The 1851 & 1861 Irish Censuses have the Spiddal Village population at 111 and 195 people, respectively.

Inside The Spiddall Old School House
(from *The Reformation in Iar Chonnacht*,
sketched by Patrick Tully Schoolmaster)

We see about two dozen children, sleeping on straw spread on the floor. James McCready's solicitation for donations cited the absence of bedding, furniture etc. He added a postscript: "Since the foregoing statement was prepared, I have learnt that the nuns of Galway, have taken a house in this village, for the purpose of opening a school for the children of the poor, and likewise an industrial school." He is patting himself on the back, as I believe he feels his success in Spiddal has the RC authorities rattled.

On 8 November 1853, the assessor Thomas Quinn signed off on the valuation of Spiddal Village buildings. Were there children present when the new large building was assessed, I assume it would have been referred to as an orphanage. What eventually would be the orphanage building was assessed, and then devalued slightly, for "want of proper finish inside." We'll assume this means the building wasn't occupied (or shouldn't have been occupied) late in 1853.

An image in my copy of *The Reformation in Iar Chonnacht* has an obscured date, with a last digit for the year possibly being a '5'. So we'll say the orphanage opened very late in 1853, or in 1854. In his August 1853 tour that visited Spiddal, the American Episcopalian Rev Dr Tyng makes no mention of an orphanage.

On 7 August 1856, an abduction occurred in Spiddal. In the dead of night, the Rev Mccredy gathered up three children from Spiddal, along with three other children removed from the Aran Islands. All were transported to Clifden, to be delivered to ICM facilities in that vicinity.

The Spiddal children were Michael, Martin, and Bartholomew Egan, aged five, seven, and nine years, respectively. Their mother had been dead four years, while their father had been dead for some years as well. They were truly orphaned, but were under the care of their maternal Aunt Biddy Tolan.

It is interesting that three children from Spiddal, a village with an orphanage, along with three Aran children who have been taken to a village with an orphanage, were all hustled up to an orphanage in Clifden, 49 miles (79 km) distant.

The six children were spotted the next morning by the Clifden parish priest, wearing ICM "scarlet merino" schoolchildren garb. Independently, the children's aunt and guardian Biddy Tolan had tracked them to the Clifden area. The Clifden parish priest P M'Manus also brought the matter to the attention of the Clifden Petty Sessions. Patrick Lyons was contacted, as the Egan children were from Spiddal.

One of six magistrates sitting at the Petty Sessions that day was the Rev Hyacinth Darcy, the Rector of Clifden. He was the son of the founder of Clifden, John Darcy. Hyacinth Darcy inherited much after his father died, and lost it by 1850. He might have had some prior knowledge of the abduction.

Two things saved the day. It seems the Galway solicitor Mr Rochford was in the Clifden Court, and was sought out by Biddy for advice. No lightweight solicitor, but a person "with the utmost zeal and powerful ability." I believe he represented James Kyne in the 1851 Loughaunbeg "Jumper" case. One can imagine Mr Rochford was outraged at the situation Biddy described. Consequently, he interrupted the Court's regular business. That the press found out about the affair didn't help the abductors either.

The Rev Mccredy stated he had a "letter" from the Spiddal parish priest. The letter's contents weren't revealed, but the insinuation seemed to be that the Spiddal parish priest approved of the children's transport, as if he had the authority. About the children, the Clifden magistrate Colonel Shaw's claim was, "we have no authority." Mr Rochford's response was that if a Spiddal cow or heifer had been stolen, and taken to Clifden, the magistrates would have been all over it, to ensure justice. The Rev Darcy was induced, by the other magistrates, to relinquish control of the three children.

After the three children were reunited with their aunt, a subscription was started to cover transportation costs back to Spiddal, and to ensure Biddy had some gelt to help her care for the children. There was no mention of what happened to the three Aran children. The Rev Lyons' August 11 1856 response to the Clifden's Father M'Manus stated that "the imported souper children" were not from his Spiddal-Tuam (Knock) parish. Thus, they were from the Spiddal Village area, east of the Boluisce River, or possibly from Minna. He then continues:

.....The village of Spiddal is in the Diocese of Galway. When funds were available for the propagation of souperism a large establishment was erected here, intended as a factory, but the only goods now manufactured in it are some few Catholic paupers, who, deprived of the guardianship of their parents, are seduced by the plausible bait of food and clothing, and immured by those kidnapping agents in those dreary dungeons...............................

The "large establishment," whose walls were 107 feet long by 22 feet wide by 18 feet tall, is listed in the 1853 VOB (page 87), and is depicted on page 98. It would seem this building was meant to replace the (presumably) smaller "Spiddal Industrial School" whose woven tweeds were so highly praised during the 1853 Dublin "Great Exhibition." It seems the building became an orphanage.

In 1860 the Spiddal Orphanage was back in the news. An incident was passionately but not entirely consistently reported, in the Irish and English newspapers.

William Sherwood, a seaman, was injured in April 1859 at or near Bermuda (the East Indies, in another account), and succumbed to his injuries in Dublin in August 1859. He left behind his wife Ellen, and four children: William (ca 9 years old), Anne (ca 7), Joseph (ca 5), and Teresa (ca 4).

By the end of 1859, Ellen Sherwood was overwhelmed providing for the children, and gave the children over to Mrs Ellen Smyly of Merrion Square Dublin. On 14 March 1860, Mrs Smyly had the four siblings, along with two other children, siblings, put on a train bound for Galway, to be met there by Mary Hartnett, matron of the Spiddal Orphanage.

Two Dublin gentlemen, ostensibly travelling to Galway on legal business, encountered the four Sherwood children unaccompanied in third class. The children revealed that they were Roman Catholic, were uninterested in becoming Protestant, and were undoubtedly not happy to be bound for a Protestant orphanage in Spiddal. One of the girls indicated she was to have made her confirmation the next day, at St Andrew's Catholic Church, on Westland Row, Dublin.

One of the men, John O'Connor, decided something was amiss. At the Galway Train Station, he removed the four Sherwood children from Mary Hartnett's custody.

After the children had a sojourn at a Galway rooming house, Mr MacRobins, the other Dublin gentleman, repatriated them to Dublin. MacRobins and the children were previously acquainted. Hmm. At Ellen Sherwood's rooming house, Mr MacRobins left the childen in the custody of Catherine Davis (William Sherwood's paternal second cousin) and Ellen Blake (Ellen Sherwood's mother). Mr MacRobins stated expectation was that the children would be delivered to their mother. Instead, the children were spirited into the Wicklow Mountains, never to be recovered by the authorities.

On 17 Mar 1860, in the Galway Assizes, a writ of Habeas Corpus was issued by Justice Hayes. Of course, the children were not produced. At least two individuals were incarcerated. They were John O'Connor, who removed the children from Mary Hartnett's custody, and Denis O'Connor, who owned the Galway rooming house.

In the Ulster press, Ellen Sherwood was honoring her late husband's wish that his children be raised in the 'Established Church'. The 23 March 1860 issue of *The Londonderry Sentinel* had an article titled: *Romish Kidnapping*, describing the kidnapper as "a monk named O'Connor, a faithful imitator of Pio Nono [Pius IX], at the same description of sacred theft." Enter *Edgardo Mortara* into a search engine.

In the press with Catholic sympathies, the late William Sherwood was RC, whose children were being raised as Catholics. The claim being that a stressed Ellen Sherwood was exploited by predatory zealots hunting for young religious recruits. In a *Galway Vindicator* article is a reference to "thirty pieces of silver," and a rant that: "These men of God.........remind us of the slave hunters in *Uncle Tom's Cabin*."

The RC parish registers, at the National Library of Ireland, reveal that William Sherwood married Ellen Blake in a RC ceremony in the Parish of Wicklow on 14 June 1847.

The children were baptized in RC ceremonies either at St Andrew's Church, Westland Row, Dublin, or in the RC Parish of Wicklow. I found two more siblings, John and George, not in the newspaper reports. Were they alive in 1860, George (3 years old) would have been too young for the Spiddal Orphanage Home, while John (aged 15) likely would have been too old. In the 1901 Spiddal Orphanage Roster, there are no male children over the age of eleven.

There were conflicting attestations. Ellen Sherwood stated that her late husband was a member of "the Established Church" (the Church of Ireland) at his death, and wished his children be raised in his faith. Catherine Davis attested that William Sherwood was a practicing Catholic, and died a Catholic in St Vincent's Catholic Hospital in Dublin in August 1859, after reportedly receiving last rites.

Mrs Sherwood left Galway, and returned to her Dublin rooming house. Of course, the children were gone, courtesy of their maternal grandmother and her extended family. According to the Rev Alexander Dallas, a mob gathered, windows were broken, then large stones and a burning straw padded chair were thrown into her room. It was said that Ellen Sherwood ended up in Scotland.

The remaining two children, escorted by Mrs Hartnett from the Galway Train Station to the Spiddal Orphanage on that 14 March 1860 day, were also Catholic, given up by their mother after their father was imprisoned. A visiting reporter informed the incarcerated father of the children's transport to a "proselytizing school." The reporter wrote the father "exclaimed that, unfortunate as he was, he could not permit his children to be damned." What the incarcerated father managed to do, we do not know.

At his 1862 Spiddal Orphanage visit, the Rev Garrett stated: "I found FORTY-SIX resident children in this home, who are joined by others from the village during school-hours."

In the 19th Century, Spiddal was an isolated place, which was why it was chosen to have an orphanage. Yet this facility was well known, even in London, and was a very controversial place. It was not placed in Spiddal to serve any local need. Below are some excerpts from a December 1867 essay: *Irish Points For English Meditation*, Vol VII (No. XLII, page 481) of the Jesuit magazine *The Month*, published in London. John Henry Newman was a contributor. Our essayist is unidentified.

.......Thus the Spiddal Orphanage in Galway was found by a lady who lately visited it to be filled chiefly with the children from Dublin, sent there to be "out of the way of the priests," and of Catholic relatives. This Orphanage may indeed be considered to express with singular adequacy the aims of the class of religionists who promote these undertaking.....

...A lady who has recently visited the institution gives us the following account of her conversation with this person [an orphanage official]: A conversation now ensued between myself and the official who was showing me over the place.

Q. ' Where do your children come from? A. ' Chiefly from Dublin. 'Q. ' Why are they sent so great a distance? A. ' To hide them out of the way of the priests. ' Q. ' I suppose also out of the way of their Catholic friends?' A. ' Yes' (with a smile); ' it is a long time before the friends find out where they are. Many of these children are those of mixed marriages, and the Catholic friends try to get them. '

Q. ' Do not the Roman Catholic children say Catholic prayers when they come?' A. 'Yes, and we let them do so at first, till we prevail on them to give them up. 'Q. ' Have you any trouble in making the Roman Catholic children Protestants? A. ' O, indeed, the greatest. I like to have them as young as possible. I would rather have 150 young children to manage than one Roman Catholic child of 12 or 13. They fight every step of the way, and won't give up a point of their religion: but we go on at them. In school and out of school our whole conversation runs on the controversy; we bring it into everything, and at last we end by making those children who were so earnest better Protestants than any of the others. We had one girl here once, and she came from a nunnery, and she was so determined that she not only ran away herself, but took another girl with her, Next day they were both brought back, but the Committee met and decided that as she was irreclaimable she was to be expelled. 'Q. ' Why do any Roman Catholic parents send their children here? is it from poverty?' A. ' Yes, they are very poor —a widow, for instance, with several children; it is such a thing to get one or two of them off her hands for life.'

A Roman Catholic child would be raised Protestant, unless they were expelled. The abductions seemed to continue. On 27 April 1868, the Clifden parish priest Patrick M'Manus wrote to the *Freeman's Journal*:

......Not later than last Saturday, the 25th of this month, Mrs Browne, from Kingstown [Dún Laoghaire], Dublin, took out of the Clifden Bird's Nest three orphans to whom she is aunt and guardian. This noble-hearted lady, after a painful search during the last year, found out that her kidnapped proteges were in one of the Dublin Bird's Nests; but whilst she was procuring a legal order for their deliverance they were transferred to Clifden. After another torturing search, and incurring vast expense, she traced them to Clifden, and thus her meritorious efforts were in the long run crowned with success.....

Catholic children were sent to Spiddal from Dublin for the same reason the Egan children and Mrs Browne's "protégés" were removed to Clifden; to separate them from what the evangelical Anglicans thought were unwholesome influences. Namely, their friends and extended families.

The Anglican Rev Richard Rudd, who succeeded the Rev McCready in Spiddal in 1862, was an agent provocateur. Twenty years after the notorious 1849 Dolly's Brae riot, Spiddal had its own Orange incident. From the 17 July 1869 issue of *The Galway Vindicator and Connaught Advertiser:*

THE TWELFTH OF JULY IN SPIDDAL

While the reports of the Orange demonstrations in the North show a comparative immunity from the usual outrages which characterize the annual celebration of the Battle of the Boyne, our readers will no doubt be surprised to learn that, nearer home, a demonstration which, were it not for the prompt and active measures to repress it, would have led to a serious disturbance, was indulged in Spiddal, as in some other parts of Connemara, there exists a receptacle of proselytism, ycelpt [by the name of] "the Bird's Nest" and on Monday morning the good people of the sequestered locality were surprised to see an Orange flag flaunting in the breeze from the pinnacle of the building.

A holiday, too, to commemorate "the twelfth" was given by the Rector, Mr. Rudd, to the inmates of the Bird's Nest, who walked through the village in procession, decorated with Orange ribbons, etc. The labourers, working on the new Pier now being erected, naturally became exasperated at such a wanton insult, and had it not been for the timely interference and influence of Mrs. Murray, wife of Captain Murray, Sub-Inspector of the Constabulary, who was absent on duty in the North, they would have demolished the structure, and wreaked vengeance on those who had the temerity of outrage the feelings of a Catholic community. As it was there were only a few panes of glass broken. The offensive emblems were removed, and tranquility was restored before nightfall.---Correspondent

On 12 July 1869, the Rev Rudd has the orphans marching through Spiddal Village wearing "Orange ribbons" and other regalia, while the "Orange flag" was flying over the orphanage. What could possibly go wrong? One hundred or more strong men (including my great grandfathers), would have been working on the nearby Spiddal New Pier (Céibh Nua). It would have been quite a mob. The correspondent downplays the orphanage damage, as "there were only a few panes of glass broken."

As the panes broke, likely the orphans inside weren't as sanguine as the *Vindicator* correspondent.

An ICM propaganda publication: *The Banner Of The Truth In Ireland* (aka *The Banner),* announced in its 1 July 1870 issue, that fifty-seven children were resident in the orphanage, and that, in the previous decade, one hundred ninety-five children came through the orphanage/school.

About this time, Michael and Mary Hartnett's association with the Spiddal Orphanage, as master and matron, was to end. Mary Rachel Brew married Michael Hartnett on 15 Aug 1859 in the St Nicholas Collegiate Church in Galway. On 13 Apr 1868, their daughter Catherine was born in Spiddal. Late in 1868, before Catherine's first birthday, her father Michael Hartnett (aged 31) died. The three-year-old Catherine, seemingly alive in 1871, was orphaned when her mother Mary Hartnett died of fever on 15 May 1871. Thirty-six orphans who contracted the same fever seemed to have survived. Over time, there must have been orphan fatalities, and one wonders whether any of the mounds in the Martin Chapel, mentioned by Timín Curran, could be orphanage children.

Through the 1850s and 1860s, the orphanage was struggling. In 1862, the Rev Garrett stated:

..........I perceived a new kitchen, which the comfort and health of the whole institution calls for, stopped in process of erection from want of funds. I wish I could lead some kind friends to assist in its completion; they may send their aid to Mrs. Darley, Bohona Lodge, Spiddal, Galway, whose heart is deeply engaged in supporting this most important refuge for children in danger.

A genealogical narrative about Margaret Lappin states that the ICM closed the Spiddal Orphanage in 1873. However, it seems the orphanage was rescued, by affiliating with the Dublin evangelical, Ellen Smyly. A newspaper announcement in the 30 March 1874 edition of the *Dublin Daily Express* seems to confirm this:

SPIDDALL ORPHAN HOME

COUNTY GALWAY

This valuable Home for 60 destitute little Boys and Girls must be closed unless £400 can be contributed to pay the necessary expenses of 1873, and friends be raised up to subscribe and collect funds for 1874.

Contributions will be thankfully received by Mrs Smyly, 35, Upper Fitzwillam-street, Dublin, and by Miss Franks, 21, Lower Fitzwilliam-street, Dublin. A Friend has offered to give £100 at Easter [5 Apr 1874] in aid of the above institution, if £200 more can be collected or contributed by that time.

Dublin Daily Express
March 30, 1874

In late April 1874, it was announced that, although only half the required funds were raised, the Spiddal Home would remain open another six months, while fundraising continued. In Dec 1875, Miss Franks publicly acknowledged a £5 donation toward the home, indicating that it remained open through 1875.

The Quiver magazine was started in 1861 by the evangelical John Cassell. Below are various excerpts an article (Vol XVII, 1882) written by a Spiddal Orphanage partisan. This document resides in the University of Michigan Library (digitized by Google). The home was referred to as *The Bird's Nest*.

'The Quiver' (Vol XVII, pg 603, 1882)
THE "BIRDS' NEST" ORPHANAGES

Spiddal is an obscure fishing village on the west coast of Ireland. The neighouring country consists of little more than bogs and stones, and is very unproductive. A small river, with wooded banks, which flows from a lake two miles distant, joins the sea here. The shore consists of hard sand and rocks. The beautiful mountains of Clare can be seen across the bay, and the Island of Arran seawards. The scanty population are mostly engaged in fishing, while the women spin, weave, and dye the coarse flannel of which nearly all their clothes are made. They are very poor and ignorant. The potato crop here is uncertain, and when it fails "yellow meal" forms their principal food. Their religion consists in a firm belief that, provided they pay their dues, the priest can save their souls.......

In addition to isolation, the rural location had another advantage:

.....Food, too, is here much cheaper than in many other parts of Ireland. Thus, potatoes, eggs, and milk can be had for little more than half their cost in Dublin. A dinner of fish can be prepared for sixty children for two shillings and sixpence, and it is still possible to feed a child for £6 a year at Spiddal......

THE FIRST MISSION-HOUSE AT SPIDDAL.

It is many years since a clergyman [In 1847, the Rev James McCready, I suspect.], struck with the destitution and ignorance of these poor villagers, hired here, as a school and mission-house, a cottage, a little better than the rest, for, although it only had a clay floor, it actually possessed a door, windows, and a chimney. It was four yards long, and a little more than two and a half wide........

.......For some months school was held here daily, and a service once on Sundays; but this effort was not destined to be encouraged, and the owner of the cottage [Morgan Darcy, I suspect] very soon forbade its use for such a purpose. In spite of this opposition, however, the school was kept together, and at length a sufficient sum was collected to build two cottages. From these small beginnings, the present home at Spiddal eventually resulted.

THE PRESENT MISSION-HOUSE AT SPIDDAL.

During a period of famine, the necessity for finding food and shelter for homeless waifs and strays was keenly felt in the neighbourhood of Spiddal, and collections were made to support the starving children who thronged the school-house.....

.........The Little Children's Home at Spiddal as now been in existence for many years, but the collections for its support gradually became so small, that they would not supply the needs of more than twenty or thirty children, although there was room for seventy. Through the death of the lady [Mary Hartnett, I suspect] who had long made it her care it fell into the hands of those ladies [the Smylys] who manage the Birds' Nests at Kingstown.

The services of a master and mistress were secured, while the number of children was increased as the other Homes became too full. So Spiddal became a mother, supported by her child; and now so greatly have the affiliated Homes been extended, that it is like a good, kind, indulgent grandmother, with a family of happy grandchildren........

The ICM had a periodical for juveniles: _Erin's Hope_. Now follows an October 1882 article. This document resides in Oxford's Bodleian Library (digitized by Google). Orphanage life is discussed, along with how the orphanage occupants interacted with the local people and the Spiddal RC parish priest. There was tension. I suspect the author of this missive and the preceding _Quiver_ article are the same person.

"NEAD LE FARRIGE"
THE NEST BY THE SEA SPIDDAL JUNE.1882.

In the _Dictionary of Irish Architects 1720-1940_ the civil engineer and architect Benjamin Thomas Patterson is cited as having an 1882 commission to enlarge the orphanage. Halloran was the builder.

At the rather whitewashed west wing (right side) of the structure, notice, between the ground floor window and the first floor window, a little smidgen. It represents a tablet, displaying the orphanage motto: "Jehovah Jireh," that is, "The Lord Will Provide."

By 1882, the "Nead le Farrige" was a substantial complex. From the Oct 1882 edition of _Erin's Hope_:

Our picture [above] represents The Nest by the Sea, as it appeared on the 7th of June, from the top of the turf-stack just inside the gate leading into the road, only the monthly rose by the hall-door is not yet planted.....

.........On Galway market-days, the people passing to-and-fro on the road look respectable enough, with their good home-made red petticoats and blue cloaks; the clean white cap-border around the face, and the head comfortably wrapped up in a bright-coloured shawl.

But at home they look very poor, and the children seem content with one garment of white or red flannel, worn night and day, until it is unwearable. They are a kind-hearted people, and if left to themselves, would do all in their power for the inhabitants of "Nead le Farrige.........

......But the priest [Thomas Curran], a native of the place, and knowing all the people well, tries to prevent any kindness being shown. His house overlooks the Orphanage, and he can see all who go in or out.

In the chapel, he threatens the people with all sorts of trouble if they sell us milk or turf, and so terrifies them, that they scarcely dare speak openly; but through all the months of last winter some were faithful to us; turf was brought in the night, and little cans of milk.......

Our *Erin's Hope* correspondent, Sarah Davies, continues:

.....Miss Franks and I spent some days at the Orphanage early in June. One day we took a long walk with Mr. Staunton. We were going along a very narrow lane, when we saw a man and woman working in a potato-field. Mr. Staunton saluted them in Irish. The man answered loudly, and in a cross voice. A conversation was entered into, and the tones of the people seemed to grow more and more harsh, and the man shouldered his fork, and came over into the road, walking along with us, his wife following. I should have been alarmed, had I not seen Mr. Staunton's calm face and frequent smile. Soon we came to the cottage where these dwelt, and were offered a drink of milk, and they shewed us the old-fashioned mill-stone, where two women sit to grind, as described in St. Matthew's Gospel.

After we had left them, Mr. Staunton said they had only been talking about the School. He had been offering a good, free education, instead of the one the man could not afford to pay for. The man was only "barking."

But now let us return to the Orphanage and the children. Look at it! The piece with a gable-end is the old part of the house; it extends a long way back; the school room is at the end of it, towards the sea. The girls' dormitory extends the whole length of this part of the building. *Just above the parlour-window is* [See previous page] *a stone tablet, with the words," Jehovah Jireh," the motto of the institution.......*

....But now about the children. We have not quite filled up the house yet —for their maintenance, funds are very low; but we have between eighty and ninety boys and girls. Some came from Dublin when we were there—homeless children, received into the Elliott Home, and sent on to Spiddal.........

Surely it is not the will of our Father in Heaven that one of these little ones should perish. "Jehovah Jireh" is still our motto. We will trust, and not be afraid.

Sarah Davies
35, Upper Fitzwillam-street, Dublin

"Franks" was the maiden name of the benefactor, Ellen Smyly. We will learn more about her shortly. "Miss Franks" could be a sister of Ellen Smyly.

It is possible that the "very narrow lane", just referenced, could be either Bohoona (see the arrow on the page 60 map) or Cnocán Glas (about five hundred meters farther west). A maternal great grandmother of mine, Kate Folan, came from Bohoona. She was three years old in 1882. Thus it's possible that Mr Staunton was conversing with her parents, Michael Folan and Margaret Folan (née Lydon), my maternal great great grandparents. We will return to Kate Folan later.

In 1883, boycotting was still an issue. From the 35th Report of The Irish Church-Missions: "...Attempts were made by the priest of Spiddal and a young Roman Catholic curate, to Boycott Protestants, and thus to deprive even the children in the Orphanage of the necessaries of life. But the decided action of the local magistrate put an end to such illegal practices......." Likely this "decided action" was quietly informal, off the record. I checked.

The Spiddal Orphanage was back in the news in 1886. In Dublin in September 1886, a Dublin solicitor, Mr Kehoe, was in court representing Mr James Mahon, the father of five missing children. His three daughters were baptized at St Andrew's Catholic Church, Westland Row.

Apparently the married James and Margaret Mahon had separated. After Margaret's death, her sister, Mrs Anne Bell, claimed custody of the girls; Mary, Margaret, and Bella, all under ten years of age, and hid them away. A writ of habeas corpus issued for Anne Bell was found impossible to serve, as she had skipped the country.

In August 1886, seemingly some of his children were spotted at the Spiddal Orphanage. Mr Mahon visited and was turned away. In court, Mr Kehoe produced the affidavit of Mr Patrick M'Donald of 16 Tara-street, who knew the children. The deponent stated he saw them at the Spiddal Orphanage.

Mr Kehoe then obtained a conditional writ of habeas corpus against Mrs Ellen Smyly, the Rev George Shea, Mr Myles Staunton, and Mrs Anne Bell. Mrs Smyly denied any knowledge of the children, who were never produced. The writ was then quashed. It's good to have friends in high places.

One day James Mahon's missing son John turned up at his father's Dublin door, stating that he had just escaped from the ICM's Townsend St schools, leaving his brother James behind. Townsend St is north of Trinity College, between the College and the Liffey, and is about a five minute walk from St Andrew's Church, Westland Row. Mr Mahon obtained custody of both sons.

Mrs Anne Bell was discovered to be back at 98 Lower Leeson-Street, her old residence. On 27 March 1888, Mr Mahon and Mr Kehoe were at the Queen's Bench seeking a new writ against Mrs Bell. Mr Mahon testified that in November 1885 he saw his daughters at one of the Dublin "Bird's Nest" facilities (likely in Kingstown). Mr Justice Murphy renewed the original writ against Mrs Bell to produce the three girls, giving her a week to comply.

I found nothing more, so perhaps Anne Bell produced the three girls. One can only wonder what all this did to the children. Shortly, we'll learn their likely fate, had they remained at the Smyly facilities.

Myles Staunton and Catherine Staunton (née Darcy) were the Spiddal Orphanage Master and Matron until 1890, when Myles Staunton died young, aged 49. They married in Clifden in 1865, and might have arrived in Spiddal shortly after Michael Hartnett's death late in 1868.

A <u>Galway Advertiser</u> (GA) article discussed the ICM, and displayed a July 1896 photo of the Spiddal Orphanage's occupants, about 55 children. In the GA, see *Old Galway* and *Galway Diary*.

I found the 1897 edition of the Charities Register and Digest, published by Longmans, Green & Co of London. There is a reference to the Spiddal Home.

The Spiddal Orphans 1896
(Courtesy of the Galway Advertiser)

1897 Charities Register And Digest

Bird's Nest and Mission Ragged Schools (1859), Kingstown, Dublin.
Object. —Home for destitute children of both sexes.
Admission. —By application to Hon. Sec. for form.
Age at least 6. A few younger, but no babies.
Admission free, but 'should friends desire to pay, £7 a year is the sum required for food.'
Marriage of parents must be proved, also freedom from bodily defect and disease.
Children brought up as Protestants, 'and if old enough will from the first be sent to church.'
Subscribers have claim for admission. *Management*. —By Committee.
Income (1895). —Charitable contributions, £3.870; sale of work, £137.
Inmates. —203 (including workers) in the Bird's Nest; 86 at Spiddal Home, Galway,
which is partly supported by Bird's Nest funds. Bankers, Ulster Bank, Lower Baggot Street,
Dublin. Secretaries, Miss E. S. Smyly, 35 Upper Fitzwilliam Street, Dublin; Miss Shepard,
Bird's Nest.

Interestingly, the admission requirements are spelled out. Disabled bastards need not apply. One could characterize this as *conditional* charity. We see that for 1897, the Spiddal Orphanage was only partly financed by the Smyly organization, suggesting that the ICM was still involved. There is indirect evidence of this in the 1901 Irish Census.

An 1884 charities report has 80 children present in Spiddal. The above report has 86 (perhaps including staff) present in Spiddal for 1897. *Burdett's Hospital and Charities Annual Report* for 1898 cites 53 orphans, close to the number in the July 1896 photo, which might be cropped a bit on the left.

On page 1371 of *Thom's Official Directory of the United Kingdom of Great Britain and Ireland, 1904* is the synopsis of the Dublin Mission Homes and Ragged Schools.

It refers to the '*Nead le Farrige*' and its 80 occupants. I take this to mean that, in 1904, the orphanage is still in Spiddal. The 1906 edition of Burdett's Hospital and Charities Annual Report (page 937) indicates that, into 1905, the orphanage was still in Spiddal, with 99 residents. A late October 1905 newspaper announcement seems to indicate that the orphanage was still in Spiddal.

The 1908 edition, seeming (?) to cover 1907, has the orphanage in Sandycove Dublin. So, circa 1906, the Spiddal Orphanage moved to Dublin. See Appendix I.

We know a bit about about a subsequent owner of the (former) orphanage building, Peter Folan, thanks to Mícheál Ó Droighneáin of Furbo. Ó Droighneáin the IRA man knew Folan and initially had a low opinion of him, as Folan, fluent in Irish, worked as a censor for the British administration in Dublin Castle during the War for Irish Independence.

Ó Droighneáin didn't know that Peter Folan was one of Michael Collins' inside men, spying on the British, while omitting certain details in his translations of the Irish language letters crossing his desk. Perhaps suppressing incriminating information about Ó Droighneáin, as Folan seemed to have more than insinuated to Ó Droighneáin, when one day they encountered each other at Dublin's Broadstone Train Station (in those days the station for Galway-bound trains). Ó Droighneáin shunned Folan, but:

> During the Truce afterwards, I asked Michael Collins if he knew anything about this Peter Folan.
> 'I do, well', he said. 'What was he like?' 'He was allright', he said, and he laughed.
> After that, I had more respect for the man.

Spiddal Boarding/Day School ca 1970
(Courtesy of Noreen Kennedy)

Eventually, the Sisters of Mercy acquired the building, turning it into a girl's boarding school that accepted boys and girls as day students. Cousins of mine boarded there, while other cousins attended during the day. This complex was demolished and replaced, after free secondary education arrived in Ireland. One cousin remembers that the doomed building was of fine construction. A cousin, who boarded, remembers a nun with a hammer walking around at night, disciplining the loose nails in the squeaky floorboards.

In the ca 1970 building photo, the orphanage motto tablet seems to have been plastered over. One way or another, the tablet disappeared. Then the above building was knocked.

Some time after the demolition, someone noticed something barely protruding out of the ground, and carefully excavated it. It was the tablet. The current secondary school has a fence/wall running along the footpath by the street. Tim Curran caused the excavated tablet to be installed in the wall, not far from its original location. At right is an image of the tablet at its current location.

Jehovah Jireh Tablet

The Spiddal Orphanage opened in Spiddal ca 1854, moved to Dublin ca 1906, and survived in the Dublin area until ca 1955. By the time the orphanage moved to Dublin, I assume that the Smyly organization had complete control of it.

Thus the orphanage that started out in Spiddal, ca 1854, lasted a century, in various incarnations.

In its early decades the occupancy was typically 30-60 children, rising to something like 70-100 children toward the end of the 19th Century. There is the statement, in the 1 July 1870 ICM bulletin *The Banner Of The Truth In Ireland*, that in the previous decade, one hundred ninety-five children went through the Spiddal Home.

It follows that a conservative estimate would be, over its Spiddal lifetime, as many as one thousand children could have passed through the Spiddal Orphanage.

Eventually a Bunbury woman, Susan Bunbury, married into the Palmer family of Galway, millers and brewers. Her husband died not too long after the marriage. The widowed Susan Palmer, who lived in Spiddal's east-side Manor House into her 90s, was the last of her line in Spiddal. Mrs Palmer was friendly with the MacNamaras, who were the Master and Matron of the Spiddal Orphanage in 1901.

In *Voices of Connemara* is an essay by "Anonymous," a daughter of Mrs Palmer's Irish estate manager. Her brother, a favourite of Mrs Palmer, inherited the bulk of the estate after she died in 1931.

Our 'anonymous' essayist married in 1927, and would have been born just after the orphanage's move (ca 1906) to Dublin. Thus the stories of that era about the orphanage were fresh in the mind. She mentions that the orphanage children were often close to starving, and that a local Spiddal merchant (named Francis) would toss loaves of bread over the orphanage wall at night.

Our anonymous essayist considered the question: where was the poverty worse, in the city or in the country? She wrote: "The poverty in the city was worse than in the country because it was harder to go hungry in the country. And we had the sea here."

It is a seemingly simple question. But, the more one learns, the more difficult a question it is to answer.

The Spiddal Orphanage in the 1901 Census
Staff

Surname	Forename	Age	Sex	Relation To Head	Birthplace	Occupation
MacNamara	Patrick	67	Male	Head of Household	Mayo	Master of Institution
MacNamara	Kathleen	52	Female	Wife	Tyrone	Matron of Institution
Taylor	Ammella	30	Female	Assistant	Tipperary	Assistant
Moore	Elizabeth	29	Female	Assistant	England	Assistant
Hammond	Hanna	18	Female	Assistant	England	Laundress
McCarthy	Mary	24	Female	Assistant	Dublin	Cook
MacWilliam	Hannah	17	Female	Assistant	Dublin	Nurse
Brown	Eunice A	32	Female		England	Teacher
Mellett	Julia	25	Female		Galway	Teacher

In the 1901 Census is the orphanage, with 71 orphans and 9 staff. The census enumerator used the College and Boarding School Form, crossing out the printed phrase "Boarding School," replacing it with the word "orphanage". There seem to be about 16 buildings (23 rooms in all) associated with the orphanage. The "Master of the Institution" is Patrick MacNamara, originally of Co Mayo, and is the only bilingual person. His wife, Kathleen, from Co Tyrone, was the "Matron of the Institution." There were seven other staff, including 2 teachers.

In the 1901 Census, the orphans and the two teachers are in house 20.2, while the remaining staff are in house 20.1.

Nearby, in House 19, was the 65-year-old bilingual widower Patrick Gallagher and his 15-year-old daughter Olivia. Patrick Gallagher is originally from Co Mayo, of the Church of Ireland, with his occupation listed as 'Mission Agent', implying there was still a connection to the Irish Church Missions.

In the 1901 Census, the Anglican Vicar of the Killannin Parish, residing in Inverin, was the 41-year-old Dublin born William Colgan (B.A., Trinity College Dublin). His wife was the 43-year-old Constance. Including the orphanage, in 1901 there were 106 Anglicans (103 Church of Ireland, 3 Church of England), and 5 Presbyterians in Spiddal (Spiddal Town, Spiddal Middle, and Spiddal East).

In the 1901 orphanage roster, which follows, only one orphan, Lizzie Johns (age 13), is from Galway. Hers is a surname I've not encountered in Spiddal. I found no Irish civil birth record or baptismal record for her. But, there were Coastguards named *Johns* in the area. William Johns in Barna in 1878, John Johns at Costello Bay in 1882, and Thomas Johns in Kilronan in 1901. They are not in the GENUKI Coastguard database.

It would seem at most there was perhaps one 1901 orphan from the Spiddal area. The Spiddal area never suffered from a lack of orphans. One inference I took from the essay, *Irish Points For English Meditation*, was that there were few if any native Spiddal area urchins in the Spiddal Orphanage in 1866. Of course, this isn't surprising, given the sectarian emphasis at the facility.

1901 Spiddal Orphanage Roster--Girls

Surname	Forename	Age	Birthplace
Glynn	Maggie	15	England
Maher	Susan	16	Dublin
Waters	Lousia	17	Dublin
Hamilton	Georgina	16	Wicklow
Magrath	Frances	16	Dublin
Harris	Mary	15	Dublin
Jones	Frances	16	Dublin
Jones	Lizzie	14	Dublin
Patterson	Mary A	15	Cavan
Nicholson	Lilly	13	Wicklow
Nicholson	Mina	11	Wicklow
Johns	Lizzie	13	Galway
Miller	Lizzie	13	Dublin
White	Mary	10	Cavan
Hammond	Emily	10	Dundalk
Owens	Mary	12	Dublin
Owens	Katie	10	Dublin
Fitzgibbon	Lena	9	England
Garrett	Irene	11	London
Byrne	Margaret	11	Kilkenny
Vantreen	Rose	11	Dublin
ONeil	Lizzie	9	Dublin
Savage	Margl	8	Dublin
Cairnes	Katie	12	Dublin
Byrne	Florence	8	Wicklow
Riordan	Maggie	5	Dublin
Cairnes	Mary	8	Dublin
Byrne	Sarah	10	Dublin
Byrne	Lizzie	6	Dublin

1901 Spiddal Orphanage Roster--Boys

Surname	Forename	Age	Birthplace
Moore	Arthur	10	Dublin
Scott	Charles	11	Wexford
Cullen	Thomas	11	England
Clarke	William	10	Dublin
Dower	Michael	10	Dublin
Luke	Richard	9	Dublin
Falkner	Charles	11	Drogheda
Beamish	William	11	Dublin
Kelly	William	9	Dublin
Rorke	Harry	11	Dublin
Lambert	Thomas	10	Waterford
Falkner	John	9	Drogheda
Gough	James	10	Antrim
White	John	8	Cavan
Karney	John	9	Dublin
Savage	Edward	9	Dublin
Curry	William	9	Dublin
Moore	George	10	England
Hunt	William	7	Dublin
Gough	Stephen	8	Antrim
Moore	Patrick	10	Dublin
Moore	Thomas	8	Dublin
Harmsworth	Arnold	10	Wicklow
Scott	Alexander	8	Wexford
Williams	George	10	Belfast
Perkins	John	10	Dublin
Perkins	William	8	Dublin
Babster	Thos	8	Dublin
Beamish	Charles	7	Dublin
Leathem	Joseph	8	Dublin
Larvin	James	8	Dublin
Harmsworth	Gilbert	8	Wicklow
Clarke	Thomas	7	Dublin
Davis	Frank	8	Dublin
Vantreen	Abraham	9	Dublin
MacDuff	Jack	9	England
Riordan	John	6	Cork
Byrne	William	6	Wicklow
Jones	Alfred	6	Dublin
Browne	Ernest	10	England
Carson	Christopher	9	Belfast
Coote	Ernest V	6	Dublin

Shortly, we'll learn a bit about the lives of the children highlighted in the above table.

The Spiddal-Dublin-Canada Orphanage Connection

What eventually happened to the children? This orphanage was part of an international network, and this played a crucial role in the children's ultimate fate. In pages following, an extraordinary resource has been the British Home Children in Canada (BHCC) Website: <u>British Home Children In Canada</u>. Ellen Smyly (née Franks, 1815–1901) of Dublin, was an evangelical Irish Anglican. She started a home/school ca 1852, and by the mid-1870s was supporting several homes:

> Smyly Mission Homes and Ragged Schools of Dublin
> Smyly Orphans Homes of Dublin
> Smyly Coombe Boys' Home and Mission (in Dublin)
> Bird's Nest Home (Dún Laoghaire)
> Elliott Home (Bray, Co Wicklow)
> Nead le Farrige Home (Spiddal)
> The Coombe (Hespeler, Ontario, Canada, opened in 1905)

Reportedly Ellen Smyly's efforts inspired the Rev Thomas John Barnardo (1845-1905) to organize a similar network across England, starting in East London. William Quarrier similarly started in Glasgow Scotland in the 1860s. Ellen Smyly's daughters Ellen and Annie continued her work.

The number of pauper children overwhelmed these homes, and eventually emigrant children's programs came to be regarded as the solution. Pauper families and pauper children went to Australia, New Zealand, Rhodesia, South Africa, and Canada. Canada, and Ontario in particular, came to be popular. Initially, many of the so-called Smyly, Barnados, and Quarrie children went to Canadian receiving homes operated by the likes of Maria Rye and Annie MacPherson. Eventually many of the British organizations acquired their own Canadian receiving properties. In 1905 the Smylys purchased a house and 12 acre farm in Hespeler, Ontario, naming it *The Coombe*, after a Smyly Dublin property. Newly arrived children resided there for up to a year, received training, and had time to acclimate.

Some children were exploited and abused. Maria Rye removed a twelve-year-old Elizabeth Lynes from the Wolverhampton workhouse, and resettled her with a Canadian farming family. Lynes was beaten, prevented from communicating with her brother, and in 1873 at age 16 was impregnated by her master's son. Her master gave her a few dollars, paid her passage to Liverpool, and left it for her to find her way to the Wolverhampton workhouse. ~~In 1873 she gave birth to a son, John Lynes~~. See page 203.

Numerous reports of abuse resulted in an 1874 enquiry, and an 1875 report by the English inspector Andrew Doyle. Consequences of the Doyle Report were supposed to be better sponsor vetting, and subsequent monitoring of the children. But, after abusing and exiling Elizabeth Lynes, the same Canadian family in 1881 had another servant girl, the thirteen-year-old Annie Ross.

Juveniles, abandoning their assigned family, fed-up with their mistreatment, would be targeted for deportation by the Canadian authorities. Catch-all charges were feebleness, sickness (TB guaranteed deportation), vagrancy, or being a public charge. John Maloney was a stunning case; sent to Canada from Ireland in 1928 by the Catholic Emigration Association. In 1930, at age 18, he was deemed insane, but was declared fit to travel alone to his deportation, presumably back to his mother in Cork.

Apparently Canadians were misled into believing most emigrant children were orphans. The claim is, by modern standards, only about 2% were actually orphans. Likely it was truly a small fraction.

Abraham & Rose Vantreen

Within the Spiddal Orphanage, many children were from Dublin. As the crow flies, it is about 126 miles (202 km) from Dublin to Spiddal. A simple journey now, but an arduous journey back then, especially the last leg from Galway to Spiddal. Those Dublin children were effectively far from home.

I've often wondered about these children. What were their lives like before Spiddal? How did they come to be there? What happened to them after Spiddal? As I learned more about the Smyly organization, I started to have an inkling about what happened to them after Spiddal.

As they weren't local children, none of the names resonated with me, so I decided to choose an orphanage child at random for further investigation. There were a number of pairs of siblings present, and I decided to constrain my choice to someone with a sibling present.

I chose Abraham Vantreen (aged 9 in 1901), and his older sister Rose Vantreen (aged 11 in 1901). I like the name 'Rose' (okay, another constraint). I highlighted them in the orphanage roster (page 113). Is it possible they are in the 1896 photo? Rose would have been 7 years old. Abraham would have been about 4 ½ years old. For Rose, yes. For Abraham, possibly.

As Abraham and Rose Vantreen came from Dublin, let's take the rocky road to Dublin.

The available historical information shows a hard-scrabble existence spanning generations.
In 1850, Abraham Vantreen, the children's paternal grandfather, was booked into Newgate Prison, charged with felony theft of a gold ring belonging to Thomas Ralph. In short order the twelve-year-old Abraham was tried and acquitted of the charge, and was released from Newgate Prison.
By 1862, things were looking up for Abraham, as he is listed in _Thom's Irish Almanac and Official Directory Of Ireland, 1862_ as an ivory turner (who fashioned objects using a lathe). He did business at 2 Exchange St, Upper, next door to H Lazenby's pickle and sauce manufacturing operation.

Abraham's and Rose's father, John Vantreen, the first-born of eleven children, was born to Abraham Vantreen and Margaret Vantreen (née Norman) on 28 March 1860. A number of John's siblings died young, from smallpox and tuberculosis etc. John's mother Margaret died young (aged 42) in 1883. On Christmas Day 1887, at St Werburgh's Church Dublin, the widower Abraham Vantreen (the children's grandfather) married Prudence Bouchier, a spinster. They had no children.

A workhouse entry log shows, in January 1872, the seven-year-old Rosanna Hudson, the future mother of Abraham and Rose Vantreen, entered the workhouse alone, afflicted with smallpox. The log states Roseanna was Roman Catholic, and that she remained in the workhouse for two months.

On 6 Oct 1889, John Thomas Vantreen and Rose Hudson married in a Church of Ireland ceremony at St Werburgh's Church, very close to Dublin Castle. Too close to Dublin Castle.

John and Rose Vantreen had four children: Rose (b. 26 Aug 1889), Abraham (b. 23 Jan 1892), Margaret (b. 20 Oct 1894), and Martha (b. 29 Aug 1896). Rose, Abraham and Martha are in the Anglican St Werburgh's parish register, while Margaret is in the Anglican St Audoen's parish register. For the four baptisms, four different residential addresses are listed, which doesn't suggest social stability.

The infant Rose Vantreen spent a significant part of her first year or so of life in the workhouse. A 27 June 1890 workhouse entry log shows that Rose Vantreen (née Hudson) entered her ten-month-old infant daughter's name as *Rose Emma*.

In the late spring of 1901, when Rose and Abraham Vantreen are in the Spiddal Orphanage, their father John is in Mountjoy Prison for assaulting his wife. Their mother, their two sisters, and their maternal aunt (Kate Hudson) were in the South Dublin Union Workhouse. I suspect the children Margaret and Martha entered the '*orphanage*' system in 1902 or 1903.

John and Rose Vantreen, and their two younger children, Margaret and Martha, are absent from the 1901 Census. The simplest explanation is that they were sleeping rough. Workhouse records show that John Vantreen slept rough on occasion.

On 31 March 1901, Irish Census Day, when Abraham and Rose Vantreen are residing in the Spiddal Orphanage, they are not orphans, as both their parents were alive.

Workhouse records indicate that, by 1903, the children's mother Rose Vantreen (née Hudson) contracted TB. Rose left the workhouse for the last time on 26 March 1904. On 6 April 1904, at the Harold's Cross Hospice in Dublin, a 39-year-old Rose Vantreen (née Hudson) of 19 Garden Lane (in *The Liberties*), died after months of affliction with tuberculosis and asthenia.

The senior Abraham Vantreen and his second wife Prudence are present in the 1911 Census as Vantree. The Vantreen family still lived at 22 Werburgh Street. Present were Abraham Vantreen aged 74, a caretaker, and Prudence, his wife, aged 63. They stated they were married 16 years (24 years in fact) and had no children. They were involved in St. Werburgh's Church/School for many years.

In 1911, also resident with Abraham & Prudence was John Vantreen, son, aged 45 according to the Census (actually 51), a grocer's packer and a widower (since 1904) born in the City of Dublin. This John Vantreen is the father of Rose, Abraham, Margaret and Martha Vantreen. Prudence Vantreen would be the children's step-grandmother. In 1911, there are three adults and no children residing in the Vantreen household. What happened to the children?

In the 1911 Census, the Spiddal Home in Sandycove Dublin had a cook. The cook was the 21-year-old Rose Vautrau. This is Rose Vantreen. The 15-year-old Martha Vautreen was in the Ellen Symly's Bird's Nest Home on York Rd, in Kingstown. There were about 120 'orphans' in the facility. I couldn't locate Margaret Vantreen, or her brother Abraham Vantreen, in the 1911 Irish Census. Eventually I did find them.

St Werburgh's Church, which figured so prominently in the Vantreens' lives, has an interesting history. See Frank McNally's 9 September 2015 *Irish Times* article: St Werburgh's Church. The most famous occupant of this church/cemetery would be Lord Edward Fitzgerald, who was interred there, after his violent 1798 demise.

Within the church's graveyard are memorials to the brothers Guinness; Benjamin, Edward, and Hosea, the sons of the brewer Arthur Guinness. The eldest son, the Rev Hosea Guinness, was a rector of St Werburghs. There is a memorial to Anne Lee Guinness (1774-1817), first wife of Arthur Guinness II. She also has a memorial in the Mount Jerome Cemetery, which opened in 1836, well after her death.

Arthur Guinness Senior favored Catholic Emancipation, and the Guinness philanthropy is well known.

But, the 1852 edition of *The Banner* lists an "Arthur Guinness Esq" [*Arthur Guinness II*], pledging £200 to the *Irish Church-Missions to the Roman Catholics*. I hesitate to call that philanthropy. I'm reminded of that when a fresh pint of Guinness approaches my parched lips.

St Werburgh's proximity to Dublin Castle had tragic consequences for Abraham & Prudence Vantreen.

From the *Dublin Fire Brigade Ambulance* log notes: "26 April 1916 10.07am Werburgh Street 'Ambulance returned left Prudence Vantreen 60 of 22 Werburgh Street dead in Mercer's Hospital.' "

Prudence Vantreen, shot in her left forearm, hemorrhaged to death and became one of the civilian casualties of the 1916 Easter Rising. Prudence Vantreen's name is on the Easter Rising Memorial Wall, somewhere in Glasnevin Cemetery. She is buried in the Mount Jerome Cemetery Dublin. The widower Abraham Vantreen, aged 83, a caretaker living at 22 Werburgh Street, died at the South Dublin Union Workhouse on 28 June 1919, from senility and heart failure.

Now let's return to the Vantreen children. Earlier, I couldn't find the young Abraham Vantreen in the 1911 Irish Census. That's because he wasn't in Ireland.

Arrival 12/5/1906 TUNISIAN
James Abbott, George Baker, Thomas Burns, George Corbett, Abraham Dantreen, Ernest Dixon, Albert Duffy, John Forbes, Charles Gill, Bertha Holms, Elizabeth Keith, John Lowe, Joseph Shaw, Bertram K Sweeny, Robert West, Samuel Wheller, John Wilson, There are 17 children noted on the LAC Database for this group.

THE ARRIVAL OF THE LAST PARTY OUT.

Abraham Vantreen in Halifax Canada--1906

The captioned photo comes from the British Home Children in Canada website. The caption lists some of the SS Tunisian passengers onboard when the ship arrived at the port of Halifax on 12 May 1906. I found the passenger manifest.

"Abraham Dantreen" is a passenger manifest misentry. This is the 14-year-old Abraham Vantreen. The group's final destination is Hespeler Ontario, the location of the Smyly Coombe Home. These were Smyly children, and likely Abraham Vantreen is one of the lads in the photograph. In the photo, presumably there is one box per child, each box containing a child's worldly possessions.

Abraham Vantreen is in the 1911 Canadian Census (as Vantrsen). His three sisters; Rose, Margaret, and Martha, arrived together (recorded as Vautran) in Ontario in May 1911 on the SS Tunisian. They were part of a group of 100 MacPherson Home youths. Given her age, nearly 22, Rose Vantreen may have been functioning as a chaperon. In the 1911 Canadian Census (started 1 June 1911), Abraham (age 19) and Margaret Vantreen (age 17) are in Ontario, residing in the Wilison household, listed as laborer and servant. So, a few weeks after the 2 April 1911 Irish Census, Rose, Margaret, and Martha Vantreen left Dublin for Canada, arriving in time for the June 1911 Canadian Census. Eventually, Rose Vantreen married Abraham's 1906 travelling companion, Charles Gill.

Curiously, the 20-year-old Abraham Vantreen arrived in Liverpool from Quebec, on the Empress of India, on 22 Nov 1912, final destination unknown. To see his father John? I suspect so. I also suspect Abraham arrived in Dublin with enough money for two fares back to Canada. There is a John Vantreen departing Liverpool alone, for Quebec, on the RMS Laurentic on 27 May 1913.

I don't know when Abraham returned to Canada. But he did return to Canada, enlisting to fight in the Great War. At Kingston Ontario on 1 Nov 1915, an unmarried Abraham Vantreen enlisted in the Canadian Expeditionary Force. He shipped abroad as a driver for a Canadian Field Artillery Regiment. He survived the war, arriving back at Halifax on 2 July 1919.

When the unmarried Abraham joined the Canadian Expeditionary Force on 1 Nov 1915, he had to provide a name for next of kin. He listed his father, John Vantreen, giving his father's address as Campbellville Ontario. Thus, by Nov 1915, John Vantreen and his children are reunited in Canada.

The 1911 Irish Census shows John Vantreen in Dublin. Abraham's 1915 enlistment document has John in Campbellville Ontario. The 1921 Canadian Census states that *John Vantreen immigrated to Canada in 1870.* In the 1921 Census, he was residing in the Ontario sub-district of Nassagaweya, which contains the rural community of Campbellville.

I searched, unsuccessfully, for a John Vantreen doppelganger. I didn't find John in the 1871 Census. Taking the 1921 Canadian Census entry at face value, in 1870 it seems the ten-year-old John Vantreen was of an early emigrating generation of British Home Children. Returning to Dublin from Canada, he married Rose Hudson in Dublin on 6 Oct 1889. They started their Dublin family, tragedy intervened, and their four children were part of the next generation of emigrating British Home Children.

On 17 Sept 1921, Abraham Vantreen married Isabel Paisley (1895-1978) in Waterloo, Ontario. Isabel had a hard Dublin childhood, spending time at a Henrietta St tenement, and the workhouse. Her Belfast-born father, a Dublin waiter, died from TB when she was a child. Was Isabel a British Home Child? Possibly. Probably.

Abraham Vantreen died on 10 Apr 1939, and is buried in the *St. John's Anglican Church Cemetery* in Campbellville Ontario. Rose Vantreen Gill (1889-1961) is buried in the *Mount Pleasant Cemetery*, Toronto Municipality, Ontario. John Thomas Vantreen died in 1925, and is buried in the same Ontario cemetery as his son Abraham. John T Vantreen's Dublin birth is noted on his headstone.

Other Spiddal Home Orphans

In the Spiddal Orphanage roster are William Perkins (b. 5 April 1892 in Glasnevin, Dublin), James Gough (b. 28 December 1890), and his brother Stephen Gough (b. 15 June 1892). The Gough brothers were born in Larne, East Antrim. These three lads enlisted in the Canadian Expedition Force, and two perished in the Great War. James Gough (d. 3 October 1916) is commemorated at the Vimy Memorial, Pas de Calais, France. A twice-wounded Stephen Gough survived the war. He died in 1972 at the age of 80, and is buried in St Mary's Cemetery, Perth County, Ontario Canada. William Perkins (d. 29 March 1916) is interred in the Ridge Wood Military Cemetery Ypres, West Flanders, Belgium.

William Beamish (b. 8 Apr 1890) and Charles Beamish (b. 21 Feb 1893) were born in the South Dublin area to William Henry Beamish & Margaret Beamish (née Parke), who married on 25 October 1882, while residing in St Fintan's Parish Howth Dublin. Early in 1904, Margaret Beamish was a cook-housekeeper at the Royal Engineers' mess hall in the Curragh (Co Kildare).

A 30 January 1904 coroner's inquest revealed that she succumbed to burns sustained in an accident in the mess kitchen on 28 January 1904. After a perfunctory mourning period, William Henry Beamish remarried on 9 June 1904. In 1901, William and Charles Beamish of the Spiddal Orphanage were not orphans.

A grand-niece of Charles and William generously provided me with information about them, including a caseworker's notes on Charles.

In the 1911 British Census, the unmarried William was residing in Wiltshire England. He was a decorated veteran of the British Army (1916-1920), who married Ethel Palmer in Wiltshire in 1919. They had nine children. William Beamish retired as a Head Groom in Maiden, Bradley, Wiltshire, and died in Birmingham on 12 Jan 1968.

Charles Beamish left the Spiddal Home on 19 May 1904, and then left Liverpool on 28 July 1904, arriving in Quebec on 4 August 1904, bound for Miss MacPherson's Home in Stratford Ontario. In January 1905, the twelve-year-old Charles is residing in the home of J J Reid.

The 1907 caseworker notes documented the 14-year-old Charles' concern, after his father stopped answering his letters.

In the 1911 Canadian Census, the eighteen-year-old Charles was a servant residing in the Ontario farm home of James & Mary Johnston. He is absent from the 1921 & 1926 Canadian Censuses. Charles is not in the 1939 England and Wales Registry. Charles Beamish, a retired farm hand, died on 15 June 1980 in a Reading Berkshire UK nursing home.

Which is sadder; to be truly orphaned, or to be treated like that by your father? Before thinking ill of the father, who may deserve it for how he treated his son, first direct ones disdain toward those who regarded the parents with contempt, and who treated the children as an export commodity.

It's time to ramble back to Cois Fharraige.

The Spiddal Fishery

FOURTH ANNUAL REPORT of the Commissioners of Public
Works in re the Fisheries of Ireland 1846

The Spiddal River.

James Tracy, sworn.—Lives at Spiddal, and is employed by Mr. FitzPatrick. He is acquainted with the Spiddal river about fourteen or fifteen years. The fishing always commenced in June and closed in October; that was the latest month he ever knew the river to be fished. They always caught good fish, and in fair quantity, up to the 15th October. Ho has opened the fish caught in September and October, and found some small in pea and others far advanced. This is more a Salmon than a Trout fishery; it is sometimes, but very seldom, fished by a weir: this weir is about thirty yards from the sea, and the high tides come up to it. The fish caught are not sold. The bottom of the upper part of the river is rocky and gravelly, and there are a great many streams running into that part, so narrow that one could step across them; so that the fish could be most easily caught there. From the sea to the source the river is about twenty miles in length, but he does not think it possible to protect it in the higher parts, there are so many small, narrow, and shallow streams. He has seen good fish taken in this river in October every season he fished in it. Mr. FitzPatrick wishes that the season should extend to the 20th September. The natural obstruction, beyond which it is impossible for the fish to pass, is about two miles from the sea. There was a passage made through it once, but the fish which went up never returned. The land along the river from the sea to the source is the property of different persons. The obstruction is a solid rock, and the passage to which he alluded as having been made at one time was a little bye way, which was cut round by the rock. If the proprietors above got a share of the fish they might protect for one or two years, but as they would not be remunerated they would not continue that protection.

In an appendix is a description of the obstruction:

There is an impassable barrier on the Spiddal, two miles from the sea; it is fifteen feet in height, and consists of solid rock, fine lakes and breeding places in the upper part of the river: it is fished with rods and nets.

Now back to the main testimony:

Martin Morris, esq., J.P., having been sworn, deposed that he was acquainted with the river Spiddal these forty years. The obstruction alluded to is a natural one of solid rock. The fishing always commenced in June and closed in October. The latest time he has seen season fish in this river was about the 6th October. The 20th August is too soon to cease fishing on this river. He has a Salmon weir on it, but it is now seldom used. About thirty years ago he and Sir Robert Staples made a cut round the natural obstruction with a view to the improvement of the fishery, and the result was that the next year the fishery was very bad; it was quite inferior to that of former years both in the number and the quality of the fish. They observed the fish going up when the passage was opened, and they must have been destroyed above, as they were not seen returning.

The removal of the obstruction would certainly benefit the fishery, but great expense would be necessary for the undertaking; and in consequence of the number of branching rivers in the upper part, it would be impossible to preserve the breeding fish without a very great outlay: the property above is much subdivided, and the people could not afford to meet the necessary expense—first, of removing the obstruction, and afterwards of preserving the fishery. His only objection to the removal of the obstruction is in consequence of the great expense necessary. There would still be destruction of the fish, and the entire cost of protection would fall on Mr. FitzPatrick. When the passage was made it was kept open for two years, and neither the supply nor the quality of the fish was so good as before; and since it was closed, there is a great difference in the number and quality of the Salmon. He has seen 200 Salmon killed in this river with the rod by one party in a season; he cannot say if there were ever 500 Salmon caught in the year....

Martin Morris's above statement, about his work thirty years earlier (ca 1816) with Sir Robert Staples, is the earliest reference I have about human intervention on the Boluisce River. James FitzPatrick, who would would have been the FitzPatrick controlling the Spiddal area properties, died in 1828, with no male heir. Thus the Mr FitzPatrick referenced above is not James FitzPatrick.

The meeting continued with similar testimony from Edward O'Malley, who was concerned with the area around Boluisce Lake, as his family had land there (see Boliska Oughter & Eighter, page 7).

There were large fish in the Boluisce, and all sorts of arguments about who had the right to take them.

ANGLING

Mr. Blake, of Furbough, killed with rod and fly
in the Spiddal river, on Friday last, 21ˢᵗ inst, a
a salmon, which weighted 24 ½ lbs.

Galway Vindicator and Connaught Advertiser
22 July 1848

On the front page of the 24 December 1853 issue of the *Galway Mercury* was extensive coverage of the preceding Wednesday's sitting of Spiddal Petty Sessions. From the *Mercury*:

The Magistrates in attendance were---Andrew W.
Blake, Martin Morris, Patrick Blake, R. A. Kirwan,
John B. Kernan, R. M., and John Scully, R. M., Esqrs.

.

All the minor cases having been disposed of, and
and only one at the suit of A. W. Blake v. Michael
Morris, Esq, being remaining.

One of the minor cases disposed of was that of the Rev Coleman Connolly and his ferocious dog.

Of course, Michael Morris is the son of one of the magistrates, Martin Morris, and was being taken to court by another magistrate, Andrew W. Blake. Awkward.

The Chairman, R. A. Kirwan, wanted no part of this:

> The Chairman said he would be very glad if some
> other gentleman would take the chair while trying
> that case. He also observed that he would not take
> any part in the proceedings except with the
> approbation and desire of both the complainant and
> defendant.

The immediate issue concerned the validity of summons that were served to Michael Morris on behalf of Andrew Blake. The underlying issue was fishing on the Spiddal River. Andrew W. Blake alleged:

> ....that you [Michael Morris] did during the said month [Sept]
> and on or about the fifteenth day thereof, at Spiddal
> aforesaid, direct and encourage certain other persons
> to wit, Martin Folan, Patrick Folan, John Connor,
> Peter Feeney, Michael Conneeley, Thomas Conneeley,
> Mark Curreen, and others, to commit a breach of the
> peace generally, and particularly towards said comp-
> lainant, and that from said grounds, as well as from
> other information, which has been communicated
> to the complainant, and which he believes to be well
> founded, he is apprehensive of you committing and
> inciting a general breach of the public peace generally,
> and especially towards complainant, and has, therefore
> prayed that you may be held to bail to keep the
> peace, and be of good behavior towards all her Majesty's
> subjects generally, and particularly towards
> the complainant. This is to command you to appear
> as defendant, on the hearing of said complainant, at
> the Court of Petty Sessions, at Spiddal in said
> County and district, on the 22nd Day of December,
> inst., 1853, at 11 O'Clock, forenoon, before such
> Justices as shall be there.
>   (Signed)
> JOHN SCULLY, Justice of Peace for said County,
> Dated this 10th day of December, 1853.

Andrew Blake is continuing to fish the Spiddal (Bolsuice) River without permission. Of course, if in the past you had caught a 24 ½ lb salmon on the river, you wouldn't stop either. The Bohoona lads; the Folans et al, who are mentioned in the complaint, would seem to be Michael Morris's fishery wardens, his muscle on the river. I wonder who was keeping an eye on them. Apparently they made an intimidating impression on Andrew W Blake on or about 15 Sept 1853.

Either the Martin Folan or Patrick Folan just mentioned is possibly my maternal great[3] grandfather. One way or another, I am related to them, and undoubtedly to some of the other muscle as well.

Whatever threats were made weren't idle ones. A newspaper account related a earlier incident, involving a Mr O'Flaherty fishing on the river, that led to bloodshed.

Two summons were served to Morris, one at his Temple St Dublin residence, and one at his Wellpark Galway residence. Michael Morris claimed a Galway JP had no authority in Dublin, and also claimed the Wellpark summons was improperly served to a servant. One retort to him was, valid or not, he obeyed the summons and showed up in court. Michael Morris also objected to John Scully's involvement. It goes on and on. The Court agreed with Michael Morris. The summons were not properly served. Morris knew the law. He became Attorney-General of Ireland in 1866.

The matter dragged on inconclusively in the Spiddal Petty Sessions. At the 21 December 1853 session, only two magistrates were on the Bench, with opposing opinions about whether Morris should be ordered to keep the peace. Thus no order was issued. On the last day of 1853, Blake and Morris were trading barbs in the *Galway Mercury*.

The matter had become an unseemly public spectacle, and was sent to the January 1854 Quarter Sessions. There, an affidavit from Morris was produced and read in Court, stating it was never his intent to "commit a breach of the peace or incite others to do so..." This reassured Andrew Blake, who requested that the case be dismissed from the Quarter Sessions, which the justices were happy to do.

Everyone climbed down. A Quarter Sessions ruling would have only concerned ordering Michael Morris keep the peace, and wouldn't have addressed the fundamental question of fishing rights on the river. That question was settled in a subsequent case. Let's head back to Court.

Farrer a. Blake

This was an action brought against the Defendant for taking fish in the river of Spiddal, in the county of Galway, the river alleged being the exclusive of several fishery of the plaintiff.

It appeared in evidence that Mr. Morris, who holds Spiddal lodge under lease, and who claims the exclusive right to fish the river under a lease made to him by a Mr FitzPatrick, leased the lodge and the right to fish to a Mr. Moore, who resided for some years in Spiddal lodge. In 1852 the plaintiff purchased the lease from Mr. Morris for £650, and thought he had been purchasing the exclusive right to fish; but in a short time after he came into possession he found that Mr. Blake claimed the right to fish there also,----

Several witnesses were examined for the plaintiff, but they all admitted that defendant always, for years, fished the river without asking the permission of any person.

The case having been fully investigated, was sent to the jury, and the found a verdict for the defendant with costs.

Counsel for plaintiff---Messrs. Fitzgerald Q. C., and
Robinson Q. C.   Agent—Mr. Todd.

For the defendant---Messrs. Bourke Q. C., Kelly
and Concannon. Agent---Mr. J. C. O'Shaughnessy

Mr. Beytagh attended to watch the proceedings
on behalf of Mr. P. S. Comyn, who also claims a right
to fish in the disputed part of the river.

Galway Mercury and Connaught Weekly Advertiser
March 22, 1856

Andrew Blake won. Peter Sarsfield Comyn owned the Spiddal West townland, part of whose western boundary was the Spiddal River. He claimed the right to fish from a section of the east bank of the river.

The *Mercury* article is interesting because it states Morris held Bohoona Lodge, and the fishery, "under lease." It seems the Morrises are dealing in leases in the same fashion as the Comyns. I suspect the original land lease goes back to John FitzPatrick of Loughmore, who may have leased it from Robert Martin (of Ross) prior to 1700. FitzPatrick's daughter Catherine married George Morris in 1684. It's said some Spiddal lands came to Morris as the dowry, but, apparently not Bohoona Lodge, as the news article states that Morris held it "under lease." Or perhaps, somehow, the lease was the dowry.

The FitzPatricks of Loughmore (aka the FitzPatricks of Aran) were a junior branch of the Fitz-Patricks of Upper Ossory. The James FitzPatrick of Loughmore, who *d.s.p* in 1828, was the last male in the FitzPatricks of Loughmore line. His estate passed to a male in the FitzPatrick of Ossory branch.

John Wilson FitzPatrick was born as John Wilson. He was the illegitimate son of the 2nd Earl of Upper Ossory. He inherited some of his father's lands, and managed to assume the FitzPatrick name. As we're about to see, John Wilson Fitzpatrick held fishing rights on the Boluisce.

Who held what interest, how, when, and on what part of the Spiddal Fishery, was complicated.

Martin Morris had seen 200 salmon taken in a season, but couldn't say if 500 salmon were ever taken from the Spiddal River. In 1842, nearly 7800 salmon, weighting over 51,000 lbs, were taken from the much larger Ballynahinch Fishery, along with nearly 20,000 lbs of trout. In 1845, Mr Tracy testified that the caught Spiddal River fish weren't sold. That seemed to continue down through the years.

For the Morrises, the rod seemed to be much preferred over the net. Given its limited extent, the Spiddal Fishery was a sport fishery, and not a commercial fishery, as was Ballynahinch.

After losing to Andrew Blake, Captain John Farrer must have been annoyed with Martin Morris, after paying good money for exclusive fishing rights, that turned out to be not so exclusive. Unsurprisingly, John Farrer took Martin Morris to court. The Mr Moore mentioned in the previous page was the Anglican cleric who owned the Spiddal yacht called *the Daw.*

COMMON LAW REPORTS,

QUEEN'S BENCH, COMMON PLEAS, EXCHEQUER,

COURT OF CRIMINAL APPEAL

FARRER v. MORRIS.

H. T. 1857.
Jan. 13.
On a motion to set aside plead ings as embar rassing, costs are discretion ary with the Court, and will be awarded, though not de manded by the notice of mo tion, if the Court think it a fit case for costs.

[H. T. = Hilary Term]

This was an action for breach of a covenant for the enjoyment of an exclusive right of fishery. The summons and plaint set out an indenture of lease, dated the 18th of August 1834, by one Martin Morris to John Moore, of the house and lands of Spiddal Lodge, " together with the exclusive right of the fishery in the river Spiddal," for three lives; by which indenture Martin Morris covenanted with John Moore, his heirs, executors, administrators and assigns, " That he John Moore, his heirs and assigns, should " and would have full and free liberty and power, and the sole " and exclusive right of fishing in the said river Spiddal during the " continuance of the said demise." The summons and plaint then stated an indenture, dated the 21st of August 1854, between John Moore of the first part, John Wilson FitzPatrick of the second part, and the plaintiff of the third part, whereby John Moore conveyed, and John Wilson FitzPatrick confirmed, unto the plaintiff the said lands and the fishery for the same lives as in the indenture of 1834. It then stated a breach of the covenant. To this the defendant pleaded, first, that Martin Morris, at the time of the making of the said indenture of the 18th of August 1834, had the exclusive right of the fishery in said river of Spiddal, so as to enable him to make such indenture of lease. Secondly, that John Moore did not grant or convey to the plaintiff the sole and exclusive right of fishing in the said river Spiddal, as same was demised by the said Indenture of the 18th of August 1834 by the said defendant to the said John Moore.

H. T.
1857
Morris
v.
Farrer

Todd moved to set aside the defences, as being embarrassing, and because they tendered immaterial issues.

Blake (with him *M. Morris*), contra.

Per Curiam.   The pleas are clearly embarrassing, and must be set aside.

Morris.   The Court will not give costs of the motion against defendant, no costs being demanded.

Per Curiam.   Costs are discretionary. Allow the motion, with costs.

Three lives means the lease will last as long as the longest-lived of three named leaseholders. An *embarrassing plea* contains unverifiable assertions, ambiguous or unintelligible or irrelevant information, or some combination of the preceding. The Morris legal team was in trouble.

If Capt Farrer lost, he would have been stuck with the existing situation. Had Farrer won, resulting in an invalidated lease, presumably he would have received his money back from Morris (plus costs). Farrer would have vacated the property, and they would have gone their separate ways. It would seem that Capt Farrer won:

AUCTION
AT
BOHONA LODGE, SPIDDAL,

(late the residence of Captain Farrer),

On WEDNESDAY, The 22ND INST,

The FURNITURE of Two Sitting Rooms, and
Six Bed Rooms, fully Furnished with every
necessary for a Gentleman's Country Lodge.
An Elegant Piano Forte,
Kitchen and other Miscellaneous Articles.
A Fat Cow, etc etc

WITHOUT ANY RESERVE

SALE AT TWELVE O'CLOCK
E. STAUNTON, & CO.,
AUCTIONEERS

Galway Vindicator and Connaught Advertiser
11 April 1857

I'm sure I haven't uncovered all the litigation involving the Boluisce. There is a saying in the American West: *Whiskey is for drinking, water is for fighting.* As is the case in Ireland.

Eventually, in 1862, it fell to J B Bunbury to deal with the fifteen-foot-tall impassible solid rock barrier:

No. 2.--SPIDDAL WEIR   [1867 Fisheries Report]

The blasting of the rocks at Spiddal Waterfall was commenced by J.B Bunbury, Esq., in June 1862, and performed according to the plan sent from the Board of Works. The act and plan could not be properly carried out before the floods came on, so that the work was obliged to remain unfinished till June 1863, when it was again commenced, and the ladder made and put up by the end of September. The work was examined and approved as of being according to the specification of Mr. Forsyth, the engineer of the Board of Works, by Mr. Eden, the Commissioner of Fisheries. A quantity of salmon and trout have been seen going up the ladder and into the sluice above it into the lake, particularly last year. A salmon was taken weighting eight pounds in the lake, and five others let go, also many white trout.

I am sure in August many fish may be taken in the lake.   As Mr. Bunbury wished the fish to increase, he did not wish anyone to take them this season. The ladder was made of the best Memel timber brought from Galway. A quantity of iron was used, made into braces and plates, to keep the steps firm. Much lead was also used, and about six barrels of gunpowder. All those cost about 60 ℓ; the blasting and labour over that, say about 70 ℓ; total, 130 ℓ. The cost of carrying in the materials by men added much to the cost; and if J. B. Bunbury had not acted as engineer it would have cost far more.
[ℓ = librae; £]

J B Bunbury seems to be neither a sibling nor a child of Thomas J Bunbury. How did J B Bunbury's June 1862 project turn out? By 1867 the Spiddal River was on the angler's map. In the Harvard College Library is Dr W Peard's 1867 journal of his Year of Liberty. I'm guessing he was a bachelor:

CHAPTER XXIX
Spiddal—Costello--Screebe--Furnace--Kilkerrin Bay—Biterbury Bay--Roundstone—Ballinahinch--Clifden--View from Urrisberg.

August 3

POST TENEBRAS LUX---Heath after sickness, joy after sorrow, day after night, are each in their way delightful, and doubly so from the mere force of contrast.....

.......A charming drive of ten miles along a coast road of marvellous beauty brought us to the little village of Spiddal, through which the stream hurries, and at once plunges into the sea....

......The comfortable lodge belonging to "the fishery" stands on a lawn that slopes down to the river, on the opposite bank of which rests the village, whilst between the lodge and the church the road to Costello, crossing the river at its mouth.....

.....The view of Galway Bay from the house is very fine, nor need the stranger fear for bodily starvation whilst banqueting on the beautiful, for in the village he will find good bread, butter, mutton, eggs, and fowls; and what more can a sportsman desire?

....The length of the Spiddal is about twelve miles, but until very recently a waterfall, situated about three miles from the sea, barred the further progress of the fish, and so practically reduced the river to a fourth of that extent. Now however, a passage has been made which gives the salmon free access to the head waters , and the benefit of the extended franchise is already beginning to be felt. The water is well preserved , as the proprietor told me he employs eight keepers — a very strong staff considering the length of the property to be watched [see page 122]......

...The scenery on the banks of the Spiddal is very lovely . As I saw it, there was a crystal stream fretting and murmuring at the mighty granite blocks that offered a hindrance to its passage; blooming heather, pleasant woods, and three miles from the sea a waterfall of exceeding beauty; then came a lake of considerable extent, then another stretch of rivulet, then another smaller lake, and so on to source. In wet weather the best angling will be found on the river; in dry seasons on the lakes; the fish are fine, the salmon running from 5lb . to 18lb., the white trout from 1lb . to 6lb . Four or five of the former and a dozen of the latter would be a fair day's sport on the Spiddal; the proprietor, however, assured me that as many as eleven salmon had been killed in one day by a single rod . Many of the casts are very large and deep, as the Blue Pool, House, Weir, Wood , and Waterfall pools.

The river, though very low, was regularly tempting, and had there been a fresh I should have desired nothing better than a day or two on its banks; but there was no chance of such a thing, so I could only hope for better fortune on some future occasion . The rent of house and angling is 100ℓ. Per annum; and what a holiday station for any overworked dweller in our great and busy cities ! Why a turn on the lawn, the music of the waterfall , the purple moorland, the sparkling ocean , the profound quiet, and the delicious air , would be agents more potent for the restoration of health than all the tonics in the pharmacopoeia; and had I one foot in the grave I should deem that a three months' sojourn in such an angler's paradise would restore me to pristine vigour of brain and body.

Boluisce Waterfall --- Post J B Bunbury
Courtesy of Seán Ó Neachtain

Our diarist was besotted with the Boluisce. The big rock above would seem to be a remnant of the fifteen foot (4.6 meter) rock wall, that in 1863 survived J B Bunbury's six barrel gunpowder assault. When the flow was relatively low, sheltering nooks at and near waterfall would appear. Ideal for the poachers. Not that I would know anything about that. A ca 1900 complaint of Lord Kilannin was that poaching made the fishery a shadow of its former-self. Knowing that local people occasionally gaffed a fish to feed their family, the lore is that the third Lord Killanin (1914-1999), up to a point, turned a blind-eye. A subsequent owner had an eagle-eye, and a shotgun.

The ultimate demise of the fishery might have commenced in the years after Ireland's 1973 Common Market entry. In the latter part of the 20th Century, a dam was constructed just below the mouth of Boluisce Lough. This allowed the diversion of water to a nearby water treatment plant, to provide the domestic water for the area. Undoubtedly this affected the lough's ecology. It must have altered the river's flow characteristics and the downstream ecology.

An ca 1851 account exists, <u>A Week in the West of Ireland</u>, describing the Spiddal area. Curiously, the anonymous author states that Bohoona Lodge was owned by Lord Netterville, a new one for me. There were Nettervilles, descendants of a Co Meath peer, likely Roman Catholic, who settled in East Galway near Mountbellew (Netterville Lodge), in the 18th Century. In 1806, we had the pistol wielding Sheriff Netterville of Galway. Other than the above reference, I've not come across any other association of Netterville with Spiddal, Co Galway. There is a Spiddal townland in Co Meath, that went to the dogs, as its claim to fame was the *Spiddal Coursing Club*.

The Spiddal Old Pier

Old Pier

*From the 1837 'SESSIONAL PAPERS OF THE HOUSE OF LORDS (Vol XLIII), an APPENDIX TO
THE FIRST REPORT OF THE COMMISSIONERS OF THE IRISH FISHERIES* contains two accounts of the
1822 construction of the Spiddal pier.

The first appendix (XVII), is Mr Alexander Nimmo's *Coast Survey of Ireland*, and is fascinating
reading in general. I reprise just his account of the Spiddal Pier:

From the south of Costello Bay there is a road along the coast to Galway, which has been greatly
improved and rendered fit for carriages by the Government grants. Two points on this coast attracted
attention in 1822, as a half-way station for the boats passing to Galway; of these Inveran Creek has
been improved by the proprietor, Mr. Blake, and now affords shelter to small boats. The other station
adopted by the Fishery Commissioners is Spiddle.

This place is situated half way between Costello Bay and Galway, and a rude pier was once
attempted here, which, when I saw it, was a ruin. It is a sandy cove among the low granite rocks, near
the mouth of a small river, on which there is a good Salmon fishery.

The deputation of the Commissioners of Fisheries in 1822, having appropriated £150 towards the
building of a pier here, and having the promise of a contribution from some neighbouring proprietors, I
had the work begun by day labour, under the management of Mr. Morris of that place, and workmen
from Dunmore Harbour [Waterford].

When the fishery grant was expended, a further aid was obtained from the Government funds, of
£262, and a subscription of £100 from Sir Robert Staples; the other subscriptions were not made
good. Mr. Morris, however, contributed his time and attention.

This harbour is dry at low water, and has about ten feet at high water; the entrance is about one hundred and fifty feet wide, between rocks, dry at low water; then rounding the pier-head we have a clean sandy cove of about one acre and a half. The quay is of rough granite, and it is well protected to seaward, by some rocks only covered at spring tide. This harbour is much frequented by the coasting and fishing craft, but on account of the minority of the proprietors, Messrs Comyn, there has not yet been any increase in the neighbouring village. A new road has been made by the Government from this harbour across the great moor of Jar Conaught to the ferry on the middle of Loch Corrib; and whenever leases can be obtained, I have little doubt there will be speedily a thriving village built. Some of the best Turbot banks of the Bay of Galway lie just in the offing.

The second Appendix (XVIII) of the 1837 document, by a Mr. Donnell, states:

Spiddle pier is on the north coast of Galway Bay, about ten miles west of Galway, adjacent to the fishery village of Spiddle, on the property of Mr. Comyn, a minor.................

.............The harbour is occasionally useful; but being considerably within low waterline of spring tides, it is in general only accessible to small craft. In 1822, £138 9s. 3d. was allocated to this work, which included £41 78. 1d. from the funds of the London Committee, and £34 12s. 4d. from the Government. It appears that Sir Robert Staples subscribed £100 (Irish) which was paid to Mr. Nimmo; and Mr. FitzPatrick £25 (Irish) which was paid to the resident overseer; and also that £176 3s. 5d. (Irish) was charged to Government, making the total sum of £416 9s. 4d. from public and private sources.

Based on Alexander Nimmo's previous testimony, I suspect the overseer was Martin Morris. I believe that Mr FitzPatrick is James FitzPatrick (who died in 1828). After cobbling together a partial FitzPatrick family tree, I concluded that Martin Morris and James FitzPatrick were third cousins.

The monies mentioned above, spent in 1822, are given in both Irish and English Pounds. Thus, in the end, the Spiddal gentry contributed about 25 percent of the total pier construction cost. Nimmo's account indicates that a number of gentry promised financial support, but only Sir Robert Staples honoured his promise. Mr Donnell states that Mr FitzPatrick also contributed (perhaps later), with the £25 sum going to the resident overseer (likely Martin Morris). Perhaps James FitzPatrick ensured the pier's completion by honouring an earlier promise of support, or was merely helping out his cousin Martin Morris.

One of the minor Comyns is Peter Sarsfield Comyn. In 1822, he would have been sixteen years old, having inherited from his father Laurence Comyn after 1820. An interesting question is: who was making decisions on P S Comyn's behalf? I suspect Martin Morris was somehow involved. Peter's older brother Francis would have been perhaps 20 years old. John S Comyn would have been about 12 years old. From the various court documents, it's clear that the Morris and Comyn families were close.

Sir Robert Staples died at his lodge near Spiddal on 5 September 1832. Most newspapers noted that it was "under circumstances peculiarly afflicting to his family." One newspaper, the *Roscommon & Leitrim Gazette*, noted the above, and added a sentence at the end: "He shot himself." There is some oral history that he shot his dogs too. For more information about him, see Appendix X.

I've found no information about the extent of his Spiddal estate.

It seems that, for the Autumn of 1850, Spiddal had its fair share of bad weather. The blurb below appeared on 28 Dec 1850 in the *Boston Pilot*, the newspaper of the RC Archdiocese of Boston.

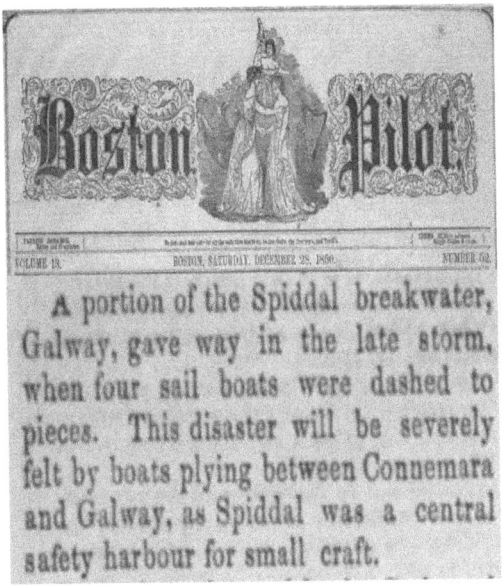

A portion of the Spiddal breakwater, Galway, gave way in the late storm, when four sail boats were dashed to pieces. This disaster will be severely felt by boats plying between Connemara and Galway, as Spiddal was a central safety harbour for small craft.

Spiddal 1850

The "Spiddal breakwater" (*An tSeancéibh, The Old Pier*) is Alexander Nimmo's work. I believe the breakwater was breached on Monday evening 18 Nov 1850. The storm lasted three or four days, and caused widespread damage along the west coast of Ireland.

Given the significant Irish immigrant population in Boston, the Boston Pilot would summarize noteworthy articles from the various Irish newspapers, such as *The Galway Vindicator* and *The Galway Mercury*.

The Boston College Libraries have digitized 1000 editions (1838-1857) of the Boston Pilot, and this provides additional information about 19th Century Ireland.

The were other things to worry about, out on Galway Bay, when fishing for hake:

A Shark Caught In Galway Bay

A young shark, of the blue species, was taken by the crew of a Claddagh fishing boat, off Spiddal, on last Thursday night. The scourge of the deep having taken one of the baits was hauled to the surface of the water, when, by it furious resistance it became entangled in all the lines, which were thus formed into kind of a rope, by means of which it was hauled into the boat, when a curious scene commenced. The little monster almost bit away the arm of one of the men while it was being lifted over the side, and the crew was more than once alarmed for the safety of their bark, fearing it would be stove to pieces by the action of the sharks tail......

Freeman's Journal
Sept 15, 1851

It was a six foot shark, whose tail was lopped off to stop the thrashing. The shark was taken to the Claddagh Piscatory and Industrial School for display.

The Spiddal New Pier

Trá An Tobar and the Spiddal New Pier

A very useful reference is: <u>Humble Works for Humble People</u> – a history of the fishery piers of County Galway and North Clare in the period 1800-1922, by Noël Wilkins. There is a local historical account (in Irish) of the pier's construction: <u>Céibh an Spidéil 1867-1871</u> . In this latter article, "Tom Éamainn Ó Céide as Sailethúna" is my paternal great grandfather.

The Spiddal New Pier is about 400 yards southwest of the Nimmo Pier. It is located near where the Boluisce River empties into Galway Bay. This newer harbour was created by constructing a 950 ft long stone pier during 1867-1871. In the foreground in the above photograph is Trá An Tobar. No one seems to know where the well (*An Tobar*) was.

Controversy preceded the pier's construction, a different controversy dogged it during construction, and yet another controversy plagued it after its 1871 completion.

Initially, when pier proposals were considered, no Spiddal proposal was submitted. There was a submission to build a pier in the Knockaille (Cnoc Aille) area (about 3 miles west of Spiddal), at a place called *"An Aill Fhinn, "* where it was claimed the water was deep. Father Patrick Lyons, still the Knock parish priest, championed this proposal, along with the local landowner, Francis Comyn.

I can't find this Irish place name on any of the Ordnance Survey maps. But it's in the Irish place names website <u>logainm.ie</u>, as An Aill Fhinn, located in the Knock South (An Cnoc) townland. The Knock South townland runs down to Galway Bay, narrowing as it reaches the water. This narrow shore of the townland is just south of the Knock cemetery. The satellite imagery seems to show deep water there.

What next happened might be described as political influence trumping good engineering. Michael Morris wanted the pier in Spiddal. By contributing £300 toward the £8000 cost, he got to choose the location. Another £1700 came from the Barony of Moycullen. This seems to have been a government loan, to be paid back by the Barony cess-payers in small annual installments. Morris chose a location about 500 yards south of the front door of his residence, Spiddal House.

It's not clear how much consideration the An Aill Fhinn proposal ever received. Francis Comyn was surprised at the turn of events in Spiddal's favor, and wrote to the *Vindicator* pointing out that the general opinion along Cois Fharraige (excepting Spiddal), the Arans, and even as far as Clifden, was that 'An Aill Fhinn' was the preferable location. The Clifden mariners were mainly interested in the new breakwater as a port of refuge between Clifden and Galway Town.

Michael Morris and Francis Comyn were relatively minor landed gentry, but I suspect Michael Morris's political connections vastly exceeded Francis Comyn's. In 1866, Morris was named Attorney-General of Ireland. In 1889 he joined her Majesty's Privy Council. And Morris was willing to pony up some of his own money (and more of his tenant's money), unlike apparently, Francis Comyn. Michael's brother George Morris became Galway Borough MP in April 1867. That didn't hurt. And so Spiddal it was.

On 2 July 1867, at a Barony ratepayers meeting at the Spiddal Court House, the final plans for the pier were ratified, and much celebration ensued, with an evening bonfire and salutes to the Morrises that lasted through the night. A 3 July 1867 *Galway Vindicator* article stated that nearly three hundred men were working on the road to the pier. The correspondent's (naive) opinion was that the pier would be completed by the end of the year. Of course, construction would have slowed in the spring, when seed had to be sowed, and again in the autumn, when the harvest came. Apparently the harvests were very good over this 1867-1871 interval.

Pier construction provided significant employment for the local people. Significant strife arose over exactly who was 'local' (and would get paid), and who wasn't 'local' (and wouldn't get paid). Lands several miles west, such as Sellernamore (including Knock, Aille, and Loughaunbeg), were not local. They lost out twice. First, no pier for their neighbourhood. Second, in Spiddal, those folk were unwelcome outsiders, and were referred to as *Gang na bPortán*, the *Crab Gang*, as they worked anyway, down at the slippery and dangerous water line. The Knock parish priest, Patrick Lyons, wrote in vain to Dublin, complaining about his parishioners' treatment.

In November 1868, two bottle-nosed whales wandered into the basin that formed with the construction of the pier. The project's chief engineer procured a curragh and a harpoon, and killed one of the inquisitive creatures. It was fourteen feet long, with a seven foot circumference at its thickest part.

In late January 1869 came a storm of varying intensity lasting several days. Initially, there was limited pier damage. But, on Sunday 31 Jan 1869, coincident with an especially high tide, the storm intensified and the pier was "altogether swept away by the violence of the waves last night."

The extensive widespread damage revived memories of 1839's *Night of the Big Wind*. According to a brief 3 February 1869 *Galway Vindicator* report, the Furbo bridge was destroyed, and human remains in the Minna graveyard were exposed. The OS show no burial ground in Minna. The 1893 OS shows a "burial ground" on a sandy shore in the Loughaunbeg townland. Father Steve Donohue informs me the area is Taughmore (*An Teach Mór*), and that the burial ground is a cillín known as *Dumhach na Leanbh (Dune of the Babies)*. A number of men worked two days to rebury the exposed remains.

After the pier's 1871 completion, there was a subsequent sequence of other damaging storms. Within about a decade of its completion, £20,000 had been spent on the pier. As the extra funds (ca £12,000) were diverted from other projects around Galway Bay, much resentment was generated in other villages. Then, in 1883, there were public hearings...., and a rebuke.

Cavenue & An Aill Fhinn

Decades prior to the construction of the Spiddal New Pier, there were discussions about a potential harbour out west of the Claddagh, and west of Spiddal.

Just prior to 21 Sept 1844, the *Galway Bay Fishery Committee* met

> ....to devise means for the improvement of the Fishery of this town, and the deplorable condition of the Claddaghmen, held their first meeting last week.......and as a commencement to useful labour for the end in view, he [the Rev T Rush], with MR BARRY Inspector of Fisheries, CAPTAIN WHYTE, Local commanding Inspector of Coast Guards, and one or two more gentlemen, proceeded on Friday last, to a place called GREEN POINT, on the property of that patriotic gentleman, FRANCIS COMYN, ESQ, Woodstock, about two miles north [we'll say he meant west] of Spiddal, to see if it would answer for a new Fishery Station, upon which a portion of the population of the Claddagh might be located with benefit to themselves and that district. They were glad to find, that it would most admirably suit for about two hundred Fishermen, if a pier and other conveniences were erected and formed for them— as deep water for trawling purposes lay immediately before it, and it being excellently situated for the taking of large fish, which abounds in the district.....

The *Galway Vindicator* article went on to state the Mr Comyn was enthusiastic about seeing the project proceed. There is no mention that he was enthusiastic enough to promise even token financial support. Nothing came of this, for on 4 October 1845, the *Galway Mercury* covered the *Tidal Harbour Commissioners---Galway Inquiry*. There was discussion of the lack of an "asylum harbour." Captain Whyte proclaimed:

> .....There is a place called Greenbanks, or Alween, about a mile and a half beyond Spiddle, which could be made a splendid asylum harbour for about £3000; thinks if a portion of the fishermen were removed there, it would be of vast advantage.....
>
> Captain Washington—Are not the fishermen of Galway a very well conducted, hard and laborious people?
>
> Captain Whyte—Not more so; the same harbour would be of great advantage to the turf boats, as many of them are injured from the want it it; on the 23rd of April, 1841, a large number of the hookers were lost on the bay in a gale of wind, not having an asylum harbour to run to: There [are] 2000 fishing boats, hookers, and yawls in his district.....

On a fine summer's day, Galway Bay could have been a very crowded place. I believe the above distances are Irish miles, so two miles west of Spiddal Village is 2.54 English miles.

On 13 October 1845, the Fisheries Committee met in Galway, and the meeting was covered by the Galway Mercury. The meeting started with a discussion of £5,000 that had been allocated in 1822, as a loan fund, to improve the lot of the Claddagh fishermen. By 1845, not a shilling had been loaned, and the saga of ascertaining the fund's fate ensued. This involved communication with the Exchequer bureaucrat Charles Trevelyan (a sidekick of Lord John Russell, the Prime Minister at the height of the Great Famine). The upshot was that it was foolish not to have used the money 23 years earlier.

There was an extended discussion about improving the lot of the Claddagh fishermen. Sounds familiar. Near the end of the October 1845 article is the following:

> ....There was a plan suggested some time ago
> for the formation of a colony on the estate of Mr Francis Comyn,
> near Spiddal, and if that were carried out and a pier erected in
> the neighbourhood at an expense of about £400, they would be so
> much nearer the fishery ground, while Galway would remain the
> market for the sale of the article. He, (Professor Kane) most deeply
> sympathised in the sufferings of the people, and was anxious
> to do all in his power to ameliorate their condition...................

It seems the expectations deflated, going from a £3000 pier to a £400 pier.

An Aill Fhinn is about 2.5 English miles west of Spiddal Village. Thus it's tempting to assume that Green Point, Greenbanks, Alween, and An Aill Fhinn (anglicised as Alween) are the same place.

So we know that, in 1844, there was a proposal to place "a colony" on Francis Comyn's land, to exploit An Aill Fhinn. Including the families of 200 fishermen, per the 1844 proposal, over 1000 people would have been involved.

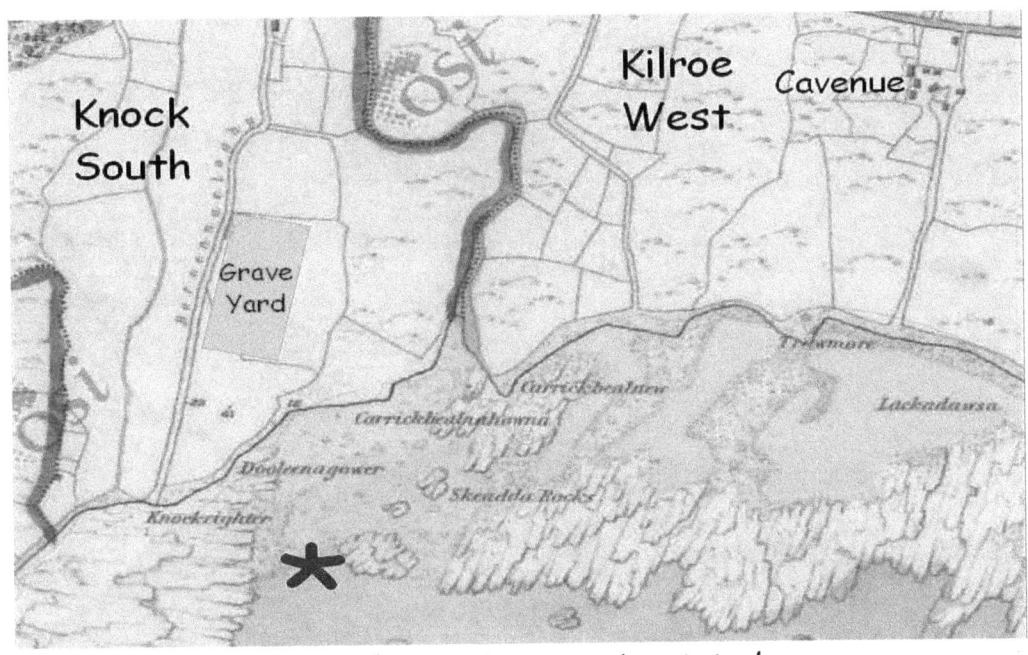

1838 Ordnance Survey – Annotated

In the 1893 OS, a few miles west of Spiddal is a hamlet Cavenue, not on Galway Bay, but close enough. Initially I thought that perhaps the hamlet was named (or renamed) ca 1867, in anticipation of a pier going in at An Aill Fhinn. We have: 'Cavenue' → ' Céibh Nua ' → 'New Pier.' But, in the 1838 map on the previous page, one sees the hamlet of Cavenue (relabeled by me for clarity). Thus Cavenue's existence predates the 1844-45 and 1867 efforts to build a new pier somewhere along Cois Fharraige.

The map on the previous page shows the southern part of the Knock South townland, and to the east, the Kilroe West townland containing Cavenue. The Knock cemetery didn't go in until ca 1906, but I've indicated its approximate location within the Knock South townland.

South of that, with an asterisk, I've indicated where the deep An Aill Fhinn water seems to be, based on an examination of the satellite imagery. One notices the high tide line indicated along the shore. I chose the candidate location because it was deep water with the shortest distance to the high tide line, and because it lies within the Knock South townland.

At the bottom of Cavenue's associated boreen is a strand known as Trawmore. Near it is a wide flat feature called "Lackadawsa." Tim Curran told me that, in the old days, céilís would be held there (at low tide I assume).

Ca 1822, Alexander Nimmo was interested in building at least one pier somewhere along Cois Fharraige. Likely he would have started by consulting the local folk as to where the deep water was, before making his own inspections. I'll speculate that An Aill Fhinn was on his shortlist, and that the local folk were aware of that, hence the anticipatory name "Cavenue."

The Servant Boy

In the Petty Sessions, one sees a particular kind of employment dispute, involving the *Servant Boy*.

On 21 April 1859, we have the case of

Thady Concannon, Bohoona West, Killannin, yeoman, Complainant

vs

Thady Conneely, Shannagurran, Moycullen, Servant Boy, Defendant

for the Defendant unlawfully leaving the Complainant's Service on the 20th March 1859, at Bohoona-West in Said County.

Andrew W Blake was the hearing magistrate.

Maternally, I descend from the Conneelys of Shannagurran, thus I am related to Thady Conneely.

In the village of Salahoona of the townland of Bohoona West in 1853 were three Concannnon households, including Thady Concannon's. The Concannons are said to be the second family into Salahoona after the Battle of Aughrim. My father was born nearby, in another part of the village. The plaintiff, Thady Concannon (1827-1907), was married to Bridget Keady (1833-1913). My paternal Great Great Grandfather Eamon Keady had a brother Thomas. Thady Concannon's wife, Bridget Keady, was Thomas's daughter.

I should tread carefully.

In those days, a servant boy hired out to a farmer, was fed and lodged by that farmer, on a verbal 9-11 month contract, with a December payoff. If it was actually a minor boy (or minor girl, yes, there were servant girls) the money went to the parents. According to the *1715 Servants Act (Ireland)*, and an 1842 modification of it, one month's notice was required to leave such service. Otherwise the employer (referenced as; *the master,* in the legislation) could withhold what wages had accumulated. It was not the same as being a simple (day) laborer. The worst thing a servant boy could do would be to fall in love with the farmer's daughter.

The word *boy* is a bit misleading. When the poet Seamus Heaney was a child, Ned Thompson, a stooped old man, would occasionally arrive at the Heaney kitchen. Ned Thompson would recount stories about most of his life spent as a *servant boy;* who treated him well, and who didn't etc. Ned Thompson was an inspiration for Seamus Heaney's poem *Servant Boy.*

Thady Conneely of Shannagurran was dissatisfied with his employer. Sadly, the court ledger doesn't include the specifics of Thady Conneely's grievances. Likely he quit without giving one month's notice. The lack of notice would be the legal basis for Thady Concannon taking his servant boy to Court. The court record indicates that the Defendant is "to return to his [the Complainant's] Service." Perhaps the airing of his grievances in court was enough to improve Thady Conneely's circumstances.

My best guess is that Thady Conneely was about 20 years old. I believe Thady Conneely is a son of my Shannagurran maternal Great[3] Grandfather Martin Conneely, and that he ended up out at Knock.

The *Irish Times* edition of 25 Nov 2004 noted the Taoiseach, Mr Bertie Ahern, <u>announced</u> that the *Servants Act of 1715* would be purged from the *Irish Statute Book.*

The Spiddal Races

We know, from the Rev John Garrett (of Penzance), that there was horse racing in Spiddal during the summer of 1862. Garrett spent one Sunday out west of Spiddal, visiting the Anglican Clynagh outpost beyond Costello. Returning to Spiddal on Sunday afternoon:

"As I returned, the road presented a very animated appearance: crowds of the people were to be seen hastening to a spot, where four roads meet, which had been appointed as the place where the Sunday afternoon was to be spent in horse-racing! This was not like an assembling of openly-declared infidels, who regard not the advice of any teacher; but it was the gathering together of a naturally docile people, whose religious teachers boast of their influence and control over them. I felt glad when I found that the police, under the orders of Captain Murray, had prevented the races from taking place, and the Sabbath was so far preserved from desecration."

No fun for the "naturally docile" Spiddal folk on Sunday. Captain Murray is Captain Pulteney Murray, who had a military career that took him to the West Indies. At age 29, he left the military and joined the RIC, much to the consternation of his family (who fancied him becoming a general). Early on, he was bit of a disciplinary problem for the RIC. But, he hung on long enough to get good service pay, and in 1869, his £180 pension. He, and his wife who defused the Orange Day unrest in Spiddal on 12 July 1869, resided in the Rose Cottage in Spiddal. As for the races, there seems to have been a quiet time of several years, until 1868. The 1870 Spiddal Races featured a donkey race, more my pace.

SPIDDAL RACES

These races, established last year, are fixed to come off over the Ballywilliam Course, adjoining Spiddal, on Thursday, 15th inst. It is anticipated that they will prove a success.

Galway Vindacator and Connaught Advertiser
September 8, 1869

THE SPIDDAL RACES, 1879.

To come off on **THURSDAY, 31ST JULY,**
Over the old-established Spiddal Course.

STEWARDS

Thomas Lyons,	|	William Ahern.
James Madden,	|	James Folan.
John Wallace	|	_____ Elder

Starter and Hon. Sec.---T. B. Brodie Esq., M.D.,
Treasurer---M. J. Lynch Coleman Esq.

1st RACE—1 o'Clock sharp--£3 0s. 0d.
Open to all horses the bona fide property of farmers
paying under £30 a year rent. About 2 Miles,
over Steeplechase Course.

2nd RACE—2 o'Clock sharp.
The Spiddal Plate of £8 0s.0d.---Open to all horses
the *bona fide* property of Tenant Farmers or
Shopkeepers. About 2 ½ Miles, over Steeplechase
Course.

3rd RACE—2 ½ o'Clock sharp.
The Tallyho Plate---Open to all *bona fide* hunters, the
property of Gentlemen, to be ridden by their
owners. About 2 ½ Miles, over Steeplechase
Course. The winner to get Three Cheers.

4th RACE 3 o'Clock sharp.---£2 0s. 0d.
Open to all Connemara Ponies, the property of Tenant
Farmers. One mile. Over the Steeplechase Course.

5th RACE---4 o'Clock sharp ---Bridle and Saddle.---
Open to all Connemara Ponies. One mile.

RULES

1st. ----All disputes to be settled by the majority of
Stewards present, whose decision shall be final, and
from which there shall be no appeal to a court of law.

2nd.----The Stewards reserve the power to postpone
or alter the Races and may remove objectionable
parties off the course.

3rd.----Four horses to start for each event, or else
only half prize money will be given.

4th.----No money for a walk over.

5th.----All entries to close at 12 o'Clock (noon) on
Race Day. All Entrance Fees to be paid, which
go to the Race Fund.

6th.---- No saddle horses allowed on the course,
except those going to run, and for use of the
Stewards.

7th.----Previous to any objection being raised, 10s.
must be lodged with the Secretary, and should the
Stewards deem it frivolous, the sum shall be forfeited
and go to the Race Fund.

8th.---No horse of pony can run two races.

9th.---Entrance Fees—2s. 6d. For Spiddal Plate.
5s. For the Tallyho, and 1s each for the others.

A BRASS BAND will (probably) attend and a
grand display of FIREWORKS will (if possible) be
set off at 9 o'Clock.

Galway Vindicator and Connaught Advertiser
July 23 1879

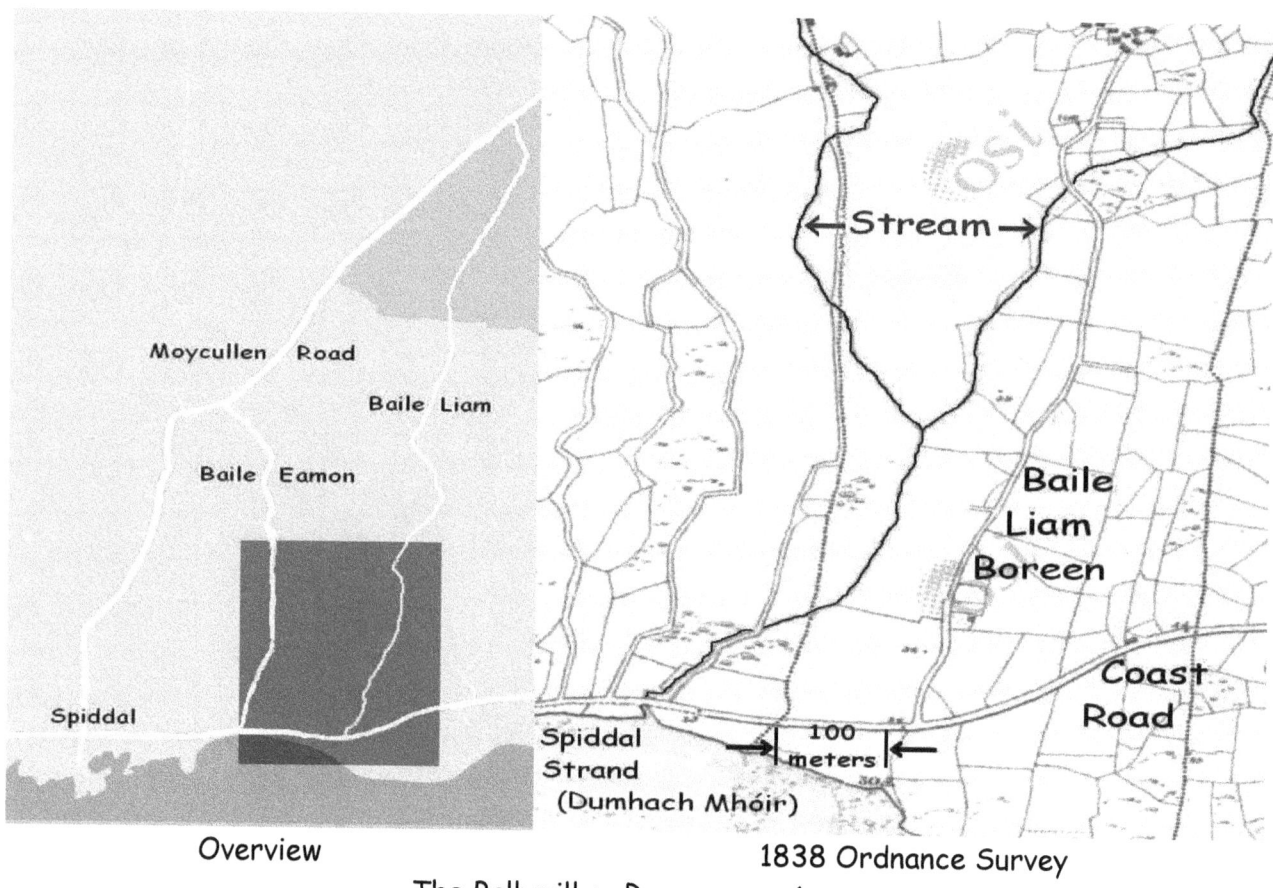

Overview

1838 Ordnance Survey

The Ballywillam Racecourse Area

The Rev Garrett mentions the 1862 races occurred "where four roads meet." This would seem to be the intersection of the Coast Road and the Moycullen Road, at the lower left in the left panel of the above maps. This suggests the 1862 racecourse came through the centre of the village.

In the right panel above, structures near the top right edge of the map mark the southern outskirts of the village of Baile Liam. Oral history, from Seán Ó Neachtain, is that somewhere along the Ballywilliam (Baile Liam) stream (indicated above right), which goes to the sea at "Dumhach Mhóir" (Big Sand Bank), was an (improvised) bridge called "Tochar a' Chláir (the boarded culvert) in olden times as it had boards over the stream to facilitate the Races." West of Baile Liam, where the stream flows, would seem to be the area. Usually a race was two laps around the course. Likely the "about 2 ½ miles " are Irish miles. "Gentlemen" were charged five shillings each to enter the "Tallyho", and got "Three Cheers" for winning. Thus the gentry helped finance the Spiddal Races' purses (using the tenants' rent payments, no doubt).

The Starter and Honorary Secretary for the 1879 races, Dr Terence Benjamin Brodie, the area doctor, along with the steward (and publican) James Madden, are rather tragic figures, as we will see. The less than £30 a year rent stipulation, for the first race, is interesting as it indirectly suggests the rents may have been several times the annualised valuations in the 1855 Griffith's Valuation for Galway

Cois Fharraige: Later 19th Century & Early 20th Century

COUNTY GALWAY,
SALMON FISHING.--SEA BATHING

TO BE LET. From the this date until 1st August, or for the months of June and July, SPIDDAL LODGE, fully Furnished, and beautifully situated on Galway Bay. It is nine miles from Galway, and Spiddal River, cele- brated for Salmon and White Trout Fishing, flows through the grounds. The tenant will have the privilege of rod-fishing, and the exclusive use of the crib at the mouth of the river, etc, etc.
   For terms &c, apply to the Rev. John Darley, Cootehill, Co Cavan, or
   Messrs JOY and SIMMS, LAND AGENTS
   33 Dawson-Street, Dublin.

Dublin Daily Express May 13, 1862

COUNTY GALWAY,
SALMON FISHING, SEA BATHING

TO BE LET, from the 1st of May till the 1st of November, or to be Sold, Spiddal Lodge, fully furnished, The House contains- parlour, drawing room, six bedrooms, &c, with out-offices; it stands in a picturesque lawn of several acres, with a beautiful view of Galway Bay, and is but 9 miles from Galway; Spiddal river, celebrated for Salmon fishing, flows through the grounds; the tenant will have the right of rod-fishing, and the exclusive use of the Salmon crib at the mouth of the river. For terms &c, apply to the Rev John R Darley, Cootehill.

Irish Times March 16, 1863

We see that, for some folks, Spiddal and Bohoona Lodge continued to be a summer attraction. John Darley had the property by 1862 (and probably by 1858). The Anglican clergy connection to Bohoona Lodge, that existed over a number of decades, is especially interesting.

Eventually (in 1874), the Rev John R Darley (1800-1884) was the Anglican Bishop of United Dioceses of Kilmore, Elphin and Ardagh. He was cut from different cloth relative to his contemporaries, especially compared to his second wife's uncle. When the coal dealers of Cootehill were gouging the poor, Darley proceeded to the railroad yard, bought coal himself and sold it locally at a fair price. He wrote two plays that are archived at the National Library of Ireland. The national school in Cootehill is named after him, and there is a biography, which I've borrowed from, at the school's website.

Rev Darley's first wife Ann died suddenly in 1850. A year on he married Nanette Plunket, daughter of the eventual 3rd Baron John Span Plunket. Her uncle, Thomas Span Plunket, the 2nd Baron Plunket from 1854 on, had ambitions to convert his Tourmakeady Co Mayo area tenants to Protestantism. His leverage was the threat of eviction, to be conducted if the tenants failed to send their children to the Protestant-controlled schools. Evictions came during 1860-1862. There was resistance, including an eviction backlash, which wore the Baron down, and led him to sell-out and retreat to Tuam in 1863.

His proselytizing ambitions were understandable, as Thomas Span Plunket was the Anglican Bishop of Tuam, and was a Vice-President of the ICM at its creation. He consecrated St Joseph's Church in Spiddal, on 20 August 1852. His sister Catherine had 1000 acres in Mayo, and was active in the ICM.

The Rev John Darley remarried well. Nanette's brother William, eventually the 4th Baron Plunket, in 1863 married Ann Lee Guinness, daughter of Sir Benjamin Lee Guinness. Yes, those Guinnesses.

A 1900 Land Commission document, about summer of 1899 judicial rent adjustments, twice lists Nanette Darley as a landlord in Grange Park, Ballymena, Co Antrim. My impression is the Rev Darley's main interest in Spiddal was as a holiday destination.

In February of 1861, the Anglican Rev Richard Rudd posted a letter from "Bohona Lodge." Was he residing there? For a time, I suspect. By 1863, he was residing in Inverin, at what eventually was called "The Vicarage. " Perhaps construction of the "The Vicarage" was motivated by the 1860 destruction of the Inverin Lodge, then occupied by the Rev McCready.

COUNTY GALWAY
TO BE LET,

For such terms as may be agreed on

A HOUSE AND OFFICES at
Spiddal, with about 14
Acres of Land, and Seaweed shores,
Turbary is most convenient and attached.
Application to be made to
Rev. JOHN GERAGHTY P.P.,
Schrule, Headford; or

GEORGE MORRIS Esq.,
Wellpark, Galway,
Thomas Dillane, Caretaker, will show the place.

Galway Vindicator April 15, 1865

SEA BATHING AT SPIDDAL

TO BE LET FOR THE SUMMER,

A HOUSE IN SPIDDAL,
CAPABLE of accommodating a family, with Stabling, &c. Most desirably situated for the Bathing and Fishing Season.
Apply to
Mr PATRICK MORRIS
Upper Dominck-street, Galway

Galway Vindicator August 31, 1867

One might wonder how much the lodge and angling would cost. Writing in 1867, the good Dr Peard stated (page 128) that "the rent of house and angling is 100l per annum." [l = librae; £]

George Morris is a son of Martin Morris (d. 1862). "Turbary" refers to the right to cut turf. John Geraghty was the Spiddal parish priest from 1862 to 1864, and may have been the priest organizing an 1862 orphanage boycott. There are other references to the Morrises being in Dominick-Street (then a western suburb of Galway). The Comyns might have been neighbours on Dominick-Street.

In the 1860s, east of Spiddal Village, was the 1336 acre estate of Cecilia and Isidore Lynch JP (son of Arthur Lynch of Petersburgh Castle), who were childless I believe. On Friday 15th November 1867, Cecilia Lynch died in Spiddal. From the 21 Nov 1867 edition of the Freeman's Journal:

DEATH OF MRS. LYNCH, OF ARRANDALE, SPIDDAL

We regret to have to announce that Mrs. Cecilia Lynch, the beloved wife of Isidore Lynch, Esq., J.P., died at her residence, Arrandale, Spiddal, country Galway, on Friday the 15th inst. The deceased estimable lady was for several years in a declining state of health.................
..........Her premature loss was deeply deplored in Spiddal, more especially by her own tenantry, to whom her life was an exalted pattern of virtue......

..............High Mass was offered by the Rev Martin Phew,
P.P., assisted by the Rev. Peter Dooley as deacon, and
Rev. John Dooley as sub-deacon. Immediately after mass
the coffin was removed from the church to the late residence
of the deceased, where all those-- rich and poor-- who had
come to pay their respects to her memory were entertained
at luncheon..............
..........................At three o'clock the large and respectable
funeral cortege moved off from Arrandale to Galway........, where
arrangements were made for the conveyance of the remains by
train to Dublin, for interment in the cemetery of Glasnevin.......
May she rest in peace.

The 1 Nov 1878 edition of the Freeman's Journal reported the 29 Oct 1878 marriage of Isidore Lynch of Arrandale Spiddal, the only surviving son of Arthur Lynch of Petersburgh Castle, to Ellie Maria Coleman (née Byrne) of Bansha, County Tipperary. Both had been previously widowed.

For the early 1880s, I located the summer rental property advertisement, for "Arrandale", apparently about an Irish mile east of Spiddal Village. From the 25 Apr 1883 Galway Vindicator:

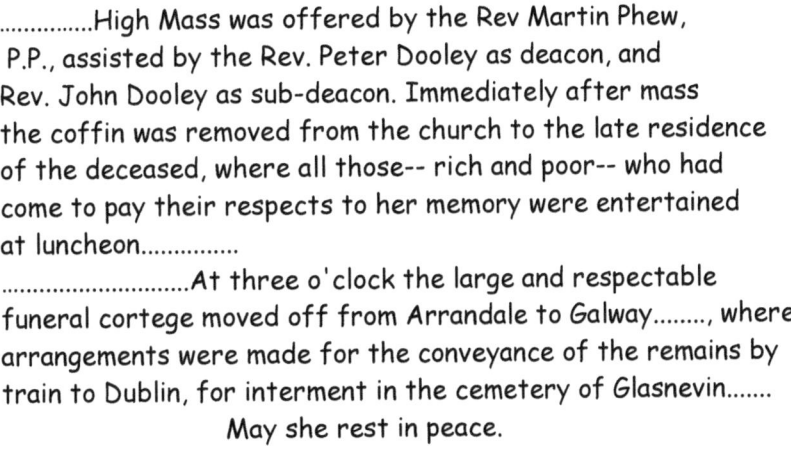

Arrandale, Spiddal
SEA-SIDE SUMMER RESIDENCE

To Be Let for four Months, from 1st April to 1st August next, within one Mile of Spiddal and eight of Galway. Dining and Drawing Rooms, four Bed-rooms, Servant's Rooms, etc, fully furnished, well-stocked Garden and the use of one Cow (if required). Splendid sea bathing and delightful situation. Sea, River, and Lake Fishing—white trout and brown.
Stabling for three horses will be let by the month.
Apply to
LYNCH COLEMAN, Esq., J.P.
Renmore Barracks, Galway.

N.B.--Roman Catholic and Irish Churches in Spiddal, Postal Telegraph office, etc.

Distances above are Irish miles. I suspect this Lynch-Coleman is a son of Ellie Maria Coleman, who married Isidore Lynch in 1878, and could be the treasurer for the Spiddal Races.

An 1879 famine didn't produce severe widespread hunger, but was severe enough in parts of Galway/ Mayo, and resulted in an uptick in emigration from there. The number of those in rent arrears rose. Tenants agitated for rent reductions, and even started withholding rents.

On 1 November 1879, the *Weekly Freeman's Journal* published a plea, to Francis Laurenzo Comyn, by his Knock area tenants:

MR. F. COMYN'S TENANTRY

The following is the memorial of the tenants of Selerna, parish of Spiddal, county Galway, to their landlord, Francis L. Comyn, Esq., J.P. :---

We, the tenants of your property at Selerna, feeling, like every other tenants in this district, the very great depression of the times, the total failure of the potato crop, which (you know) was at all times our own special food, and that of the pigs, intended to meet the landlord's rent: even in their rotten state, they will scarcely keep us from actual starvation up to the Christmas time.

We beg you to say that we never directly refused to pay you your rents; your respected agent, Mr. Reddington, will acknowledge our last November rent was paid, with the exception of about £30, out of a rental of £1000 a year---a small arrear out of so large a rental. The Spiddal October fair was held here on the 20th instant. We brought our stunted, poor cattle there, and were never asked what brought us to the fair. Unless some public works are opened immediately for the employment of the people here, both by the Government and landlords, our fate will be as bad as it was in Skull and Skibbereen in the famine times. The landlords here are giving a reduction in the rents from 20 to 25 per cent. We hope you will not be an exception to the rule, as we looked upon you at all times as an indulgent landlord. We beg also to say that our rents were raised in the year 1856 about 16 per cent in some villages, and more than that amount in others. We certainly are not in a position at present to pay this half-year's rent.

Unless you help us to pass over this year of the most direful distress we do not know what will become of us. We trust that you, like other benevolent landlords who are making reductions in their rents, will kindly consider the justice of the present memorial, and in duty bound will ever pay.

We, the priests of the parish where memorialists live, are quite satisfied that every matter alluded to in the memorial is perfectly true:--
Patrick Lyons, P P, V F, Spiddal, county Galway: Patrick Mannion, P P, V F, do.

The above purports to be signed by 130 tenants.

Weekly Freeman's Journal
November 1, 1879

The day the "half-years's rent" was due was called "the gale day." What subsequently transpired between Francis L Comyn and his tenants is unknown. His position became clear the following month. At Knock, on 10 Dec 1879, twenty-nine ejectment processes were to be served by John & William Tully, father and son (or vice versa), who met significant resistance, and were roughed up by a crowd of about two hundred. Initially, it was thought a head injury to one of the Tullys would prove fatal.

On Tuesday 6 January 1880, about 75 RIC were assembled to escort one of the Tullys, who apparently had fifty to sixty ejectment notices to serve. They were met on the road by a crowd of one thousand, near the residence of the Rev Patrick Lyons, who counseled the crowd not to assault the police, or cause any other disturbance. At this point, Tully wisely got cold feet, and refused to proceed. He and the RIC turned around, and the unserved Knock ejectment notices expired.

In March 1880, there was a trial of nine men for the December 1879 assault of the Tullys and RIC officers. Two men were acquitted, and the rest were convicted, although their sentencing was deferred.

Resistance to the evictions on the Kirwan lands in Carraroe (just west of Cois Fharraige) necessitated RIC reinforcements, and Cois Fharraige residents did their best to thwart the RIC. An *Irish Times* special correspondent wrote of what awaited the Galway RIC reinforcements when they arrived in Spiddal in early January 1880, on their way to Carraroe:

> Early the next morning an additional party of sixty men, from different parts of the country, arrived at Spiddal, and went on to the seat of war, where it is expected there will be bad work before all is over. There are large boulders, almost rocks, rolled onto the roads, which are also extensively torn up. It is an extraordinary circumstance that at Spiddal none of the shopkeepers will send any provisions to the police, as they have been stopped, turned back, and threatened by the people.

By 8 Jan 1880, thirty RIC remained in Carraroe, after ninety RIC men boarded a steamer for Galway, with some fifty of those dispatched to Headford for more of the same. Some locals were willing to provision the remaining Carraroe RIC men, with "butter being 2s 8d per pound, and whiskey 32s per gallon."

The war resumed on 10 June 1880. To avoid road sabotage and harassment, the authorities placed the process server and 200 RIC men on a ship, with two days provisions, and steamed to Carraroe, where the ejectment notices were served without incident.

Michael Davitt documented his visit to the Carraroe area in '*The Fall of Feudalism in Ireland*' (page 213 therein). He mentions it was Kirwan's agent Mr Robinson's practice, when a tenant's son married without Robinson's permission, to jack the tenant's rent by £5. Feudal indeed.

There was an American organization called the *Irish Catholic Colonization Association of the US*, one of whose supporters was the Irish born Bishop (later Archbishop) John Ireland. In the late 1870s, he was recruiting immigrants to settle and farm newly available lands in Minnesota. Hundreds of thousands of acres were available because the Native American inhabitants had been vanquished and evicted. Déjà vu.

The Liverpool born and based priest James Nugent collected alms in Liverpool, and travelled to the west of Ireland to distribute the alms. He convinced Bishop Ireland to allow him to recruit 50 Irish families from near Spiddal and points west and northwest for resettlement on the Minnesota prairie. Below is an excerpt from a *Galway Vindicator* article that was reprinted in the 15 June 1880 issue of the *Londonderry Sentinel*:

The Distress In Ireland
INTERESTING SCENE IN GALWAY

The Austrian, steamer of the Allan Line, which
called at Galway for the Connemara families whose
passages have been provided by Father Nugent,
sailed on Friday for Boston. The emigrants arrived
on Thursday evening in Galway, each company
headed by its own pastor. The Rev. Father Grealy
P. P., Carna, had ten families averaging nine each
family. The Rev. Father Millett, P. P., Killeen, had
thirteen families, averaging eight each family.

The Rev. Father Stephens, C. C., Augha, county Mayo,
had five families, averaging ten each family; and five
families, averaging eight each family, came from
Clifden in charge of Mr. Thomas Campbell, Secretary
of the Temperance League of the Cross, Westminster,
who has been engaged by Father Nugent to accompany
the emigrants to their new homes in Minnesota.
Besides the families there was a large number
(between fifty and sixty) unmarried young men and women.......

......Most of the people, especially the children, were
poorly clad, but Father Nugent had several large packages
of clothes, which Mr. Campbell will distribute amongst
them during the voyage. They all seemed very happy,
but wept bitterly on parting from their clergymen.

The *Irish Times* special correspondent who covered the June 1880 events in Carraroe also noted:

"Some of the people whom those [Carraroe] ejectments are to be served are among the fifty families who are to go by the Austrian Steamer of the Allan line from Galway to Boston on Saturday next, and whose passages have been provided for by Father Nugent. They will go to Bishop Ireland's colony in Minnesota."

The SS Austrian manifest survives. Fifty-seven passengers boarded in Glasgow, twenty-four boarded in Moville, while in Galway 337 persons boarded. Mr Thomas Campbell of London (the 419th passenger) was the group's escort. The ship departed Galway on Friday 11 June 1880 with 419 passengers and six Galway stowaways. It arrived in Boston on the evening of 22 June 1880, and the passengers disembarked on 23 June 1880. It's not clear how many of those who boarded in Galway were headed to the Minnesota prairie via Chicago.

A *Boston Globe* reporter boarded the SS Austrian upon its evening arrival in Boston. He found there "were 100 young men and women between the ages of twelve and twenty-one years of age, a hundred children under twelve years and twenty-one babies, under one year." He found four Spiddal families along with six families from Carna. The reporter interviewed Mr Thomas Campbell, the group's escort to Boston, who it seemed visited Spiddal and points west prior to the voyage, and bore witness to the dire situation there.

That evening of 22 June 1880, on the SS Austrian, the *Boston Globe* reporter described "the women as buxom and rosy and the men ruddy and stalwart." Days later, a representative of a local Chicago RC charity met with the immigrants, and was appalled at their condition.

The Commonwealth of Massachusetts (MA) Passenger Manifest Lists (1848 - 1891) show 228 passengers disembarking, and not the 419 passengers and six stowaways listed on the ship manifest. The *Globe* reporter stated that 300 immigrants were to proceed west, while the *Boston Pilot* indicated that 200 immigrants would proceed west. Having multiple reports about an event is good. It's even better when they are consistent.

A steerage fare on the SS Austrian, Londonderry to Boston, was £6 6s. Assuming Father Nugent paid the full steerage fare for each of his charges, it cost about £2100 to get the group as far as Boston.

Probably there were discounts for the young, infants, etc, so that the actual cost was less. According to the *Globe* reporter, the group was to travel to Chicago on half-fare, and from there to St Paul Minnesota for free. A discounted railroad fare was good public relations. Facilitating the homesteading of the Minnesota prairie was also in the railroad's best economic interest.

A Loughaunbeg family, who boarded in Galway, was Lawrence Flaherty, his wife Mary (Myra) Flaherty (née Conneely) and eight children. The youngest child was Bridget, an infant when she arrived in Graceville Minnesota in late June 1880. Bridget's granddaughter Bridget Connelly, Professor Emerita of Rhetoric at the University of California Berkeley, has written about the immigrant Flaherty's lives in Minnesota, and her discoveries about their lives prior to immigration, in *Forgetting Ireland*.

Mary (Myra) Flaherty (née Conneely), came from Shannagurran, and had a brother Nicholas Conneely, my maternal great great grandfather. Professor Connelly and my mother are third cousins.

During the construction of the Spiddal New Pier, Lawrence Flaherty was a member of the "Gang na bPortán," the 'Crab Gang,' and would have interacted with "Tom Éamainn Ó Céide as Sailethúna" my paternal great grandfather. They would have been acquainted with each other prior to the construction.

There is indirect evidence that, well after 1880, the Flahertys of Graceville Minnesota kept in touch with Shannagurran. Myra Flaherty (née Conneely) had another brother, Seán Conneely (maternal grandfather of Máirtín Ó Cadhain), who married and stayed in Shannagurran. In 1906, his nineteen-year-old daughter, Nora, immigrated to Graceville Minnesota. In late May 1906, two weeks after her arrival, she was caught in a prairie storm and died. See *Forgetting Ireland*.

The English Quaker, James Hack Tuke, organised an assisted immigration effort that, for 1882-1884, helped 9,482 people emigrate, mostly from around Belmullet, Clifden, Newport, and Oughterard. The Clifden and Connemara Heritage website has a Tuke 'Assisted Emigration' database. There was a demand for his services. For May 1882 alone, a parliamentary report stated that 698 families were (officially) evicted across Ireland. Who knows many unofficial unrecorded evictions occurred.

A significant portion of this emigration (over 3300 people), involved the SS Austrian and other Allan Line ships, departing from *Blacksod Bay* in Co Mayo. On 27 Feb 1883 in Carna, ca 400 area folk, desiring to emigrate, lined up to be interviewed. I do not know how many were selected, or when they might have emigrated.

Dublin Castle was constantly issuing "Castle Circulars." One seemed to decree that the local Boards of Guardians had been too liberal about who qualified for workhouse aid.

That and other repressive directives left the able-bodied with no aid and no work, with only the prospects of emigration or starvation. Another circular, uncovered by the Freeman's Journal in Nov 1883, "offered a premium to the clerks of the poor-law boards and emigration agents for every able bodied man and woman sent out of this country." There shouldn't have been any particular surprise, as the original 1838 Poor-Law legislation authorised the Poor-Law Commissioners to assist emigration.

The Poor-Law Boards in the west of Ireland weren't in the best financial condition, and likely were incapable of assisting emigration. Boards of other Unions were willing to assist. In June 1882, Mary Duffy (and her three children) of the Youghal Union Workhouse, applied for assistance so they could travel to America, to join Mary's husband there. After some debate, she was given £16. A standard steerage fare to Boston or New York was £6, with half-price discounts for children. Mary Duffy received just what she needed. In 1882, an "assisted-passage" steerage fare to Canada, for able-bodied agricultural workers, was £3. These were the fares advertised in December 1882, by a Roscrea Co Tipperary spirits merchant and emigration agent Michael Madden.

The Quaker philanthropist Jame Hack Tuke offered a sober path across the ocean. In 1883 RC clergy in various Deanerys: Castlebar, Clifden, and Iar-Connacht were writing to the newspapers, voicing their opposition to Dublin Castle's actions and emigration schemes like Tuke's. They viewed these as depopulation efforts, and had their concerns about the emigrants' fate in Canada and the USA.

In late December 1883, Tuke responded to these newspaper letters with testimonials from earlier emigrants about how well they were doing: 'The first is from "Thos. W. Boston," who sends home £3, and says he is receiving 8s a day as a labourer. ....Thos. D. Grantor gives an account of several persons, who are all in good situations, and tells of a good priest who is with them, and who once lived in Spiddal.' Tuke continued: '....Pat. F., writing from St Paul Minnesota says he is working every day. "My wages is 7s a day, and I would have more trouble sowing potatoes in one day in Ireland than I have earning 7s." ' I haven't figured out where "Grantor" is. Was "....a good priest.......who once lived in Spiddal," a Spiddal parish priest?

In the lean years, remittances from America, as mentioned above, and from England, often helped pay the rent along Cois Fharraige. Remittance details for Carna will follow shortly.

Tuke included a testimonial from Bishop Ireland about how well the Connemara/Mayo folk in Minnesota were doing. Those Galway/Mayo immigrants who stayed on their 160 acre homesteads had a very rough start in Minnesota. They arrived too late for spring wheat planting, and then experienced one of the coldest winters in Minnesota history.

The 18 January 1887 issue of the *Freeman's Journal* described an eviction that occurred on 13 and 14 January 1887, "on the Blake (minors) property, situate in the parish of Spiddal Tuam." Twenty-five families were evicted. It was said that: "The huts from which the poor people were evicted were unsuited to the housing of cattle." In 1887, the heir to the Gortnamona estate, Valentine Alexander Blake (born in 1868), was a minor. Apparently, by 1880, the Blakes were no longer in residence in Gortnamona.

The summer of 1890 was especially wet, ruining the potatoes, and was on the way to ruining the hay, oats and rye. It was impossible to dry the turf meant to be used for the coming winter. In the *Weekly Freeman's Journal* of September 13, 1890, was a special correspondent's report. Under the headline "THE THREATENED FAMINE," was an article *Glimpses Of Galway*.

DAN FEENEY'S HOUSE.

The correspondent started in "Menlough," on the lands of Sir Valentine Blake Bart., before proceeding to Spiddal: ".........at Spiddal I called on the hospitable parish priest Father Curran, who is full of anxiety about the winter and spring. He thinks the outlook is worse at all events than it was in '86....."   This is Valentine Blake, the 14th Baronet of Menlough, not to be confused with the various Valentine Blakes of Gortnamona and Tully.

A very short distance from the town of Spiddal I turned into the house of Daniel Feeney, where I found his wife at the 'merry spinning wheel,' to of his girls carding wool, and some other evidences of thrift and industry. Dan Feeney rents some seven acres of rock and bog called a farm from Lord Morris. He had an acre of potatoes planted, but they are digging so badly that he will not have half a crop. He turned up a basket of them just brought in, and it was certainly sad to see them so small and diseased. I got the occupants of this house, with the spinning wheel, to come outside to be photographed, a proceeding which seemed to amuse all of them very much.

I wonder where the photographs ended up. Seán Ó Neachtain informs me the Dan Feeney of interest lived on River Rd, and had died by 1901. In the 1901 Irish Census for Spiddal Town and Spiddal West are four Feeney families, all related to Dan Feeney. So our correspondent went north of Spiddal toward Moycullen.

POTATO DIGGING.

.....This [potato] patch was fairly well sheltered, and the soil was peaty, and the stalks seem to have grown pretty ripe. I went down to the ridges to see the tubers, and I was surprised to see several of them completely diseased.

The previous remark demonstrates that the blight never really went away, but fluctuated in severity from year to year.

A little further on I reached the house of Widow Curran (Tom), and his poor woman owns a very small holding also from Lord Morris at a yearly rent of £2 5s. Her potatoes, the only crop she had to rely upon for the support of her family of five individuals are badly diseased, and she sorrowfully remarked that she would have one-third the quantity she had last year.

I put up my camera, and photographed the house. At every house I visited, I saw one or two pigs, the rearing of which enabled the tenants to pay their rents. It must not be forgotten that these--- I can not call them 'uncomplaining brutes,' for some of them I saw complained most bitterly in their own fashion--- will suffer a great deal by reason of the 'short potatoes,' to use the expressive remarks of the peasants. But the feeding of the pigs is not now so profitable an occupation as it was some years ago; like the potatoes, a blight has also come upon this once flourishing industry........

........Allow me space for one short reflection to close with. The more I have seen of the poor peasantry in Menlough, Barna, and Spiddal, their poorly furnished houses, and their miserable surroundings, the more am I puzzled to understand how they live at all—-not to speak of paying rent---from year to year; and yet they manage to struggle on, and a complaint only goes out when the occasional wet summer destroys the potato.

As mentioned by the *Weekly Freeman's Journal's* correspondent, for many Spiddal area households, raising livestock helped pay the rent. Poultry and young livestock would be vulnerable to depredation by dogs. Losing livestock to dogs could be devastating. Sheep were vulnerable possibly because they grazed on remote semi-open or open commonage. Depredation by dogs was a significant issue in Ireland, and still occasionally makes the news even today. From an 1875 House of Commons Report:

Location	Year									
	1865	1866	1867	1868	1869	1870	1871	1872	1873	1874
Clifden	36	84	63	33	20	25	92	52	101	65
Spiddal	30	30	17	17	21	33	40	111	114	84
Tuam	-	2	6	1	-	-	4	-	-	6
Ireland	2,444	2,888	3,263	3,389	3,544	4,390	4,514	5,566	6,585	7,442

Number of Sheep Supposed to Have Been Killed by Dogs

According to the Royal Constabulary Office, over the 1865-1874 period, a total of 44,025 sheep were killed in Ireland, allegedly by dogs. Apparently Tuam dogs were well tethered, and Tuam was a relatively safe place for sheep. Spiddal, not so much, with 114 Spiddal sheep killed by dogs in 1873. For Ireland, around 1900, the estimate was that 3000 sheep a year were killed by dogs.

The Spiddal Petty Sessions records describe attacks on livestock. In June/July 1901, Nicholas Conneely and John Conneely were taken to court by John Keady (no relation to me, maybe) and Pat Madden, of Shannagurran, and by Stephen Conneely, a gabha (blacksmith) from Knock. Allegedly, on 4 May 1901, two of Nicholas and John Conneely's dogs killed a total of about 12 sheep and 5 lambs belonging to Keady, Madden and Stephen Conneely. Apparently the dogs mauled another 6 sheep.

The complainants were claiming a total of about £14 in damages. There were also assault charges and counter charges. The cases were adjourned and adjourned until it seems the charges were dismissed without prejudice. John Conneely is John Nicholas Conneely, my maternal great grandfather. Nicholas Conneely is my maternal great great grandfather. Recently, I've tentatively concluded that Stephen Conneely, the gabha from Knock, is connected to Thady Conneely; "The Servant Boy" (page 137).

Stephen is possibly Nicholas Conneely's nephew, and possibly a first cousin of John Conneely. This Stephen Conneely may have participated in the Knock eviction uprising of 10 December 1879. A Stephen Conneely of Knock was convicted in the Spring 1880 Assizes, for his participation in the uprising.

The 16 December 1896 issue of the *Freeman's Journal,* aka *The Journal* (pages 6-7, therein) had an extensive article on the 1896 situation (with some references to the 1879 situation), titled; *The STATE OF THE COUNTRY,* followed by a number of subtitles including, *THE CONDITION OF CONNEMARA,* and *WIDESPREAD FAMINE THREATENED.*

Michael Davitt's characterization of the landlord-tenant system as *feudal* was spot-on. One suspects that the *Freeman's Journal* correspondent who visited Spiddal in 1890 agreed. The landlord-tenant system contained the seeds of its own destruction. Over time, Cois Fharraige tenants' rents increased much more precipitously, as did the population, than did the soggy and boggy and rocky land's productivity.

A series of Land Acts, from 1870 through 1909, were designed to curb landlord abuse and encourage tenant acquisition of their holdings. The 1870 Act required departing tenants (in good standing) to be compensated for property improvements. There was an ineffectual provision to limit rent increases. There was also a provision ostensibly enabling tenants to buy their holdings. Assuming the owner was amenable, a much too hefty 33% down payment was required, with the government providing a 35-year 5% loan.

Legislation passed in 1881 prevented landlords from factoring property improvements into rent increases. Given the failure of the 1870 Act to mitigate rent increases, a Land Commission and Land Court were authorised, along with judicial appeal of rents and rent abatement. By 1881, the rents had significantly exceeded the property valuations. In 1882, nine of F L Comyn's Loughaunbeg area tenants filed for review of their rents. On 13 Dec 1882, the Land Commission announced 10-30% rent reductions for them. One lucky fella named John Keady had his rent reduced by 40%.

In June 1882, in Waterford, the Duke of St Albans and about 30 of his tenants agreed to arbitration. There were nearly factors of two rent reductions for many of these tenants. One tenant's rent was slashed by a factor of 3.4. I suspect these generous cuts were an anomaly, with 10-20% rent reductions more the norm across Ireland.

Early in the 20th Century, Patrick Conroy of Garrafin rented 109 Irish acres for £90, while the valuation was £35. An area parish priest, Father Newell, felt the rents were 300% above normal. Thus incremental rent reductions are of little help if the rents are factors of two or three too high. This situation in turn spawned *proposals* about alternatives to judicial rent revisions, such as the compulsory purchase order. Initial *attempts* to allow for compulsory purchase orders were unsuccessful.

The Congested Districts Board (CDB), which, after a time, had considerable influence along Cois Fharraige, came into existence in 1891. The CDB's creation was said to be motivated by Arthur Balfour's alarm after he visited the west of Ireland in 1890. If the rateable property value of district, divided by the district's population, was less than £1 10s, then the district was "congested."

The 1903 Act (aka the Wyndham Act) offered incentives to landlords to voluntarily facilitate land sales to their tenants, and was perhaps the most successful of the various Land Acts.

On Tuesday 24 September 1907, a hearing was held at the Spiddal Schoolhouse, before the <u>Royal Commission on Congestion in Ireland</u>. Witnesses were invited, and significant testimony was heard. Usually a synopsis of a witness's testimony would be presented, followed by the extended testimony. Earlier the Commission took testimony in Carna, while the following day they were in Oughterard.

Some of the testimony came from the expected sources, the area's parish priests: Mark (Marcus) Conroy, John Flatley, Thomas Hosty, Redmond McHugh, and Michael McHugh. There was also testimony from a number of Spiddal area residents: Patrick McDonagh of Spiddal, farmer, Michael A Lyons a Loughaunbeg farmer and farmer organiser, Peter Costello a Loughaunbeg farmer and shopkeeper, Patrick Curran, a Cloghmore farmer, and a land agent, Henry Robinson. My belief is that Michael Lyons is something like a grand nephew of the Rev Patrick Lyons. The witnesses could make an opening statement, if they wished, before answering questions from the commissioners.

Mr. Henry A. Robertson examined.

54643. Chairman—You are a land agent ?—Yes. I know this district, and I wish to give my views on rundale or intermixed plots. I have brought a map that I could show to the Commission if they liked. (Map produced.) This is Rossaville, a very bad place, further west. There is a townland called Parke quite close to here, on the Blake Minors' property under the Lord Chancellor.

I have authority to give you any information that you wish.
This is a bad estate in rundale ?—Yes. a £3 holding there might be fourteen different bits.........

In this testimony, "here" is the Spiddal Schoolhouse, and "Parke" is the Park townland, a mile or so east of Spiddal village. See page 6. Park is where the historian Roderic O'Flaherty, son of Hugh O'Flaherty, spent his last days in penury. "Under the Lord Chancellor" means the estate is in the Encumbered Estates Court. For those "fourteen different bits" a few might be mostly soil, but most were varying combinations of rock/bog/soil, with the emphasis on rock and bog.

The 1907 Royal Commission testimony extensively covered Loughaunbeg:

Mr. Peter Costello examined.

54781. CHAIRMAN.——Where do you reside ?
—Loughanbeg, Inver, Spiddal.
54782. Are you a farmer—Yes, and a shopkeeper.
54785. What do you want to tell the Commission ?
—We want some roads built up to the mountains, and to buy the estate. We want some roads and piers, and to get fishing boats there.
54789. Sir JOHN COLOMB—Would it be the big or the small men who would be willing to migrate ?
—The small men.
54790. Most Rev Dr. O'DONNELL.—They are in most need—is that your point ? —Yes.
54791. CHAIRMAN—Do you think the people are worse off than they used to be ? ---Far worse off.
54792. What is the reason of that ? --The families are big and the lands are small.

Peter Costello testified that, for the twenty years he had his shop, he never instigated any court action to recover a debt. Nor did he ever charge interest on the £400 to £500 the local people owed him. About the tenants indebted to him, Costello continued: "Some of them come to me in the summer time and tell me they were three days fasting with the hunger, then I give them goods." In 1907, there is still hunger along Cois Fharraige. Peter Costello indicated he had a 'license', to sell alcohol I assume, and felt he couldn't survive without it.

There is the thread about the phenomenon of *An Spailpín*. Seasonal migrant laborers. In our case, the seasonal Iar-Connacht labor migration to East Galway.

Costello remarked: "I often saw from 60 to 100 of them on Friday morning going to meet the train at Galway to bring them down to Woodlawn." Presumably Peter Costello was in Loughaunbeg when he observed these men. From Loughaunbeg to Barna, and from Oughterard to Galway, would have had large groups of migrating men as well. Historically, *An Spailpín* were much exploited.

Accounts (www.oughterardheritage.org) indicate that the Iar-Connacht laborer – East Galway farmer relationship was, by and large, respectful and mutually beneficial. Many Iar-Connacht workers would link up with the same East Galway farmers year after year. What might have eventually doomed the collaboration was the combination of relentless emigration and agricultural mechanization. Compared to Iar-Connacht, much land in East Galway was/is especially amenable to mechanised farming.

Repeatedly referenced at the 1907 hearing was the disposition of the Cois Fharraige Comyn and Blake Minor Estates. The Cois Fharraige Comyn Estate had two distinct components. The "Sellernamore" (Loughaunbeg area) part, and the "Spiddal Estate" (the 1222 acre Shannagurran townland, up by Boluisce Lake, and Spiddal Middle).

Royal Commission testimony that day indicated that some tenant farmers in these areas were in direct discussions with the gentry landlord about purchasing their tenant holdings. These tenants, who had no capital, approached the various agencies about financing.

In the Spring of 1884, and through 1903, Francis Laurenzo Comyn Esq was the incumbent of the Comyn lands. He was an absentee landlord, residing in West Hampton, Terenure in 1884.

My maternal Great Great Grandfathers Seán Caulfield and Nicholas Conneely of Shannagurran had some dealings with him. In the Spring of 1884, they were caught (presumably by Comyn's agent) illegally cutting turf on Comyn's land up by Boluisce Lake. Francis Laurenzo Comyn took them to Court. Seán Caulfield paid a fine, and, apparently, Nicholas Conneely didn't show up in court. Seán's son, Joseph Caulfield, would also deal with F L Comyn.

Apparently, not too many years after its 1891 creation, the CDB was approached about purchasing the Sellernamore property, and declined to do so. Ironic in that Loughaunbeg and adjacent townlands were the perfect definition of a 'Congested District.'

The agencies resisted acquiring land between Spiddal and Lettermore, because they thought the land was of poor agricultural quality. Thus they declined to help Loughaunbeg area farmers. At least initially.

Next, in 1897, the Sellernamore tenants went to the Land Commission, and were not well received. Commissioner O'Brien noted ".....the holdings consist of so many scattered plots, and the tenants are so poor, the rents have been so badly paid, that it appears to the Commissioners that the holdings would not be sufficient or satisfactory security for the advances applied for." According to Michael Lyons, the tenants were given bad advice by the parish priest, offering to pay too much for the land. Likely the parish priest had a somewhat different opinion.

Joe Folan of Bohoona showed me a tattered 1902 Irish Land Court document, about the matter of F L Comyn; *A Vendor of Land.* F L Comyn might have winced at that characterization, a mere *Vendor of Land.* Involved were the Shannagurran and Spiddal Middle townlands. In 1901, F L Comyn had come to agreement with some of his Shannagurran and Spiddal Middle tenants about purchasing their plots.

Perhaps he realised the jig was up, and decided that it was better to cash-out sooner rather than later.

The front page of the document lists five Shannagurran tenants (including Joseph Caulfield, my maternal great grandfather), along with some tenants from Spiddal Middle etc, who applied to the Land Commission for advances.

Oral history has Joseph Caulfield involved in a confrontation with the authorities. The story goes Joseph stood on one side of a Shannagurran stone wall with a rifle, warning the authorities not to come over the wall. Apparently they didn't. It's hard to believe they simply went away.... Afterwards he was asked if he would have actually shot anyone. He responded no, for he had no ammunition for the rifle!

On 25 Sept 1901, the Land Commissioner Mr O'Brien refused the tenants' applications for advances. An appeal was filed on 19 Oct 1901. The tattered legal document announces the intent, on 16 Apr 1902, to obtain a court decree overriding the refusal of the advances. If the motion was successful, my maternal Great Grandfather Joseph Caulfield would have become a Shannagurran landowner in 1902.

It's not clear that the legal motion succeeded. One reason for the uncertainty is that the Land Commission archive is closed to the public, and to researchers. Efforts to provide access seem to be slowly afoot. Apparently the (possibly 12 million item) archive contains more than just deeds. There is also supporting documentation, such as family trees etc.

Later, F L Comyn sent a statement to the Estates Commissioners, about the state affairs as of early 1904, referring to ".......the Spiddal Estate [Shannagurran] comprising 1,222 acres, of which 1,038 were mountain, and the remainder being in the hands of 18 tenants, the latter being the unsold residue of this part of the estate." I suspect the 1902 legal motion failed.

The "Sellernamore" tenants did not give up their quest for mortgages, and next went to the Estates Commissioners, who apparently knew the previous history, but did send their own representative(s) to inspect. In March 1905, the Estates Commissioners decided to make no offer. However, the Rev Hosty testified to the 1907 Royal Commission that the Estates Commissioners indeed made an offer for the property, a low-ball offer designed to be summarily rejected by the owner, so as to allow the Estates Commissioners to walk away.

That was untrue. Later, the Rev Hosty amended that part of his testimony, which was based on hearsay.

About this time, the Sellernamore (Loughaunbeg area) tenants were unaware that their parcel had been advertised for sale in Dublin. It was sold out from under them to Mr Davy, or Mr Darby, or Mr Dally, his name, depending on who was testifying. Apparently the new landlord Mr Davy did forgive the debts on the rents in arrears.

In his 1907 testimony, Peter Costello stated that "there had been a lot of arrears, some people owing £150 and £200, which he [Mr Davy] had wiped off." This level of debt was illustrative of the shortcomings of the various Land Acts, and was evidence that the system was coming a cropper.

Once established in America, many immigrants sent remittances back to Ireland to help their families. At the 1907 hearings, the Carna parish priest, Michael McHugh testified: " Carna parish contained about 300 families.......[The] Congested Districts Board had purchased an estate in this district.........the tenants had purchased the holdings and lived by fishing and kelp-making, depending partly also on American cheques; about £2,500 had reached the parish from America within twelve months." In 1907, that was a fabulous amount of money.

Remittances to some extent financed further emigration, which required a nontrivial sum of money, above and beyond the basic ship's fare. The US 1882 Immigration Act and subsequent legislation gave immigration officers wide latitude to refuse entry, by citing, for example, suspicions that an immigrant might become a public charge, or because of physical or mental defects. The more money in your pocket upon arrival---the better. Earlier in 1882 the US Congress passed the *Chinese Exclusion Act*. Such was the US political climate of the time.

Given the situation in the 1890s, it's no great surprise that, on 4 August 1898, my maternal Great Grandmother Kate Folan (page 108) and her cousin Annie Connolly (aka Conneely) departed Queenstown Cork, on the White Star Line's (WSL) RMS Majestic, arriving in New York City on 10 August 1898. The ship's manifest indicates that Annie was already a US resident.

The RMS Majestic's Captain for Kate's and Annie's passage was Edward John Smith, who commanded the ship from 1895 to 1904. He progressed up the WSL hierarchy, ultimately becoming commodore. Presumably, as commodore in 1912, he got to choose himself to be captain of the latest WSL super-liner, the Titanic, for its maiden voyage. Smith perished, but his WSL boss, J Bruce Ismay, who was also on board, did make it into a lifeboat. Ismay had a Connemara connection. See Appendix X.

Kate was fortunate that she already had close rather than distant US connections. Another resource was available for arriving immigrants. The *Boston Pilot,* from 1831 to 1920, had a section called *Missing Friends.* Newly arrived immigrants would advertise to find family who had immigrated years or decades earlier. In the 1840s, an ad cost about $3, when the average pay ranged from $4 to $6 a week. It wasn't cheap. Ads could be placed from Ireland. Over 45,000 such advertisements were placed between 1831 and 1920. They have been incorporated into Ancestry.com, findmypast.com, and AmericanAncestors.org.

Kate's and Annie's final destination was Oakland CA, where Annie's sister Nora lived. Kate's fare was paid by her father, and she had $25 in her purse. Annie paid her own fare, and had $6.50 on her.

Kate's pocket money was crucial to gaining her admission into the US. The money and the fare were a handsome sum for Kate and her parents, Michael and Margaret Folan of Bohoona. Some of Kate's siblings preceded her to the US, into Portland Maine. Remittances from them likely came to Bohoona.

The oral history I received was that Kate got engaged to a physician in California, but her father Michael objected to the marriage. Why would he object? Religion? Who knows. That father-daughter conversation was remarkable, as Kate's father died two years before she left for California. Kate did return to Spiddal, and was married to Seán Conneely by early 1901. Good news for me. The oral history also has it she returned to Spiddal with a wind-up record player. That I can believe.

Occasionally, no amount of pocket money was sufficient to gain US entry. Ca 1925, three nieces (sisters) of a maternal great great grandfather of mine turned up at Ellis Island. Two were admitted. The third was turned away because she was myopic. She found her way to New Zealand.

Returning to the 1907 Royal Commission on Congestion testimony, one sees that the Blakes of Gortnamona and Tully estate figured in the issue of compulsory purchase powers:

COMPULSORY POWERS FOR ACQUISITION OF LAND AND FIXING OF PRICE ADVOCATED.

Rev Mark Conroy

Where congested districts were surrounded by fertile grass Lands. as in East Galway, the congestion problem was fairly simple. but on the West Galway coast the population—despite emigration, equalling probably that of pre-Famine days—was confined between the sea and mountains on small and wretched holdings, and grass lands were almost non-existent; neither the Congested Districts Board nor the Estates Commissioners had done much for this district, where congestion was at its worst. and to ensure better results in future compulsory powers should be conferred.

51031. 54183-6.—Some landlords had been unwilling to sell for a fair price, e.g., the Blake Minors Estate had been offered for direct sale, but the parties had not been able to come to Terms, and witness believed the matter was now closed; rents were being paid—low rents— for the place was the poorest in the district; the estate was now in the Chancellor's hands, and its management by a committee made a difficulty...........

The Rev Conroy's unfavorable opinion of the CDB and the Estate Commissioners was widely shared.

In 1909, the Birrell Act provided some authority to issue the compulsory purchase orders that the Rev Conroy was advocating for in 1907.

We know Cois Fharraige gentry weren't in quite the same league as the Clanrickardes. In 1878, the 12,882 acres the Francis L Comyn controlled in Galway, Mayo and Clare, were valued at £2174. In the Comyn genealogy, David Comyn states they were sold off between 1902 and 1907.

It's said that the intransigence of the Earl of Clanricard, about dealing with his tenants, at least partially motivated granting agencies compulsory purchase power in 1909. In 1915, after a legal battle, the CDB acquired Clanrickarde's 52,000 acre East Galway estate, paying him £238,211. No need to feel sorry for him.

In 1923, an act of the Irish Free State absorbed the functions and personnel of the CDB into the newly reconstituted Land Commission. The new Land Commission had compulsory purchase powers for untenanted land, and for land owned by those who weren't Irish citizens.

Initially funds used by Irish farmers purchase their holdings flowed from the British government, under the auspices of various 'Land Purchase Acts', and represented debts owed to that government.

After the establishment of the Irish Free State, the farm buy-out money became farm annuities owed by the Irish government to the UK government. Across Ireland, one might wonder how much money was involved. A recent *Irish Times* article (14 September 2020) by Charles Lysaght provides some insight.

The suspension of the farm annuity payments was part of the Anglo-Irish trade war of the 1930s. In 1938 the dispute was resolved, and the farm annuities were terminated after one final payment of £10 million. For the farm annuities, £3 million a year had been flowing from Dublin to London.

It must have been immensely satisfying for tenants to finally get ownership of land they and their ancestors farmed across many generations. But, the underlying difficulties persisted. Rent payments became mortgage (annuity) payments. Qualifying Peter Costello's and Mr Robertson's 1907 remarks; the families were still big, the lands were still small, and were still in rundale.

And what of the Morris family? From the National Inventory of Architectural Heritage:

"Spiddal House, formerly Bohoona Lodge, is notable for being of two periods. The relative simplicity of the earlier building, constructed between 1805 and 1822, contrasts with the elaborate orientalism of the early twentieth-century addition designed in 1910 by architect William A. Scott for the second Lord Killanin. The loggias and the extension include in their design the sculptural works of Michael Shorthall of Loughrea: carved capitals, corbels and a date-stone depicting animals, foliage and sporting activities."

On 31 Mar 1914, Martin Henry Morris, the 2nd Lord Killanin, sold an estate of 2557 acres to the CDB. Ca 14 acres of the core of the estate, including Spiddal House, were retained by Morris.

An October 1924 newspaper account mentions significant 1908-1909 expenditures (£9,000 - £10,000) on Spiddal House. This would be WA Scott's work, which was probably finished by 1910. In the first years of the 20th Century, WA Scott was busy designing Spiddal's Cill Éinde.

What is shown on the modern satellite imagery is not derived from the Spiddal House of 1893 or 1910. During the evening of 28 April 1923, Spiddal House was burned to the ground by the "Irregulars," said to be from Tuam. The house contained 20 bedrooms and 5 bathrooms (with cold and hot running water). The luxury and the fishing were favorably compared to Ballynahinch Castle. Judge Powell, at the Clifden Circuit Court, awarded Lord Killanin £17,865 for the arson of his Spiddal residence.

There was much destroyed for which no amount of money was adequate compensation. Oral history has it that, shortly after the arson, an auction of the surviving furnishings occurred.

The 2nd Lord Killanin died in 1927. The present-day Spiddal House arose from the ashes, starting in 1930, to the plans of the architect Ralph Byrne. In March 1960, the 3rd Lord Killanin sold Spiddal House and much of the remaining diminished estate. The Connacht Tribune noted that included were "....the fishing and sporting rights over 8000 acres..."

Although I haven't found the legal details, I suspect that eventually those hunting and fishing rights were scaled back significantly, if not abrogated.

One of the subsequent owners was a certain Mrs Buckley, who as some of the local people know, was handy with a shotgun. Mrs Buckley's butcher was in Galway. She would come from Galway with a big hunk of suet, that she would peg down on the front lawn of Spiddal House. Then she'd retreat to the bushes with her shotgun, and wait for the magpies to gather. When enough magpies gathered, she'd blast them, and would then engage a (then young) friend of mine to clean up the bloody mess.

The house subsequently suffered the ravages of time, until it was refurbished by subsequent owners early in the present century.

Into the 20th Century, some Spiddal area farmers were in a desperate situation:

POTATOES FOR NEEDY WEST
GALWAY BOAT'S MISSION

Eleven and a half tons of epicure seed potatoes were conveyed by hooker from Kinvara (County Galway) to the Spiddal coast line, and distributed amongst the needy people at a nominal charge of 5s per cwt [112lbs].

Remarkable scenes were witnessed in the little fishing village when the first of the consignments arrived at Spiddal Pier. Hundreds of people flocked down from the mountains with no other conveyance than the donkey, across whose back were strung two creels.

The potatoes were quickly loaded into sacks, balanced on the creels on either side of the donkey, and taken across the mountain tracks to the villages of the peasantry.

Today the hooker will land at Maneen Pier, further up the coastline, near Bealdangan, with a further consignment of seed potatoes.

Wonderful progress is being made along the coast line from Spiddal and Cairagore [?] with the making of roads in places were nothing but mountain tracks had hitherto existed.

Belfast Telegraph
February 10, 1925

According to the publication '*Potatoes of Historical Interest in Ireland*', the 'epicure' is a potato of English origin, first formally documented in Ireland in 1897. Stiofán Ó Cúláin and Joe Francis inform me that the epicure is known as an early potato, a *first crop* potato, that would go in the ground in February Other common varieties of the era in the Spiddal area were 'banners' and 'pinks.' Likely the 'Aran Banner' and 'Kerr's Pink.' A cousin informs me that she always thought the banner was a 'soapy' potato.

SANITARY MATTERS

When witness [Rev John Flatley] was stationed at Spiddal,
he attended within six months sixty cases of typhus
fever, and himself superintended their removal to
Galway hospital; the sanitary conditions round
Spiddal were shocking; witness succeeded in getting
the Board to send down a committee of inspectors to
consider about buying some estates between Spiddal
and Costello Bridge, 52366.—He had met with much
opposition to this, and thought it well to inquire
whence the opposition came; Father O'Hara had
informed witness that neither he nor Lord Shaftesbury
could go to Spiddal for some time, and that
people there were anxious to defer the inspection,
52366 .—The land had not been bought, and the fever
remained rampant; it was impossible to improve
the sanitation without purchasing the estates. as the
people were huddled together on the land, 52368.—
There was no place in Ireland where sanitation was
worse than at Spiddal, 52637..

ALLEGED INSANITARY CONDITION OF SPIDDAL

Witness [Rev Mark Conroy] did not think Spiddal exceptionally
unhealthy as regarded manure heaps, but perhaps it was
in so far as the houses were huddled together, making
sanitation and cleanliness difficult; the district
had had rather a bad name, but typhus had always
come from Galway; once the school inspector had
brought it from there............

As plausible as this 1907 testimony sounds, infected Galwegians were not a significant source of typhus in Spiddal. Manure piles could be a significant factor, to the extent they attracted or harboured rodents infested with vermin.

By the early 20th Century, it was illegal to board or slaughter livestock in human habitations. But these practices continued. The vermin, on livestock and rodents, carry various Rickettsia bacterium (typhi, prowazekii, etc), and spread disease via the bacterial load in their feces. Lice crawl around on their human victims, biting as they liberally deposit their feces. The bites itch, and the victims scratch the feces into the bite wounds. Fleas can transmit murine typhus (Rickettsia typhi) in the same fashion. Now you know more than you wanted to know.

Wells or springs contaminated with human feces could harbour *Salmonella typhi* or *Vibrio cholerae*, causing typhoid (enteric) fever or cholera, respectively. Consuming tainted water or thereby contaminated food results in infection.

It was illegal not to report that a family member contracted typhus. Late in 1903 there was a significant typhus outbreak in Salahoona. In January 1904, Mike Tom Ned Keady of Salahoona was prosecuted by the Galway Rural District Council Sanitation Authority for not reporting that his younger brother Darby had contracted typhus.

My paternal Grandfather Darby Keady recovered. Eventually he married and had 14 children before succumbing to another killer, tuberculosis. His spouse Bridget preceded him in death by several years, also a victim of tuberculosis, five weeks after giving birth to twins.

The civil death records aren't fully indexed, e.g. one can't search for all examples of a particular cause of death. In the early records, tuberculosis isn't mentioned. Tuberculosis would be called "phthisis," and later "consumption." Other listed diseases, such as "brain fever" and 'worm fever' (don't ask), are now thought to be something else. A dictionary of archaic medical terms is useful.

What follows documents the devastating effects of typhus and tuberculosis on a particular family.

In the 1855 GV for Salahoona are the brothers Eamonn (Ned) and Patrick Keady. Ned is my great great grandfather. Patrick had a daughter Mary Keady who married Bartley Conroy of Creduff (the next village east). They had five children that I know of; Margaret, John, Barbara, Mary, and Nora.

The oral history is that some Conroys went to America, and that a shortfall of funds prevented the entire family from immigrating together. Some remained until their fare money arrived from America. Now comes what's been possible to document.

Nora, the youngest child, was born on 12 August 1883, three months after her father Bartley's death from fever. Her birth was registered by her mother Mary Conroy (née Keady).

Margaret (aged 20) died of tuberculosis on 24 December 1894, attended by her sister Mary (14). Their brother John (24) died of tuberculosis in early September 1899, followed three days later by Mary (19).

Their Aunt Mary Keady (née McDermott) of Salahoona (the next village west) reported their deaths. Evidence that the children's mother, Mary Conroy, was dead or incapacitated. I doubt she emigrated.

Seemingly Barbara was not in Creduff by 1899. A further search of the Irish records revealed nothing about her or her mother. I combed publicly available genealogical family trees for evidence that Barbara survived, and perhaps had left Ireland, but found nothing.

On the same mortuary registry page as Mary Conroy, was a paternal great grandmother of mine, Judy Keady (née Naughton, originally of Púirín). Three funerals in one week, a sad week in September 1899 for an extended family in Bohoona West.

Nora Conroy, alone by October 1899, would have been 16 years old. Two years later in the 1901 Irish Census, an 18-year-old Nora Conroy is listed as living alone in a windowless one room stone structure in Creduff. Nora Conroy immigrated to America ca 1905. Tragedy followed her. In 1912, she married an Inverin man in Portland Maine, and had children, including a son born in 1918, three weeks after his father died.

Decades ago, long before the Internet, TripAdvisor and Airbnb, some Salahoona families related to Mary Conroy (née Keady) did summer B&B.

One summer day an American family arrived out of the blue, and booked into one of these B&Bs, mentioning that their ancestor was a local Conroy. They were taken over to the old Conroy homestead, and the Conroy descendants spent time climbing about taking photographs.

Tuberculosis cases only started to significantly decline into the 1950s, with the advent of government schemes for improved housing, and public health initiatives championed by the likes of Dr Noël Browne. For an account, see Dr Noël Browne's autobiography, *Against The Tide*. Tuberculosis claimed his parents, four siblings, and infected him as well. He survived, and accomplished much.

Out at the new part of St Colmcille graveyard at Cloghmore (*An Chloch Mór Theas*), Dr Browne purchased two adjacent grave sites. He and his spouse Phyllis are in one plot, while the adjacent site has an engraved stone bench overlooking Galway Bay. It's a nice place to sit and think.

Some have suggested that the windowless stone structure of Nora Conroy, in Creduff, might have been windowless because of the so called "window tax." The "window tax" replaced an earlier "hearth tax."

The window tax was first introduced in England and Wales in 1696, extended to Scotland in 1748, and imposed on Ireland, by the Irish Parliament, in 1799 (39 George III c15). It was a banded tax, with a number-of-window threshold, above which the tax applied. Usually, the occupier of the structure was taxed. Window size didn't matter.

In 1799 for Ireland, the threshold was five windows, for which the tax was 4s 10½d. For six windows, the tax was 6s 6d, rising to £39 17s 4d, if your retreat had 180 windows. Dublin Castle was exempted from the tax. Seemingly as an afterthought, the last paragraph at the end of the legislation exempted the occupants of Trinity College.

Prior to 1851, there was at least one unsuccessful attempt to repeal the window tax in Ireland. The parliamentary Hansard transcripts document a May 1819 repeal attempt, mentioning that, by 1819, the threshold was seven or more windows in Ireland, while it was six or more windows in England.

Mr Richard Martin spoke in opposition to the repeal motion. Neither he nor the other Galway MP James Daly nor the Galway Borough MP Valentine Blake voted in favor of the repeal motion.

Other legislation (not the window tax) influenced the size of Irish windows. In the 18th Century, Ireland was allowed to produce glass tax-free, which lead to significant production facilities in Cork and Waterford. Between 1825 and 1845, Irish glass was taxed, with a duty that may have exceeded that on English glass.

Few or no windows kept the cottage warmer in the winter, but undoubtedly helped TB and other pulmonary afflictions thrive. In that Creduff cottage, Bartley Conroy died of "fever", likely typhus, while at least three of his five children, and possibly his wife Mary, perished from tuberculosis.

The various number-of-window thresholds etc make it difficult to see how the window tax influenced the construction of modest Cois Fharraige structures, such as the Conroy cottage.

Over the decades, precipitous increases in the rates helped finance various wars. Pressure from the medical community, and others, especially from Ireland, led to the 1851 repeal of the window tax.

There was also smallpox. The first British vaccination statute came in 1840, and was more or less ignored by the British public. In 1852-1853 came compulsory vaccination with noncompliance penalties. Systematic smallpox vaccination of Irish children commenced in 1863.

Germany passed a vaccination statute in 1874. Austria didn't pass a comparable statute. Subsequently, a classic epidemiological investigation, contrasting Germany and Austria, demonstrated the efficacy of the smallpox vaccine. It seems Austria got around to making smallpox vaccination mandatory in 1948.

The inoculation wasn't without risk. In 1880, human lymph was still used in the vaccine. A lymph donor, infected with other diseases, was a wildcard. There was a mandatory follow up visit eight days after vaccination to check for infection, and to collect lymph material from the recently vaccinated person (arm to arm vaccination). By 1899 in the British Isles, the vaccine was entirely based on purified calf lymph (calf to arm vaccination), and the collection of human lymph was unnecessary and prohibited.

Even when nonfatal smallpox could leave a person disfigured. Five years after he moved to London, a vaccinated Bernard Shaw contracted smallpox. The beard he maintained would have partially masked any facial scarring. Queen Elizabeth I preferred to have a vinegar based white-lead mascara slathered on her face.

In examining the mortuary registers that commenced in 1864, which typically have about ten entries per page, I don't recall seeing a large number of smallpox fatalities. But, the registers aren't fully indexed, ie, one can't search the register for all cases of a particular cause of death, which would be the appropriate starting point.

It seems that the Irish vaccination approach taught the British a thing or two. There is an 1871 British report about a resolution passed by the Council of the Poor-Law Medical Officers' Association, when they met in London:

......The Council [of the Poor-Law Medical Officers' Association], considering the present administrative arrangements for the performance of vaccination in the metropolis [London] where a frightful epidemic of small-pox is now raging, desire to point out that the plan adopted in Ireland has been eminently successful, whilst the mode now adopted in London has failed,................they therefore recommend that the Dublin system of amalgamating the offices of district surgeon, vaccinator, and registrar should be adopted throughout England, whereby..............small-pox be averted as completely as it now is in Ireland.....

While Ireland may have been better off than London, smallpox wasn't eradicated in Ireland. Vaccination was required within six months of birth. The noncompliance fine typically was a shilling, along with court costs of one shilling sixpence.

The Furbo Relief Officer Martin O'Connor and the Spiddal area medical officer Dr TB Brodie seemed to be especially diligent. On one May 1878 Petty Sessions ledger page were several lack of vaccination cases. In January 1879, Dr Brodie related an experience at the Galway Workhouse. He encountered

a woman with a bundle on her back, and having asked her to show its contents he found it contained the body of a child that had died of smallpox. That woman had travelled all the way from Westport, and at Spiddal, in the houses where she got lodging, there were in a few days after two cases of smallpox.

An April 1885 court action was brought by Dr Brodie against John Conneely (a brother of my maternal great great grandfather Nicholas), for skipping the eighth day after vaccination medical inspection for an unnamed child. He was fined a shilling plus a shilling and six-pence court costs. In the records, their youngest child seems to be an eighteen-month-old Bridget.

When she grew up, Bridget married into Cnocán Glas, and had a number of children, including in 1906, a son Máirtín Ó Cadhain, whose Irish language novel *Cré na Cille,* went to the booksellers in March 1950.

Measles and diphtheria were rampant. On one civil death register page, for the period 29-31 Dec 1884, I found four children, from Bohoona to Cornarone, who died from measles (or complications thereof). Dr T B Brodie certified the deaths.

Prior to Spiddal, Dr Terence Benjamin Brodie practiced out of Letterfrack. In Spiddal, on 15 Nov 1879, Dr Brodie's four-year-old son William succumbed to diphtheria. On 20 November 1879, his son John was born. On 26 November his two-year-old son Terence perished from diphtheria. A week later, on 3 December 1879, his 32-year-old spouse Frances died from childbirth complications, followed nine days later by the infant John. The Brodie's five-year-old daughter, Margaret Mary, was sent to relatives in Dublin. If one is looking for a definition of *Tragedy,* look no further. And more was to come.

In Dublin, on 11 December 1880, Mary Jane (Molly) Bunbury married the Spiddal area medical officer Dr. Terence Benjamin Brodie. In Spiddal, on 12 July 1886, Dr Brodie murdered his wife by shooting her in the face. There was a witness, Coleman Naughton, an employee of Dr Brodie, who struggled with Dr Brodie immediately after the shooting, and relieved the doctor of the gun.

Dr Brodie more or less got away with murder. His 'temporary insanity' was blamed on excessive use of alcohol. After about six years in the Dundrum Asylum, he was declared cured and released, to live off his late wife's estate, all of which must have galled the Bunburys. Brodie migrated to South Africa, remarried, started a new family, and died in 1906. A recent article in the Irish language publication, <u>*Biseach 2021*</u>, by Clíodhna Ní Mhurchú, touches on Brodie's life in South Africa. In the 1940s, his South African born son, Benjamin, turned up in Spiddal, enquiring about his late father.

The crime didn't occur in the Manor House, but in a nearby Bunbury property noted on the 1893 OS as "Pattaranga." The name (*paṭṭa:* **cloth** & *rañja:* **to dye**) connected to a South-Asian tree, *Caesalpinia sappan*, also known as: Brazil-wood, false sandalwood, or sappanwood. A red dye, extracted from the tree's wood, was used to colour clothing. A Co Tipperary area Bunbury had some Asian connection. There are Bunbury Shoals off the northwest coast of Borneo, and farther north near the Paracel Islands.

A Spiddal area resident had a Galway Bay trawler named *Pattaranga*.

Pub Life

In July 1861, a John O'Connor leased a house on a small plot, within Spiddal Village (Appendix II). Eventually, I suspect there was a public house (pub) there. Adjacent to O'Connor was Coleman Darcy.

Coleman Darcy, a Spiddal publican/shopkeeper, was a sponsor for the 7 June 1867 baptism of Mary Caufield, the daughter of Shannagurran's Seán Caufield & Margaret Folan (my maternal great great grandparents). Mary Caulfield went to America, first to Massachusetts, where she married, and ended up in Portland Maine, as did many from Spiddal. Coleman Darcy was a character, well known to the authorities. In 1861, the Rev John Darley sued Darcy over his cow grazing on Darley's Bohoona East grass. In February 1865, Darcy forfeited £100, for possessing 6 ½ gallons of unregistered spirits. Poitín? In 1865, that's a lot of money. In 1881, he was in trouble over a contract he had to maintain a section of the road approaching the Furbo bridge. Coleman Darcy ended up in the Cill Éinde graveyard:

> Lord have mercy on the
> soul of Coleman Darcy
> who died in the 1st May
> 1896 aged 60 years
> Erected by his son in law
> Patrick Concannon

Patrick Concannon took over Coleman's pub. On 22 August 1880, a Sunday, my Great[2] Grandfather Seán Caufield is alleged to have entered Kate Lydon's licensed liquor serving premises (aka a pub), when it was required by law to be closed, thereby breaching the Licensed Premises Act of 1874. Seán's first wife was Bridget Lydon. I believe the married Kate Lydon's maiden name was Lydon. I suspect Bridget and Kate are related. I like to think Seán and Kate claimed it was just a family gathering.

In 1882 there were other public houses in Spiddal. One was a combined grocery and pub, owned by Sarah and James Madden. James Madden was a steward for the 1879 Spiddal Races. Late in the day on 22 Aug 1882, two RIC men entered the Madden establishment, and found Mrs Madden behind the counter, sobbing, because she said, her husband was dying, having been poisoned while drinking at another village public house. The RIC men asked to see Mr Madden, and found him writhing on the floor in another room, covered in his own vomit. The RIC men noticed phosphorus, aka rat poison, in the vomit. Their suspicions aroused, they summoned the head constable, "who on arriving, asked Madden, as he was in a dying state, who gave him the poison, and, after repeated efforts at articulation he muttered out, 'My wife.'" Mrs Madden was then cautioned and arrested. The RIC also summoned Dr Brodie, who administered an emetic, which greatly improved Mr Madden's condition.

Sarah Madden was indicted and came to trial at the Connaught Winter Assizes in Sligo, on 15 December 1882. She pleaded not guilty, and was represented by Messrs Stritch and Bodkin. For the prosecution were "Sergeant Robinson and The McDermott." *The McDermott.* Sounds ominous. Sergeant Robinson stated that Mr Madden had an alcohol problem, but that, lately, Madden had been avoiding ardent spirits, consuming nothing stronger than port. The sergeant continued that, for some reason, the Madden marriage was an unhappy one.

Mr Madden started the morning of 22 August 1882 with two glasses of port in his own pub, before proceeding to the adjoining establishment, Lydons, where he consumed another glass and a half of port. Returning to his own place, he got into a row with his wife, who didn't want him in the shop. He got in anyway, and consumed a tumbler of wine that she gave him. Then the indigestion started. Apparently his vomit was green, and glowed in the dark. Behind where the tumblers were stored, was a box of phosphoric paste, rat poison. That summer day, Mrs Madden told the RIC that she had sent her servant to fetch the doctor. The servant, Anne Ferris, told the RIC this was news to her.

Mr Madden's trial testimony had the spousal row occurring in Lydon's establishment. Questioned by *The McDermott,* Madden said he didn't remember stating that the glass of wine was given to him by his wife. The RIC stated that James Madden wasn't sober when he said his wife gave him the poison. Madden wasn't quite the definitive witness the prosecution had expected.

Mr Lydon stated that indeed James Madden had taken a glass and a half of port in Lydon's premises, supplied from a bottle that Mr Lydon himself had sampled, with no ill effect.

Part of defence's job is to present their client in a sympathetic fashion. Sarah Madden was presented as "long suffering, forbearing, kind, and affectionate." Sarah Madden's father, Martin M'Donagh, testified through an interpreter. He "stated that his daughter had been kind to her husband. He had often known a man to be left in charge of Madden at night to keep him from doing himself injury."

A more important part of the defence's job is to sow doubt in the jurors' minds. Perhaps by insinuating someone else was capable of the deed. Mr Stritch cross-examined Mr Lydon. There is an old saw for trial attorneys: never ask a question if you don't already know the answer. Mr Stritch asked Lydon where he was the previous year. Lydon refused to answer.

Mr Stritch knew that, the previous year, John Lydon was in prison, completing a sentence for arson. The building in question, three stories tall and insured for £1,000, was in Galway; #89 High-Street. It was torched early on 5 April 1879. Most of the ground floor was a grocery, with a bakery in the rear. It was said that John Lydon was *"a merchant, carrying on a large business and a man of respectable position. Besides the house in Galway, he had a large concern in Spiddal......"* Quick action by the local citizenry limited the damage. The structure and its contents largely survived, and the fires didn't spread beyond the house.

The various newspaper accounts are not entirely consistent. Fires were started at five or six locations. Five people (three in another account) in the building at the time were arrested. They were Lydon, a Spiddal man named Curran (Corcoran in another account), two servant girls, Barbara Naughton (Knockton) and Catherine Thornton, and a child Catherine Moore. Kate Knockton was described elsewhere as Lydon's "friend." Later Curran, but not Lydon, was offered bail. By then the servant girls seemed not to be in custody, although it seems there was some residual suspicion about Kate Knockton.

It emerged that, in a previous Assizes, Lydon obtained compensation for a house he owned on Prospect Hill that burned to the ground. For the authorities, that the High-Street house and its contents were insured amounted to circumstantial evidence. An assessor retained by the Crown found the structure's meager contents to be significantly over-insured. Immediately after the fire, John Lydon's High-Street neighbours scrambled to obtain insurance for their houses.

Only Lydon was indicted. Early in August 1879, defended by *The McDermott,* Lydon was prosecuted in the Assizes, for intent to defraud and for arson of an occupied building.

A defence witness, Mr George Morris MP, said the prisoner was a man of excellent character. The jury found John Lydon guilty, and "...recommended him to mercy." Mr Justice Harrison asked on what grounds the jury made the recommendation, and the foreman was unable to say." John Lydon received a five year sentence. So much for *The McDermott.* Yet John Lydon was out of prison, and in Spiddal, by August 1882.

At the December 1882 Madden trial, in the presence of the jury, Mr Justice Lawson forced John Lydon to acknowledge his arson conviction. Thus the defence's Mr Stritch had his bogeyman. The defence's contention was that either James Madden was poisoned elsewhere, or, if he was poisoned in his own establishment, it was accidental. After all, in storing phosphoric paste, rat poison, next to the drinking glasses, something unfortunate was bound to occur.

The jury found Sarah Madden guilty, "recommending her to mercy." Sentencing was deferred until Monday 18 December 1882, when Sarah Madden was sentenced to seven years of penal servitude. There is an old trad song: *She Who Wears The Britches.* In the Madden and Lydon households, the women wore the britches.

For 1895-1904, I have about a dozen court references for Kate Lydon. Her pub closing times were very flexible, more so than the law allowed. On May 1 1895, she was convicted of being open after hours, and was fined £20 plus court costs, with a default 14 days in the Galway gaol, if the fine was unpaid. A ledger notation seems to indicate the fine was quickly paid. In Sept 1899, someone unsuccessfully objected to the renewal of her license, as she had been convicted of poitín (moonshine) possession.

On 27 Dec 1899, RIC Head Constable William Mansfield caught Kate Lydon open after hours. His evidence was the pub patron Joseph Francis. Both were charged, but the charges were "dismissed without prejudice."

In the 1901 Irish Census, the sixty-year-old John Lydon is listed as the publican, with Kate Lydon as his fifty-year old wife. The court records always refer to Kate Lydon (née Lydon) as the publican. It seems that they both died by 1911, for in the 1911 Irish Census, their thirty-three-year old son Patrick is the householder, while the twenty-three-year old unmarried Joseph is listed as the publican.

Later, Ben Harvey (a Donegal man from Dunkineely) appears, and marries a Lydon. Then the pub became known as Harvey's, which had one of the first TVs in the village, receiving English language broadcasts from RTE. A dedicated Irish language TV station, TG4, came much later. A TV in Spiddal in the Gaeltacht, blaring away in English, vexed Máirtín Ó Cadhain. One day, he found a young cousin of mine and a young friend of mine in Harvey's, watching an English language broadcast, possibly of 'The Virginian.' Giddy up. Ó Cadhain chased them out of Harvey's, all the way back to Bohoona.

In the 1901 Census is the publican Timothy Conway (building #5). The publicans Patrick Concannon, John Lydon, and Timothy Curran are side by side (bldgs #21, 22, 23, respectively). A short pub crawl. I suspect Timothy Curran was the 1901 proprietor of what was the Madden pub. The 1911 Census still has Patrick Concannon. Agnes Conway replaced Timothy Conway, James McHugh replaced Timothy Curran, and, as mentioned earlier, Joseph Lydon replaced John Lydon. In 1911, there is also the "farmer and publican" Thomas Walsh. Three of the five Spiddal publicans had a household servant. Eventually, Conway's establishment became "Tigh Hughes," once renowned for its trad sessions. Later, Harvey's was a restaurant called Boluisce, and until recently, was a place called Giblins. R.I.P. Ned.

The WWI & WWII Era

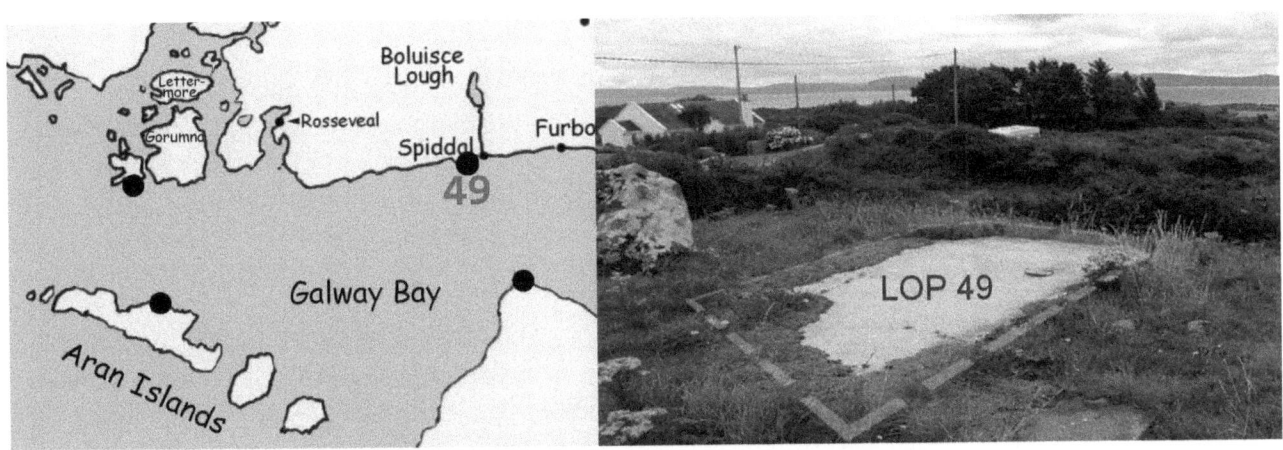

WWII Lookout Posts (LOPs) in Galway Bay.
(LOP 49 photograph, above, courtesy of Tim Schmelzer)

East of Salahoona is the Creduff Village. Down on Galway Bay, across the Coast Road from this boreen, was a <u>Coast Guard</u> watch tower used during WWII. My cousin Jerry Darby Keady found a WWII era <u>duty log</u> for the watch tower. Our paternal Uncle Stephen Keady put in time there, before immigrating to the UK. Decades later, the tower was deemed unstable, and was knocked. There are five logbooks for this <u>lookout post</u> (LOP). Often, on the ground near the tower, would be a representation of "EIRE" and a number. "EIRE" told the Allied crew they were over Ireland. The number, listed in their map book, provided a more precise location. Oral history is that the "EIRE" for LOP 49 ended up out at *An Aill Fhinn*, where the Knock cemetery (page 135) is located. The satellite imagery reveals nothing obvious, although a 2021 satellite image shows a good hint of something just outside the cemetery's southern stone wall boundary. The ca 2.5 km distance between the LOP and "EIRE" marker seems unusual. Perhaps originally the LOP was meant to be farther west.

The first page in the LOP 49 log is unusual because it was typed. I don't recognise the names on the page. Nevertheless, this first page is interesting because, on 12 Sept 1939, the lookouts spotted a naval mine, which was reported and subsequently deactivated. On 13 September 1939, they discovered a body in the water. It's since occurred to me that the first typed page may pertain to someplace else, but was included as an example of how information should be entered.

Twenty-two years earlier, there were two Galway Bay incidents involving mines that claimed thirteen lives. One can imagine the coast watching could get boring. But, from 1939 on, thanks to the vigilance of the lookouts, another catastrophe was averted.

One day in June 1917, a group of fishermen from the Loughaunbeg (*Lochán Beag*) area was near the shore, when they noticed a dark floating barrel shaped object. The object had handles and spikes, and the fisherman used the "handles" to guide the object ashore. Residents along Cois Fharraige were always on the lookout for salvage, and this find might have seemed like a good opportunity.

The men were tinkering with the object when it exploded. Nine men died. One survivor had just gone off to tend a pregnant animal, and it had dawned on another that perhaps tinkering with the object was a bad idea. He voiced this opinion as he ducked behind a large boulder moments before the explosion.

This survivor, Joe Hughie Flaherty, lived to be nearly 100 years old, and rarely spoke of the event. In Spiddal, 4 miles east, the Royal Irish Constabulary (RIC) barracks had its windows shattered. The blast was heard in Galway, 15 miles east. Some houses in Loughaunbeg must have sustained damage.

The authorities arrived and quickly scooped up the mine debris and hauled it away. A rushed inquest was held at what is now known as An Poitín Stil. A suspicious coroner summoned a Royal Navy officer to testify. The officer asserted that the mine was German, and thus absolved the British government of liability. See Appendix XIII. The victims' families had no legal representation, probably not understanding its importance, and were undoubtedly too poor to afford it.

Two of the nine men were buried in the Knock cemetery. The other seven were buried in paupers' graves at the New Cemetery, Bohermore. There is a bronze memorial embedded in a large stone at the blast site. Near the entrance to the Bohermore cemetery is a memorial plaque to the 7 men buried inside. The precise locations of their paupers' graves are unknown. The victims (including their ages and villages) were:

Mánus Ó Fatharta (20)   An Lochán Beag
Éamonn Mac Diarmada (53)
Tomás Hoibicín (30)
Seosamh Ó Flaithearta (32)
Tadhg Ó Céidigh (30)
Colm Ó Feinneadha (18)
Éamonn Ó Laoi (17)   Na hAille
Pádraig Ó Laoi (17)
Peadar Ó Cualáin (17)   An Teach Mór.

Loughaunbeg Memorial
(courtesy of Jerry Darby Keady)

Now we come to the tragedy of the fishing trawler the Neptune. A 14 Dec 2017 Galway Advertiser article by Tom Kenny, approaching the event's centenary, described the Neptune tragedy.

The Claddagh fishing trawler, the Neptune, with about a 45 ton displacement, was one of the larger boats of the Claddagh fleet, perhaps the pride of the Claddagh Fleet.

On 17 Dec 1917 it left the Claddagh with 4 men and a boy aboard. They started trawling Galway Bay late in the morning, about 3 miles off Spiddal, and unknowingly snagged a mine. The trawler was one mile off Spiddal in the late afternoon, drawing in its nets, when the mine struck the trawler. The trawler broke in two, and sank within a few minutes. There was a motor launch and another fishing vessel that proceeded to the site. At the end of the day, there was one survivor.

Appendix I
Fate of the Spiddal Home

Early into the 20th Century, the ICM's heyday was over. When the orphanage moved to Dublin, I suspect the ICM involvement with the "Spiddal Home" ended. The ICM involvement might even have ended a few years before 1906. A newspaper reference indicates that, in late October 1905, the facility was still in Spiddal.

When it left Spiddal ca 1906, the orphanage went to Sandycove, a suburb of Dublin, where the 1911 Irish Census, and a 1915 House of Commons report on charities, also place it.

The Thom's Directories were very useful in tracking the Spiddal Orphanage/Home. The Dublin City Library on Pearse St has a more or less complete set of the Thom's Directories in the open stacks. A wide-field magnifying glass is especially helpful.

Thom's Official Directory of the United Kingdom of Great Britain and Ireland, 1917, refers to the '*Spiddal Home, Sandycove, Dublin*', and its 40 residents.

For 1918, there was some consolidation of the Smyly facilities. It seems the Smyly Elliot Home (for girls) in Bray Co Wicklow, was combined (in some fashion) with the Spiddal Home. For in 1919 we have the Elliott Home – Spiddal Orphanage having 70 children (boys & girls) in Sandycove Dublin.

There is no 1918 reference to either of the Dublin or the Waterloo Ontario Canada 'Coombe Home' facilities. The Canadian Coombe Home was sold to the Waterloo County Children's Aid Society in 1917, and continued on as an orphanage. Another source seems to indicate that the Dublin Coombe Home closed in 1944.

By 1921 the "Elliott Home – Spiddal Orphanage" moved to #7,8 Charlemont St Dublin (south of St Stephen's Green), and had 70 children. There the "Elliot Home and Spiddal Orphanage" remained up to about 1950, with 70 children, according to Thom's.

In 1955, we have a reference to the "Birds Nest, Elliot Home, Spiddal Orphanage", with 100 children, in Dún Laoghaire. More consolidation. At this point in time, one might suspect that the Spiddal Orphanage had a nominal existence, at best.

In the 1960 Thom's for the Smyly Homes, the entry is a generic statement about relying on voluntary contributions to support their facilities. Oddly, I didn't find an explicit listing of the facilities.

In the 1965 and 1969 Thom's, the reference is to the "Birds Nest - Elliot Home" at 19 York Road, Dún Laoghaire. No mention of "Spiddal".

The 'Spiddal Orphanage/Home' was in Spiddal from 1854 until ca 1906, when it moved to Dublin. Eventually it was combined with other Smyly homes, but seemed to nominally exist until ca 1955.

The Smyly organization still exists, sans orphanages, as the Smyly Trust.

Appendix II
Spiddal West Townland Prospectus 1861 (*transcription*)

In the Landed Estates' Court, Ireland
COUNTY OF GALWAY
IN THE MATTER OF THE ESTATE OF
P. SARSFIELD COMYN, *owner and petitioner.*

R E N T A L
OF THE

TOWN AND ADJOINING LANDS OF SPIDDLE,

containing 727 Acres, 1 Rood, and 13 Perches, Statute Measure,

THE PARISH AND BARONY OF MOYCULLEN, AND COUNTY OF GALWAY,

Held under Lease for Residue of 999 years:

TO BE SOLD IN ONE LOT,

AT THE LANDED ESTATES' COURT, BEFORE JUDGE LONGFIELD, INN'S-QUAY, DUBLIN,

----

On TUESDAY, the 3rd day of DECEMBER, 1861, at 12 o'clock at Noon.

For RENTALS and further PARTICULARS, apply at the Landed Estates' Court; to
Messrs. MACNEVIN & WHITNEY 8, Middle Gardiner-street, Dublin; or to
The OWNER, THE FARM, Killeen, Galway.

DESCRIPTIVE PARTICULARS.

This property is situated upon the Bay within about nine miles west of Galway, and embraces the town of Spiddle or Spiddal in the barony of Moycullen,

There is a sea frontage of about a half a mile, upon which the town is built, and which contains a pier (erected by the Fishery Board), which is the only good shelter for boats on this side of the Bay, and also a Police Barrack, Coast guard Station, Dispensary, Post Office, National School, Irish Church Mission Society's Schools, and Roman Catholic Chapel, and immediately adjoining the town is a modern Protestant Church.

The bathing strand is extensive, and washed by the Atlantic, there is also a considerable extent of seaweed shore, and a large and valuable turbary partly in the owner's hands, and part of which (seaweed and turbary) the tenants are allowed to use.

The property is well intersected with public and private roads, the mail road from Galway to Costello Bay passes through it, as also the public road from Moycullen to the pier of Spiddle.

An extensive salmon river (to one bank the purchaser will be entitled) bounds the property on the west, capable of great mill power.

There are four excellent annual fairs held in the town. The tenants are well circumstanced, and have considerable interest in their holdings, for which, in the town, they pay but nominal rents.

There is an uninterrupted view of the Bay of Galway, and the American Packets pass by the shore.

With the many advantages already belonging to this property, and the increasing value of land in the neighbourhood, it may be made a most desirable investment, and is capable of producing a large income by a moderate outlay in erecting bathing and fishing lodges, and leasing the lands now held from year to year or in the owner's hands, on which are excellent sites for building.

Private offers for sale will be received by the owner or his solicitor, up to the 20th of October next.

SUMMARY

Denominations	Ordnance Survey			Ordnance Valuation			Yearly Rent		
	A.	R.	P.	£	s.	d	£	s.	d
SPIDDLE TOWN AND SPIDDLE WEST,	727	1	13	203	11	0	246	15	1

SPIDDLE TOWN and SPIDDLE WEST, situate in the Parish and Barony of Moycullen, held under Lease for residue of 999 years from 1774.

Denom- ination	Tenants' Names	Gale Days	Yearly Rent			Quantity of Land			Tenure
			£	s.	d.	A.	R.	P.	
Spiddle Town ↓	Rev C. Magrath	25 Mar 25 Sep	6	0	0	9	0	9	Lease dated 4 Dec 1850, and made by P. S. Comyn to Reverend c. Magrath, for 150 years, from 1st November 1854 at £2 a-year, of house division, therein stated to contain 2 acres Irish. The remainder of the lands in this tenants possession he holds as tenant from year to year.
	Rev James Mecredy	25 Mar 29 Sep	2	10	0	0	3	30	Lease dated 22 March, 1853, made by P. S. Comyn to Rev. James MeCredy, of house division, therein stated to contain half an Irish acre, for 300 years, at £1 10s. a-year; and further lease (as representative of Bryan Sweeny), dated October, 1842, from the owner to said Byran Sweeny, of plot of ground, therein stated to contain 13 perches, for 65 years, at £1 a-year; gale days 1st Nov and 1st May.
	John Connor	25 Mar 29 Sep	16	3	10	14	2	26	Lease for 150 years, dated 1st November 1855, and made between P. Sarsfield Comyn and John Connor, at £5 a-year, for part of Spiddle, and plot in the Village of Spiddle, therein stated to contain 1 acre and 20 perches. The remainder of the land in this tenant's possession he holds as tenant from year to year.
	Edward Connor	May & Nov	9	0	8	0	0	15	Lease of 1st Oct 1842, for 65 years, and made between P. Sarsfield Comyn and Edward Connor, at £1 a-year, for house division, therein stated to contain 14 ¾ perches. The remainder of the land in this tenant's possession is held in common with the tenants on Spiddle West.
	Denis McEntyre, representative of Michael Folan	May & Nov	7	16	0	0	0	36	Lease of 1st Oct 1842, for 65 years, and made between P. Sarsfield Comyn and Michael Folan, for house division, therein stated to contain about 30 perches, at at £1 10s. a-year. The remainder of the land in this tenant's possession, he holds as tenant from year to year, in common with the tenants on Spiddle West.
	John Davern	May & Nov	3	12	6	7	2	13	Lease of 1st Oct 1842, for 65 years, and made between P. Sarsfield Comyn and John Davern, for house division, therein stated to contain about 6 ¾ perches, at at £1 a-year. The remainder of the land in this tenant's possession, he holds as tenant from year to year.
	Stephen Toole	May & Nov	3	14	6	2	2	16	Lease of 1st Oct 1842, for 65 years, and made between P. Sarsfield Comyn and Stephen Toole, for house division, containing about 1 rood, 39 perches, at £1 a-year. The remainder of the land in this tenant's possession, he holds as tenant from year to year.
		Carried Forward	48	17	6	35	0	25	

SPIDDLE TOWN and SPIDDLE WEST, situate in the Parish and Barony of Moycullen, held under Lease for residue of 999 years from 1774.-----continued.

Denom-ination	Tenants' Names	Gale Days	Yearly Rent			Quantity of Land			Tenure
			£	s.	d.	A.	R.	P.	
Spiddle Town ↓		Brought Forward	48	17	6	35	0	25	
	Byran Sweeny	25 Mar 25 Sep	1	10	0	0	2	0	Lease dated 1st May 1856, for 65 years, and made between P. Sarsfield Comyn and Byran Sweeny, for house division, containing about 8 perches and 40 yards, Irish measure,, at £1 a-year. This lease contains a covenant against sub-letting. The remainder of the land in this tenant's possession, he holds as tenant from year to year.
	Mary Flynn	May & Nov	2	0	0	0	0	15	Lease dated 13th July, 1861, made between P. S. Comyn and Mary Flynn, for 65 years, of a house and plot, therein stated to contain about 15 perches, at the yearly rent of £2.
	Mary Folan	May & Nov	1	5	0	0	0	20½	Lease dated 1st day of May, 1861, made between P. S. Comyn Esq., Mary Folan, for 150 years, of a house and plot, therein stated to contain about 20 and a-half perches, at the yearly rent of £1 5s. sterling.
	James Hearman representative of Anthony Kean	25 Mar 25 Sep	1	10	0	0	2	20	Lease dated 24th Mar 1851, for 65 years, and made between P. S. Comyn and Anthony Kean, of plot of ground, therein stated to contain 63 Irish perches at rent here stated.
	Martin Kilroy	May & Nov	4	0	0	0	1	0	Lease for 65 years, dated 1st May, 1859, and made between Martin Kilroy and the owner. Covenant not to sublet nor to build without consent of owner, and in default to pay an additional rent of £10 sterling yearly.
	Mr. Patt McDonogh	1 Jan & 1 July	15	5	0	9	2	1	Lease dated 1st May 1861, for 300 years, and made between P. Sarsfield Comyn and Patt McDonogh., for £10 a-year, of house, police barrack, and gardens, containing about 3 roods, 12 perches, statute measure. The remainder of the land held by this tenant as tenant from year to year.
	Coast Guard	Apr, Jul Oct Jan	16	11	0	Houses, no land			Tenant from year to year, rent payable quarterly.
	John O'Connor	May & Nov	2	10	0	0	1	14	Lease dated 13th July, 1861, from P. S. Comyn to John O'Connor, of house and plot therein stated, to contain in front 76 feet, and in depth 270 feet, for 150 years, from 1st May 1861, at £2 10s. a year.
	Coleman Darcy	May & Nov	2	10	0	0	1	24	Lease dated 13th day of July, 1861, made between P. Sarsfield Comyn and Coleman Darcy, for 150 years, from 1st May 1861, containing 1 rood, Irish measure, at £2 10s. a year.
	Commissioners of National Education	25 Sept	-----			-----			Lease dated 12th October 1843, for 60 years, and made between P. Sarsfield Comyn, 1st part; the Commissioners of National Education, 2nd part; and their Trustees, 3rd part. Nominal rent.
	Widow Clancy	May & Nov	0	10	0	------			Tenant from year to year, determinable every 1st November.
		Carried Forward	96	8	6	43	3	39½	

SPIDDLE TOWN and SPIDDLE WEST, situate in the Parish and Barony of Moycullen, held under Lease for residue of 999 years from 1774.-----continued.

Denom-ination	Tenants' Names	Gale Days	Yearly Rent £ s. d.			Quantity of Land A. R. P.	Tenure
		Brought Forward	98	8	6	43 3 39½	
Spiddle Town	Roman Catholic Chapel and Grave Yard	-	------			1 1 15	To be excluded from Conveyance to Purchaser.
	Under-houses, Yards, Street, small Gardens and Strand,	-	------			6 1 35	
	Untenanted about	-	-			2 1 1½	
Part of Spiddle West ↓	Owen Naghten	1st May 1st Oct	6	9	7	--	The land included in these 670A. 1R. 2P. is held undivided, and enjoyed in rundle by the tenants. Tenant from year to year, determinable every 1st November. ↓
	John Feeny	↓	5	7	2		
	Michael Feeny		10	3	8		
	John Tearney		6	10	4		
	Martin Sweeny		5	3	8		
	John Fallon		3	16	2		
	Thomas Flaherty		8	15	7		
	Michael Curreen		5	0	0		
	Thomas Molloy		2	14	6		
	Widow Connolly		2	16	3		
	John Thornton		7	17	9		
	Murty Curran		8	17	0		
	Widow Connolly		7	18	10		
	Pat Walsh		10	18	0		
	John Walsh		11	8	0		
	Martin Kyne		4	11	8		
	Michael Connolly		4	11	8		
	Michael Lyden		2	16	4		
	John Lyden		5	0	10		
	Pat Flaherty		5	9	2	670 1 2	
	Bartley Connolly		3	13	6		
	Coleman Connolly		2	7	3		
		Carried Forward	228	15	5	727 1 13	

SPIDDLE TOWN and SPIDDLE WEST, situate in the Parish and Barony of Moycullen, held under Lease for residue of 999 years from 1774.-----continued.

Denom-ination	Tenants' Names	Gale Days	Yearly Rent			Quantity of Land			Tenure
			£	s.	d.	A.	R.	P.	
		Brought Forward	228	15	5	727	1	13	
Part of Spiddle West ↓	Peter Curran	1st May 1st Nov ↓	2	14	8				Tenant from year to year, determinable every 1st November. ↓
	Thomas Folan		5	0	0				
	Michael McDonagh		1	0	0				
	James Curran		2	5	0				
	Pat Folan		1	0	0				
	Michael Martin		1	0	0				
	Thomas Tearney		0	10	0				
	Pat Brennan		0	10	0				
	Richard Tenpenny		0	10	0				
	Widow Walsh		0	10	0				
	Michael Regan		0	10	0				
	William Barrett		0	10	0				
	Peggy Hanly	May & Nov ↓	0	10	0				
	Widow Cook		0	10	0				
	Michael Flaherty		0	10	0				
	Michael Cook		0	10	0				
	Total Amount .... Deduct Head Rent £85 15 4 Do. Tithe Rent-charge 1 10 0		246 15 1 87 5 4			727	1	13	

Deducting the head rent and tithe, the net profit on the rent is £159 9s 9d.

Typically the tenant paid the rent semi-annually, on the *"Gale Day."* Some autumn Gale Days were set at October 1, but could vary. However, the sale of mature livestock (often swine), and/or the harvest, whose proceeds would cover the rent, might not occur until after the Gale Day. A payment grace period, typically up to six months, granted by a landlord was referred to as a "Hanging Gale." Make no mistake, the legal definition of Hanging Gale was "Overdue Rent."

Noteworthy is that 1.34 acres, containing the graveyard and Colm MacGragh's 1857 church (see page 60), were excluded from conveyance to the buyer.

Appendix III
The Martyns of Tillyra
Martyn of Tillyra

EDWARD JOSEPH MARTYN, of Tillyra, co Galway, J. P. and D.L., High Sheriff 1886 b. 31 Jan 1859; s. his father 5 April, 1860.

Lineage. – This family was established in Ireland by one of the officers in Strongbow's army, Geoffrey Martyn, living in Galway about 1450. He was s. by Richard (who m. Miss D'Arcy of Kiltulla, co. Galway), who was s. by Andrew, who was s. by Oliver Martyn, M.P. For Galway in the reign of James II, who was especially exempted (by 8 Anne, Ch 3, Sec 39) from the penalties inflicted on Catholics, and was s. in direct descent by

PETER [OLIVER] MARTYN, of Tillyra, who m. Miss Browne, of Castle McGarrett, co. Mayo, and had issue, OLIVER of Tillya, m. 1748, Frances, dau. Of John Donnellan of Bally Donnellan Castle, and d.s.p.. and

JOHN MARTYN, of Tillyra, m Mary Ann Lynch, of Tubber, co. Galway, and had a son,

EDWARD MARTYN, of Tillyra, m. 1798, Mary eldest dau. Of Andrew Browne of Mount Hazel, co. Galway, and had issue.

1. JOHN, late of Tillyra.
2. ANDREW, of Spiddal, co. Galway, m. 1863, Mary, oldest dau. of Oliver Dolphin, of Turoe, co. Galway, and d. 1878, leaving an only dau. Mary.　　3. Peter, Capt. In the 88th Regt., d. unm.
1. Jane, m. John R. Corballis, Q.C.
2. Mary Anne, m. James Balfe, J.P., of Runnamoat, co. Roscommon, and d. leaving issue.

Mr. Martyn d. 1836, and was s. by his son,
JOHN MARTYN, of Tillyra of co. Galway, J.P., b. Aug. 1801; m. 17 Feb. 1857, Annie Josphine, dau. Of James Smith J.P., of Masonbrook, co. Galway, and d. 5 April, 1860, leaving issue, two sons,
1. EDWARD JOSEPH, now of Tillyra.
2. JOHN, Lieut. 3rd Dragoon guards, b. 19 March, 1860; d. 5 March, 1883.

Arms—Az., a cross Calvary arg. Between in dexter chief this sun in splendour or, and in the sinister chief the moon in crescent of the secone.　Crest ---An etoile of six points or.　Motto---Sic itur ad astra.

Seats---Tillyra Castle, Ardrahan, co. Galway, and Mount Bernard, and Ballymacquard, co. Galway. *Clubs*-- Reform, London, S.W.; and Kildare Street, Dublin.

First, a general comment about the genealogies. Sometimes one finds multiple not entirely consistent genealogies about a given family. Or one finds a court record mentioning a person, a excellent indication that they existed, who should be in a given genealogy, but isn't listed. One learns to tolerate a certain amount of contradiction.

The tree on the previous page comes from the 1898 Burke's Landed Gentry. The 1882 Burke's Landed Gentry differs in that it has no Peter Martyn, but Oliver Martin instead, marked within brackets by me.

One of the other Galway Tribes was the Blakes. Martin J Blake (1853 – ca1930) assembled the Blake Family records in two volumes. Vol. 1 covered 1315 to 1600, and was published in 1902, while Vol. 2, covering 1600-1700, was published in 1905. The two volumes have lots of interesting references to the other Galway Tribes. One never knows what one might learn. I searched the Blake Family records for references to "Tullyra", and there are some.

Blake of Ardfry Family Records - Genealogical Memoirs

Sir Richard Blake died 1663. His will, dated June 13, 1663, was proved July 20, 1663. His eldest son,
   ROBERT BLAKE of Ardfry and Wallscourt, of which he obtained a regrant by patent dated February 24, 1681. He married Elizabeth, daughter of Martin Lynch of Levally, and had issue:
1. Richard, his heir.
2. Andrew.
3. Joseph, of Grange, Co. Galway, married Mary, daughter of Ignatius Browne, fourth son of Geoffrey Browne of Carrowbrowne (see ORANMORE, B.), and had three sons:
   (I) Richard, of whom presently.
   (2) Ignatius, barrister-at-law, d.s.p. His will was proved 1780.
   (3) Henry, died unmarried. His will, dated Jan -uary 14, 1786, was proved December 21, 1789.
4. A daughter, married, December, 1685, Oliver Martin, junior, of Tullyra.
Mr Blake died March, 1697, and was succeeded by his eldest son,
   RICHARD BLAKE of Ardfry, married first, March I, 1681, Mary Magdalen, only daughter of Oliver Martyn, senior, of Tullyra, by whom he had issue:

For 1689, Hardiman has an Oliver Martin Esq representing Galway in Parliament, along with a note, that I interpret to mean that Martin also served in the earlier parliament of James II (dissolved in 1687).

There are some other accounts of the Martyns, that commence with Richard Óge Martyn of Dunguiare Castle. His father was Oliver Mór. Richard's eldest son was Oliver Óge (Oliver the Younger) Martyn, who fought in the Williamite War.

In the Down Survey for 1641, the Oliver Martin possessing the lands around Kinvarra likely is Oliver Mór Martyn, who was succeeded by his son, Richard Óge Martyn (1602-1648; Mayor of Galway in 1642). In the Down Survey for 1670, the Oliver Martin (ca 1630 – ca 1709) holding the lands around Ardrahan and Gort, is Richard's son, and grandson of Oliver Mór Martyn.

It's worth mentioning that there is a Martin genealogy: *The Martin Family* written by George C Martin (published by Martin and Alladyce, Asbury Park, NJ, 1914), that has Oliver Óge born in Ross to Robert Martin.

It appears that, for Oliver Martin (d. ca 1709), his penal law exemption arrived just in time to benefit his heirs.

There are more Olivers in the mix. There is a mid-to-late 18th Oliver Martyn, as the 1861 Chancery Court opinion on the Comyn Lands stated.:

> The lands now held by the petitioner [Peter Comyn], and by the respondent Francis Comyn, were demised in 1777, by Oliver Martyn, to a person of the name of Lynch, at a rent of £380, late currency.

Oliver Martyn married Frances Donnellan in 1748. It's also stated Oliver *d.s.p.* in 1768, which seems to be inconsistent with the 1861 Chancery Court statement that has him demising property in 1777. Presumably in 1861 the Court had access to the written land leases and deeds.

Now we jump forward in time a bit. Burke's entry references:

> 1. ANDREW, of Spiddal, co. Galway, m. 1863, Mary, oldest dau. of Oliver Dolphin, of Turoe, co. Galway, and d. 1878, leaving an only dau. Mary.

When Hardiman's tome was published in 1820, referencing "houses of Curraghmore, Ross, Spiddle and Tullyra", Andrew Martyn would have been twelve years old. '*A Statistical and Agricultural Survey of the County of Galway*', by Hely Dutton, 1824, states (pg 415) the residential proprietor of the estates of 'Tullyra, Curraghmore, and Spiddall' is 'Edward Martin', Andrew Martyn's father.

When Edward Martyn died in 1836, it seems the bulk of the estate went to his oldest son John, while the second born Andrew received the Spiddal area lands. I say this because, in 1861, it was Andrew Martyn who intervened in the Comyn Chancery Court case, in opposition to splitting the land lease.

What was the ownership situation in Spiddal by the mid-19th Century? The GV volume for Galway was printed on 7 Mar 1855, while the VOB show that the property/land assessors were in the Spiddal area during the second half of 1853.

For the Barony of Moycullen in 1853, there is no 'Martyn' listed as owning or renting property. As for 'Martin', there was a Peter Martin owning property in the Moycullen vicinity, possibly associated with the Martins of Ross. This is not the Peter Martyn mentioned in the 1898 Burke's Landed Gentry. In Spiddal Village, there was a Michael Martin et al renting a very modest house from the Anglican Rev James McCready. I doubt he's directly connected to the gentry Martins.

For Spiddal East, the major landowner and landlord was Thomas Bunbury. Anthony Donnellan (of Ballyeighter, Aughrim) is the other significant landowner who, unlike Thomas Bunbury, seemed not have a residential presence in the townland.

There were Donnellans in the Loughrea area and the Aughrim area, somehow related to each other. And there was Martyn-Donnellan intermarriage, thus I suspect the Donnellan presence in Spiddal is somehow connected to the Martyns.

Where in Spiddal would these Martins have been residing? In the historical records, occasionally one sees references to a townland; "Spiddal Martin." Mike P Ó Conaola indicates this is another name for Spiddal East, containing the boreen (and village) of Baile an tSagairt. [*priest; sagart*] Recently I came across a 1928 record containing the reference; "Ballintaggart, Spiddal Martin."

Seán Ó Neachtain kindly provided the following:

> *The Martin's are interesting in that they gave their name to a village*
> *and that name was used in the church records into the early years of*
> *the 20th century However the local name Baile an tSagairt was previously*
> *the dominant name of the village. The cleric who gave the village its name*
> *was an tAthair Mícheál Ó Luachra (Fr Michael Rush) was the parish priest*
> *of Spiddal in 1792. The official name of the village at present is Spiddal East.*
> *Why did the church use the Spiddal Martin? Folklore has it that Fr Rush*
> *fell foul of the church authorities but that is the only "nod" we have.*

In passing, I'll mention that one sees references to 'Spiddal Ned.' In the Spiddal West townland is the village of Baile Eamon (Baile Eamoinn). The diminutive of Eamon is 'Ned ', so I would say 'Spiddal Ned' is Spiddal West.

For the Civil Parish of Ardrahan in the Barony of Kiltartan, surrounding Tullyra, I estimated that Andew's brother John Martyn controlled about 984 acres. John Martyn died in 1860. Likely he had other holdings farther afield. In the 1878 Landowners of Ireland compilation, Edward Joseph Martyn of Tullyra Castle, John's son, was listed as holding 4932 acres, valued at £2424.

Rather than a physical presence, there was a continued Martyn connection to Spiddal. Edward Martyn born in Tullyra, and holding 4932 acres around Tullyra in 1878, is Andrew Martyn's nephew.

What of 'Andrew Martyn, of Spiddal' ? Andrew Martyn and Mary Josephine Dolphin, Kingstown (Dún Laoghaire) residents, married on 3 August 1863, at St. Michael's RC Church. Their only child Mary's 29 Nov 1864 birth is documented in the St Michael's baptism register.

Andrew Martin, a 'Retired Ireland Revenue Officer', aged 70, died of old age on 31 July 1878, at "Fair Hill" Galway, reported by John Martyn of Dominick Street. What's interesting is that seemingly Andrew Martyn had become a salaryman. Andrew and Mary Martyn's child Mary married well, becoming Baroness Hemphill. Andrew's wife Mary, their daughter Mary (the Baroness Hemphill), the elder Mary's sister, but not Andrew (seemingly), are buried together in Glasnevin Cemetery Dublin.

The last Martyn in direct descent, Eward Martyn of Tullyra, died on 5 Dec 1923, d.s.p.

He founded the Palestrina Choir, was the first president of Sinn Féin, and advised the second Lord Killanin about engaging W A Scott to design Spiddal's Cill Éinde.

The Galway Observer
March 15, 1930

The "Irish Times" the other day in its attractive section under the title of "Quidnunc" speaks very deservedly and properly of a now extinct Co. & City of Galway family although as regards the Tullyra branch, the oldest of the many Martins, there happily remain as representatives Lady Hemphill and her son the Hon. Martin Hemphill, B.L., now the owner of the old home at Tullyra where with his wife and child he spends a good deal of his time. He is now a member of the Irish Bar and if there were, as there should be, a Connaught Bar, would, like so many of his name in the Past, be a member of it. Our contemporary says of the Martins; —

The Martyn's of Tullyra — Notable Scions of Galway — When a King was Captured
Hon. Martin Hemphill, B.L

Amongst the notable scions of the Galwegian family of the Martins there is one that stands out in a momentary spotlight of romance with but little beside to know of him. When Richard the First was captured on his way home from the Holy Land, there was one faithful follower who shared his troubles and his castle prisons. Unfortunately, before the mission of the faithful minstrel, Blondel, who attracted him to his goal, could be brought to a satisfactory conclusion, that faithful companion was dead. It became a story, told in Galway, that the name of Coeur de Lion's friend was Sir Oliver Martyn, but in the absence of corroborating evidence, it was given so much credence as such tales usually obtain. Some few years ago, however, a document came to light in one of the monastic castles of Bohemia and therein the name of the King's companion occurs just as the story had it.

We know from our never failing authority on Galway, Hardiman, that Oliver was the first of the name that settled in Ireland, and that the name is derived from Martins, Warlike but we cannot subscribe to that theory of the origin of Martin. O'Brien and Valency derived it from the Belgian Firbolgs or Martini Martinigh, Richard Martin of Dangan or Ballinahinch was descended from the eldest branch of the family and the houses of Curraghmore, Ross, Spiddal and Tullyra were, in Hardiman's days, the chief branches, but the Martins of Ross have gone and the houses of Spiddal and Tullyra are represented in the present family at Tullyra. There was an Act of the 8th Parliament of Queen Anne specially exempting the Martins from confiscation. It recited that Oliver Marin of Tullyra was during the Rebellion a person who behaved himself with great moderation and was remarkably kind to numbers of Protestants in distress, many of whom he supported in his family, and by his charity and goodness saved their lives, and in consequence it enacted that he might enjoy his estates firm and his heirs and settle and dispose of the same to his eldest son and his heirs male. "This solitary instance" says Hardiman, "of legislative justice is particularly conspicuous because it stands alone and surrounded by the most unjust and ferocious enactments that ever disgraced the code of any civilized country." And those broad acres were kept in the Marytn family down to our day and sold by the late Ed. Martyn to occupying tenantry. The old Castle of Dungorey at Kinvara was also alienated but not in his day. He looked upon it with great interest and got it renovated inside and made fit for habitation. It was purchased by Senator Gogarty. Hardiman says that the Martin coat of arms — the splendid armoral ensigns, namely, azure, Calvary Cross on five degrees argent between the sun in splendor on a dexter limb and the moon in crescent, on the sinister or crest, an etoile wavy of six points or motto "Ausilium Meum a Deo" — are stated to have been granted by King Richard the First of England to an ancestor named Oliver Martyn who accompanied that monarch to the holy wars and distinguished himself in Palestine, but on his return was made prisoner in Germany with his master and died in confinement. Such is the story as given in Hardiman's invaluable History.

The above confirms the connection of Spiddal to Tullyra. The 62nd London edition of *'Who's Who'* for 1910 has an entry for Capt Hon Fitzroy Hemphill JP, who in 1897 married Mary, daughter of Andrew Martyn of Spiddal. I found no Irish marriage registration. I suspect they married in England, and stayed there for some time.

The article's author, Martin Hemphill, is the son of Fitzroy Hemphill, and thus is a grandson of Andrew Martyn of Spiddal. Lady Hemphill is Mary Hemphill (née Martyn), Andrew Martyn's daughter.

Appendix IV
The Martins of Ross and Ballynahinch

Then there are the Martins of Ross, near Rosscahill. In 1910, Seymour Clarke published a genealogy of the Martins of Ross.

The Martins became established in Ross with the 1592 purchase (lease) of land there by Robert Martin. He was Sheriff of Galway for 1607, elected Mayor of Galway for 1621, and died in office on the 20th of April in that year, and was succeeded as mayor by his father Richard Martin. Robert's son Jasper, who succeeded him, died in 1629, and left an infant son Robert. Eventually Robert was elected Sheriff in 1644. Robert lived to an advanced age, dying in 1700, and left behind three sons: Jasper, James (who had no offspring), and Richard (aka *Nimble Dick*). It was from this Richard from which the Ballynahinch branch of the family sprang.

Jasper succeeded his father Robert, died in 1710, and was then succeeded by his eldest son Nicholas. The 1914 Martin genealogy of George Martin, mentioned earlier, has the three sons as Jasper, Oliver, and Richard. I believe the Robert Martin who died in 1700, is the Robert Martin listed (page 7) as the 1670 owner of the Bohoona East and Bohoona West townlands.

Another resource is:

Genealogy of the Family of Martin of Ballinahinch Castle, in the County of Galway, Ireland

by Archer E.S. Martin (1865-1941) privately printed in Winnipeg 1890. His genealogy starts with the divergence of the Ballynahinch branch from the Martins of Ross. It's not a surprise to see "Winnipeg," as some of these Martins immigrated to Canada.

Occasionally, one sees a reference like "Martin of Birch Hall." The variations go like Birchhall, Birchall, Curreveha, and in Irish, *Corr a' Bheithe*, Round Hill (or Rocky Ridge) of the Birch. It is a ca 120 acre townland in the Kilcummin Civil Parish, having a narrow frontage on Lough Corrib. Nimble Dick is *said* to have built himself a mansion at Birch Hall. Perhaps he called it 'Birch Hall.'

An 18th Century Martin-O'Flaherty matrimonial connection was discussed previously (page 11).

A later matrimonial Martin-O'Flaherty connection dates to 5 Oct 1806, when Robert Martin, brother of Anthony Crosby Martin and half-brother of *Humanity Dick,* married Mary O'Flaherty, brother of Thomas Henry of the Lemonfield O'Flaherties, children of Sir John Burke O'Flaherty (1728-1806).

This brought a détente between the clans that lasted a few decades. On 8 December 1837, hundreds from both clans gathered to fight over a disputed 20 acre bog straddling the Ballynahinch estate (200,000 acres) and Lemonfield estate (2000 acres): *The Battle of Rushveala.* Thomas Barnewall Martin and an O'Flaherty received gaol sentences.

I suspect that Richard Martin, the first Martin of Ross, and the landowner Oliver Martin, listed in the Down Survey for 1641, are either brothers, or first cousins.

Appendix V
The Comyns

The <u>Landed Estates Database</u> states:

"From the mid 17th century the Comyn family were established at Kilcorney in county Clare. In 1796 Laurence Comyn married Jane Lynch of Barna and bought land in the Spiddle area from his in-laws and from the Frenchs. Beggan states that he bought more land from the Blakes of Drum in 1814."

As we learned, the Comyn's also leased Cois Fharraige land from the Martyns of Tullyra.

Sometime after 1912, David Comyn published a <u>genealogy</u> of the Comyns. A copy exists in the Limerick City Library, not surprising considering their Co. Clare connections. The genealogy seems to be an extract from a collection of articles.

One is supposed to take away that the Comyns go way back. In the narrative are references to William the Conqueror and Charlemagne. Eventually the narrative mentions the Scottish Comyns. There was a John Comyn who was killed by Robert Bruce, and there is at least one John Comyn in the narrative, but, there is no mention of Robert Bruce.

For the 18th, 19th and early 20th Centuries, the Galway/Clare male Comyns of interest to us are Laurence Comyn, his sons: Peter Sarsfield Comyn, John Sarsfield Comyn, Thomas F Comyn (who only appears once, in a court reference), Francis Comyn, and Francis Comyn's son Francis Laurenzo Comyn. Also of interest are Laurence Comyn's two daughters; Harriet and Caroline, discussed below.

Apparently the Comyns didn't shy away from a fight. Laurence Comyn's father was David Comyn [Senior], who died prematurely on 20 Dec 1775, in a duel. Moving along, from the senior David Comyn's Great Grandson David Comyn we have:

............David's [Senior] eldest son, Laurence, married (15th April 1796) Jane, the daughter and ultimate heiress of Nicholas Lynch (the Cranmore) of Barna Co. Galway. He was the Representitive of the Connaught Catholics in 1798, having represented those of Co. Clare in 1792, and was, with Lord ffrench, examined by the House of Lords on the education of Catholic Youth. He died on 28th June, 1819*, leaving three sons and two daughters. (1) Francis, his heir; (2) John Sarsfield d.s.p. , 1835**; and (3) Peter Sarsfield, D.L., d.s.p., 1866. The elder daughter married, firstly, Robert de Blacquiere, and had issue, Robert; and secondly, the Baron Cornelius von Stenz von Hagen, but had no issue by him. The second daughter, Harriet, died unmarried in 1837.

I found an 1844 reference identifying a Thomas F Comyn as a brother of John Sarsfield Comyn.

*The 1868 Burke's Landed Gentry has Laurence Comyn dying in 1820. Also, it seems he was writing to Dublin Castle in January 1820. So perhaps he died on 28 June 1820.

** John S Comyn actually died on 30 May 1834 in Piccadilly, London.

Francis, the eldest son (b. 4th Oct., 1801), married (28th April 1834) Honoria, daughter of Edward Beytagh of Cappagh, Co. Galway by Sarah, his wife, daughter of the second Baron ffrench. By her he had issue. (1) Francis Laurenzo, his heir; (2) John Sarsfield, as Hon Deputy Surgeon General, who married Sophia, daughter of Major-General Owen, C. B., and had issue. Francis Ulysses, married to Sybill, d. and h. of the Rev. Mr. Bailey (and has issue, Denis Sarsfield (b. 3rd August, 1912), and Sophy, married to Lieut. Ussher, R.N.R.; (3) Charles, for a time captain in the Emperor (of Mexico) Maximillian's bodyguard. He distinguished himself in the fighting in Central America, especially in the sorties from the city of Mexico, and with other decorations, received that of Knight Commander of our Lady of Gaudeloupe; (4) George, M.D., married to Miss O'Flynn; (5) William; (6) Henry M.D. He had two daughters; the elder, Rose, married Count Cavaliere Strozzi of Lugo, Florence, and d.s.p. 1912; the younger, Laura, married Edward Beytagh of Mannin, and d.s.p. Without issue..............

Francis died 9th June, 1873, and was succeeded by his eldest son, Francis Laurenzo (b. 12th Nov., 1835, died 13th Sept., 1903), who married (4th Sept., 1865) Cecile, d. and h. of Walter Bourke, Q.C. (the Macwilliam Iochtarach), of Carrowkeale, Co. Mayo, by Mary, daughter of Peter Blake (junior) of Tower Hill. He had issue. (1) Walter Bouke, died unmaried (26th May, 1900) at Kismayu, East African Protectorate, where he was a deputy Commissioner; (2) John Sarsfield, a lieutenant in the Royal West Kent regiment, who died unmarried at Lokoja on return from the Lepai expedition (medal and clasps) (14th July, 1898); (3) David Charles Edward ffrench, his heir; (4) Kenneth Henry, who died at Kronstad, while serving in the South African war (medal with clasps) (3rd June 1900). He also left four daughters; (1) Mary; (2) Aimée; (3) Eva, who married (1907) H. Reandy, Esq., and has issue; Barbara; (4) Dorathea.

The only surviving son, David the Comyn (b. 2nd April, 1876), is representative of the senior male line of the Comyn family. He is lieutenant on retired pay in the Black Watch (Royal Highlanders), and an F.R.G.S.; served in the South African war (two medals with clasps), and was, for some time, Bimbashi (Major) in the Egytian Army, and acting-Governor of Halfa province. He is the author of "Service and Sport in the Sudan" and of this memoir. The senior line has an unbroken record of adherence to the Catholic religion.

The narrative continues, describing the Comyns scattered across Ireland and the world, and mentions the poet Michael Comyn. There is a passing swipe at the pretenders; the various Cummins, Commons etc, who decided it would be beneficial to claim Comyn descent.

We see that it's important to marry well. The Strozzi family of Florence was, in their heyday, a major rival of the Medici. Being a captain protecting the Emperor Maximillian I of Mexico afforded only short term job security.

Our memorialist, David Comyn, was the only surviving son of Francis Laurenzo Comyn.

Buried in the latter part of David Comyn's narrative is the following:

Note.-----The Comyn estates (12,883 acres) in Clare, Galway, and Mayo (Kilcorney, Woodstock, Carrowkeale, etc) were sold in 1902-7.

Appendix VI
THE NAME AND FAMILY OF LORD MORRIS - OF GALWAY AND SPIDDAL

A Morris genealogy appeared in the 1897 'THE IRISH LAW TIMES AND SOLICITORS' JOURNAL.' I've transcribed most of it here. I added an update to take the genealogy beyond 1897.

The following interesting account of the old, well known, and respected name of Morris—-whose present representative is Lord Morris—was written and published by Charles Ffrench Blake Forster in his memorable work, "The Irish Chieftains, or a Struggle for the Crown," published in 1872. We give this singularly accurate memoir with necessary additions to bring it up to date :—

The ancient family of Morris was distinguished in Ireland since the twelfth century, Sir Harvey de Monte Maurisco, Knt., the founder of this house, having accompanied the great Earl of Pembroke, better known as Strongbow, to that country in 1172. Sir Harvey, who was one of the most accomplished knights of his time, was appointed by the Earl of Pembroke seneschal over the vast territories which he had acquired by his marriage with the Princess Eva, daughter and heiress of Dermot MacMurrough, King of Leinster, and he was afterwards confirmed in his appointment by King Henry II. Sir Harvey, who was a great benefactor to the Church, founded the large and noble Cistercian religious house of Dunbrody, which he filled with learned monks, who came from Bildewas in Shropshire. He died in the monastery of the Holy Trinity at Canterbury.............

....................In the reign of Henry VI. A branch of the Morris family settled in the ancient town of Galway, where they soon took a leading part, and several of them held the offices of Mayors and Sheriffs of that town, and were distinguished by their active and upright conduct as members of the Corporation. In 1486 Richard Morris was one of the bailiffs of Galway, which was the ancient name for Sheriffs, which better designation the bailiffs of Galway first received in the reign of King James I. In 1501 John Morris held this office, as did William Morris in 1508, and John Morris in 1515. In 1527 William Morris was Mayor of Galway, and Andrew Morris was bailiff of the same town in 1588, in which year one of the bailiffs was George Morris.............

The Galway Branch of the Morris family were of the 14 Tribes of Galway (see Hardiman's History of Galway), and from Richard Morris, who was bailiff in 1406, lineally descended William Morris, Mayor in 1529, Andrew Morris, Mayor in 1588, George Morris, bailiff in 1588, and Edmond Morris. He, with other well-known townsmen of Galway, witnessed the will of Sir Morogh ne doe O'Flaghertie in 1593, who was chief of his name, and owner of the territory of Iar Connaught.

John Morris and Andrew Morris are next mentioned. The latter took an active part under General Preston in the defence of Galway against the Parliamentary forces, and upon the surrender of the town in 1652 refused with other townsmen to sign the Capitulation. George Morris, of Spiddal and Galway, was a son of James Morris, and he served in King James' army. In 1684 he married Catherine, daughter of John FitzPatrick, of Loughmore, in the south island of Arran, a descendant of the junior branch of Ussory. 'His son, Edmond FitzPatrick, married Annabel Martin, of Dangan, of the family of Colonel Richard Martin, of Dangan, who was the founder of Ballinahinch branch.

Edmond FitzPatrick died in 1717, leaving a son Rickard. His widow married a Michael O'Flaherty, of Park, near Spiddal, son of Roderick. the celebrated author and antiquarian. Roderick outlived his son Michael [This is inconsistent with most other accounts.], and who assigned his estate of Park to his stepson, Richard FitzPatrick, who was sheriff of Galway in 1730, and M.P. from 1749 to 1761, when he died, and was succeeded by his nephew, Edmond FitzPatrick, sheriff of Galway, in 1769, 1789, 1794, and 1797. His son, James FitzPatrick, died in 1828, when the male line of this branch of the FitzPatrick family became extinct. George Morris, by his marriage with Catherine FitzPatrick, obtained the property of Spiddal, where he and his descendants, and at the house in the west suburb of Galway, afterwards called Dominick-street, have resided.

John FitzPatrick died in 1709 at the house of his son-in-law, George Morris, leaving personalty to the amount of £6,000, and £1,500 in gold and silver as appears by his will. Andrew Morris, of Spiddal and Galway, was the only son of George, and he married Monica Brown, of the ancient family of Gloves, near Athenry, leaving two sons, George and James.

George died in India, having had one son and two daughters. Edmond, an officer in the Indian army, and killed at the siege of Seringapatan; Mary (who married, first, Christopher Oldfield, Esq., of the Bengal Civil Service, and their grandson is the present Sir Richard Oldfield, and, secondly, Major Macan, of Co. Louth, by whom she had one daughter, the present Mrs. Kirwan, of Castlehackett); and Catherine, who married W. T. Smith, Esq., B.C.S. James Morris, of Spiddal, was born in 1732, and married in 1762 Deborah Lynch, daughter of Nicholas Lynch, merchant, of Galway, and niece of the distinguished diplomat, Sir George Staunton, of Cargins, Co. Galway, who accompanied Lord Macartney on his embassy to Madras and China, and was created a baronet in 1785, and was buried in Westminster Abbey in 1801.

James Morris died in 1813, leaving daughters, of whom Monica married Andrew Blake, of Galway, and had James Blake, Q.C., who died in 1841, leaving an only daughter, the present Mrs. Alymer Gowing; Henry, whose daughter is the wife of the Right Hon. The MacDermot, Q.C.; and the late Patrick Joseph Blake, Q.C., and County Court Judge; and Deborah, who married Anthony O'Flaherty, of Shrine, and had one son Christopher, who died in 1896. Another of James Morris's daughters, Mary, married R. M'Donagh, Esq., and had one daughter, who married Michael Brown, of Woodstock, Co. Mayo, and their son is the present Colonel Dominick Brown, of Woodstock.

James Morris had three sons; Ambros, a Captain in the 64th Regiment, killed at the battle of Talavera in Spain; Michael Morris, of Spiddal, who died in 1826, unmarried, and Martin Morris, J.P., of Spiddal, who, born in 1784, married in 1822, Julia, daughter of Dr. Charles Blake, of Galway, by his wife Jane, daughter of Christopher Browne, of Gloves. He was High Sheriff of the county of the town of Galway in 1841, and was the first Catholic who held office since 1690. He died in 1862, and left two sons, Michael and George, and two daughters, Jane and Lizzie.

Jane married Thomas Courtenay, nephew of Lord Chief Justice Lefroy, and had, with other children, Arthur, Master of the Court of Queen's Bench in Ireland, and Emily, who married Major William Blakeney. George Morris, J. P. and D.L., was High Sheriff of Galway in 1860 and 1861, and was M.P. for Galway, 1867-8, and 1874 to 1880, and is now Vice-President of the Local Government Board in Ireland. He married in 1875 Elizabeth, only daughter of David O Connor Henchy, Esq., M.P., of Stonebrook, Co. Kildare, and niece of Sir Thomas Burke, Bart., M.P., of Marble Hill, Co. Galway, and they have one daughter.

The Right Hon. Michael, Baron Morris, was born in 1827 [14 Nov 1826] at Dominick-street House, and was educated at Galway; entered Trinity College, where he graduated in 1847, obtaining first moderatorship and gold medal. He was High Sheriff of the town of Galway in 1849, and was called to the Bar in the same year. He became Recorder of Galway in 1857, and was the first Catholic who filled the office. He held it till 1865. He was made a Queen's Counsel in February, 1863, and a Bencher of the King's Inns, Dublin, in 1866. He was elected member for Galway town at the general election of 1865, having the largest majority any member ever was returned by.

He became Solicitor-General in July, 1866, was re-elected M.P., and became Attorney-General in October, 1866, and a member of her Majesty's Privy Council in Ireland. He was again re-elected member for the borough in 1867, and was raised to the Bench as one of the Justices of the Common Pleas in March, 1867. In 1876 he was promoted to be Lord Chief Justice of the Common Pleas, and in 1887 he was appointed Lord Chief Justice of Ireland. which office he held till 1889.

He was created a Baronet in 1885, and a Lord of Appeal in Ordinary, with the style and title of Baron Morris of Spiddal [a life peerage], in 1889, when he was also sworn a member of her Majesty's Privy Council in England. In 1890 he was elected a Bencher of Lincoln's Inn. Lord Morris is a J.P. for counties, Galway and Cavan, Chairman of the Board of National Education, and a Senator of the Royal University of Ireland, and LL.D. (Hon.) of Trinity College, Dublin.

In September, 1860, he married Anna, daughter of the Hon. Henry George Hughes, one of the Barons of the Court of Exechequer in Ireland, and has had, with daughters, four sons—Martin Henry FitzPatrick, born in 1867, B.A., Trinity College, Dublin, Barrister-at-Law, and J.P. for counties Galway and Cavan, and High Sheriff for the town of Galway 1897; George Henry, born in 1872, Lieutenant and Adjutant, 3rd Battalion Rifle Brigade; Michael Redmond, born in 1878, and entered Trinity College, Dublin, 1896; and Charles Ambrose, born in 1880."—-Tuam Herald

Update (by JJK)

The Baron supposedly once quipped that he spent his time in Dublin, during the week, putting people in gaol, while in Spiddal he had endure his tenants' entreaties to spring their family members from gaol. While a Petty Sessions magistrate in Spiddal, he would have been sentencing people to gaol, or referring them to the Assizes for more serious accusations. Rising through the judiciary, after a time he was probably incarcerating few people, although he likely had great power to influence the fate of those who were improperly prosecuted. Oral history is that, when he walked his Spiddal holdings, the only tenant who dared walk beside him was Nicholas Curran, great grandfather of the late Timín JoeTim Nicholas Curran.

On 15 June 1900, the London Gazette (issue 27202, page 3751) announced that Baron Morris was made a hereditary peer; Baron Killanin (aka Lord Killanin). He died on 8 September 1901, and is buried in Galway. Martin Henry Morris' younger brother, George Henry Morris, born in Spiddal in 1872, eventually became the Lieutenant-Colonel in command of the 1st Battalion of the Irish Guards. He was killed in France on 1 Sept 1914, during the Retreat from Mons.

Martin Henry Morris, the 2nd Lord Killanin, never married, dying childless in 1927, and was succeeded by his nephew Michael Morris (1914-1999). Michael Morris, the 3rd Lord Killanin (once he turned 21), was the son of Lt. Col. George Henry Morris, born in London, one month before his father died in France.

Julia Morris, wife of Martin Morris (1784-1862), died of cholera on 6 August 1833. Oral history is that, after her death, her young son George, younger brother of Michael (1826-1901), was a temporary resident in the Feeney Tuar Beg household. Later, one of these Feeney's, John Feeney, immigrated to Maine. There he married a Barbara (Abby) Curran (1856-1933), who hailed from Coill Rua (Kilroe), according to the local oral history. Other accounts have her coming from Kilronan. At least two of his sons (John & Francis) ended up in Hollywood, adopting the stage name 'Ford.' Apparently the film director John Ford referred to Michael Morris, the 3rd Lord Killanin, as his 'cousin.'

There may be something to the claim. Public Feeney genealogies show one set of John Ford's paternal great grandparents as Edmond Feeney (1785-1856) and Barbara Morris Feeney (1785-1856). According to the genealogy, she was the daughter of James Morris (1732-1813) and Deborah Lynch Morris (1740-1820). This is consistent with the local oral history. This would make Barbara a sister of Martin Morris. She is not mentioned in the just discussed 1897 genealogy. Her absence doesn't necessarily mean to stories are untrue. Missing siblings in these genealogies is not unheard of. According to the stated birth years, Deborah Lynch Morris would have been about 40 years old when she bore Barbara. Not impossible. There are also some uncertainties associated with those stated eighteenth century birth years as well. It is suspicious that Edmond and Barbara had the same life spans; 1785-1856.

The 3rd Lord Killanin had a number of vocations; Fleet Street journalist, a British Army major involved in planning and participating in the D-Day landing, and a film producer. He was an uncredited producer for the film "The Quiet Man", directed by John Ford, starring John Wayne and Maureen O'Hara. He was president of the International Olympic Committee (1972-1980) during a time of great tumult (Munich Massacre, Olympic boycotts etc).

His wife, Sheila Dunlop (1917-2007), was at least as interesting as her spouse. She was born in the Himalayan foothills, eventually relocating to Oughterard when her father, the Canon Douglas Dunlop, was designated Rector of Oughterard in 1936. She taught ballet in Galway for a time. During World War II, she worked at Bletchley Park, as did Alan Turing, in cryptographic intelligence, assisting in the efforts to decrypt German ciphers, many created by the Enigma Machine. She, her husband, and Turing, were made MBEs for their contributions to the war effort. Michael Morris, the third Lord Killanin, died in Dublin on 25 April 1999. Lady Kilannin's 2007 obituary stated that the Killanins sold the Spiddal House Estate in 1960.

Appendix VII
The Blakes of Drum, Tully, and Gortnamona

PATRICK BLAKE of Drum, who was Mayor of the town of Galway in 1771. He was admitted to the Middle Temple on January 24, 1777. He married, in 1774, Maria Nagle, and by her (who survived him, and remarried, in 1783, James Skerrett of Galway, and died November, 1796) had issue two sons and three daughters, viz. :

1. Valentine, born in 1780, of whom presently.
2. James.
3. Mary, who married the Rev. Lorenzo Hely-Hutchinson (sixth son of the Right Hon. John Hely-Hutchinson, Provost of Trinity College, Dublin), and had issue.
4. Margaret, who married, in 1796, Francis David Kirwan.
5. Magdalen.

Patrick Blake died September 11, 1782 (will dated September 11, 1782), and was succeeded by his eldest son,

VALENTINE BLAKE of Tully, and Gortnamona, near Ballinasloe, Co. Galway. He married Anne Burke, sister of Nicholas Archdekin Burke of Gortnamona, by whom he had issue one son and two daughters, viz. :

1. Patrick, of whom presently.
2. Mary.
3. Jane.

Valentine Blake died Circa 1819 (will dated March 7, 1819, proved P.C. February 15, 1821), and was succeeded by his only son,

PATRICK BLAKE of Gortnamona. He married Eleanor Mary Roberts, by whom (who survived him, and died June 30, 1874 ; will dated May 14, 1874, proved October 27, 1874) he had issue one son and four daughters, viz.:

1. Valentine FitzPatrick, of whom presently.
2. Frances.
3. Rosa.
4. Eleanor.
5. Mary Anne, who died unmarried on March 14, 1864 (will dated March 9, 1864, proved April 5, 1871).

Patrick Blake died July 24, 1857 (will dated May 12, 1857, proved November 17, 1860). He was succeeded by his only son,

VALENTINE FITZPATRICK BLAKE of Gortnamona. He married (settlement dated June 2, 1865) Ellen Smyth, by whom (who survived him) he had (with other issue) a son,

1. Valentine A. Blake, Captain 4th Scottish Rifles, who married, on October 22, 1902, Alison, eldest daughter of Robert Skeet of Windmill House, Bishop's Stortford, Hertfordshire.

Valentine FitzPatrick Blake died at Bray on November 1, 1870; will dated June 14, 1869, proved December 3, 1870.

The *Landed Estates Database* noted: "In the 1870s Valentine [Fitzpatrick] Blake of Gortnamona is recorded as the owner of 17,335 acres in county Galway though Walford notes that he had died in 1870 and his son, Valentine [Alexander] Blake, born in 1868, was a Ward in Chancery." It must have been the nineteen-year-old son's legal representative that conducted a Cois Fharraige eviction in January 1887.

Appendix VIII
The Blakes of Furbough

ANDREW (OGE) BLAKE, third son of Andrew fitz Patrick
Blake (see BLAKE OF DUNMACRINA AND ORANMORE, ante,
p. 211). He obtained a grant, by patent (dated July 26, 1677,
enrolled August 9, 1677) under the Acts of Settlement, of lands
in the baronies of Dunkellin and Moycullen, Co. Galway. He
married Christiane, daughter of Dominick Martyn of Iar Connaught,
by whom he had issue eight sons and three
daughters, viz. :

1. Francis, of whom presently.
2. Nicholas, a Dominican friar of the Dominican convent
    at Galway. He was living (in concealment) at
    Galway in 1705.
3. Edward, died vita patris in 1678 (will dated January 6,
    1678, proved at Tuam January 23, 1678).
4. Patrick.
5. Martin.
6. Dominick.
7. Walter.
8. Augustin.
9. Sibyl, who married (circa 1672) Peter Martyn, afterwards
    Justice of the Common Pleas in Ireland,
    tempore James II.
10. Anne, who married Dominick Bodkin.
11. Katharine, dead in 1682.

Andrew age Blake died circa 1687 (will dated October 20,
1681, proved at Tuam August 22, 1687). He was succeeded
by his eldest son,

FRANCIS BLAKE of Furbough in the barony of Moycullen,
Co. Galway. He married Jane Martyn, by whom he had issue
two sons and a daughter, viz. :

1. Thomas, of whom presently.
2. John, of Ballymanagh, Co. Galway, who married Sarah
    French of Aggard, Co. Galway, and died on November
    26, 1763, leaving issue a son:
    (1) Andrew, of Ballymanagh, who married (articles
        dated February 4, 1760) Honoria, eldest
        daughter of Michael Burke of Ballydugan,
        Co. Galway, and died circa 1781 (will dated
        September 22, 1768, proved P.C. April 25, 1781),
        leaving issue two sons and a daughter, viz. :
        (i.) John (Colonel), of whom presently.
        (ii.) Andrew, Captain in the 88th Regiment;
            killed at Talavera July 28, 1809.
        (iii.) Sarah.
        (iv.)

3· Juliane.

Francis Blake of Furbough was succeeded by his eldest son,

THOMAS BLAKE (the elder) of Furbough, who had issue two sons, VIZ. :

    1. Francis, of whom presently.

    2. Jasper.

The elder son,

FRANCIS BLAKE of Furbough (living in 1748), had issue an only son,

THOMAS BLAKE (the younger) of Furbough, who died without issue circa 1764; and the representation of the family eventually devolved upon his cousin John Blake, eldest son of Andrew Blake of Ballymanagh (see above). This

JOHN BLAKE of Furbough, Lieutenant-Colonel, was Mayor of Galway from 1830 to 1836. He married first, in March, 1789, Mary, daughter of Nugent Sylvester Aylward of Ballinagar, Co. Galway, and widow of Edmond Blake of Ballyglunin (see BLAKE OF BALLYGLUNIN, ante, p. 216), but by her had no issue. He married secondly, in 1797, Maria, second daughter of Edmund Galwey of the city of Cork, by whom he had issue three sons, viz.:

    1. Andrew William, of whom presently.

    2. Edmond, born in 1803, who was Mayor of Galway from 1836 to 1840, when the mayoralty was abolished by Act of Parliament. He married, on November 24, 1870, Anne, daughter of Christopher St. George of Tyrone, Co. Galway, and died on May 9, 1895, leaving issue by her (who survived him, and died February 1, 1904) an only child: (1) Anne.

    3. John Henry, of Rathville, Co. Galway, who married Harriet, daughter of Francis Lynch of Mount Pleasant, Co. Galway, and died June 29, 1882 (will proved in Principal Registry August 23, 1882), leaving issue surviving two sons, viz. :

        (1) Edmond, now (1905) of Rathville.

        (2) Henry.

Colonel John Blake of Furbough died on October 18, 1836, and was succeeded by his eldest son,

ANDREW WILLIAM BLAKE of Furbough. He married, on September 22, 1832, Maria Julia, second daughter of Malachy Daly of Raford, Co. Galway, by whom (who survived him, and died March 2, 1871; will proved April 3, 1871) he had issue three sons and four daughters, viz. :

1. John Archer Daly, of-whom presently.

2. Malachy J., Clerk of the Peace for County Galway, who died unmarried on May 12, 1902.

3. Andrew, married, but died without issue.

4. Julia, died unmarried June 2, 1854.

5. Elizabeth.

6. Emily, who married, on July 24, 1866, William, tenth Earl of Westmeath.

7. Charlotte, who married, on October 29, 1863, John Smyth of Masonbrook, Co. Galway.

Andrew W. Blake of Furbough died on January 27, 1868
(administration granted April 21, 1868), and was succeeded by
his eldest son,
JOHN ARCHER DALY (Colonel), now (1905) of Furbough and
of Raford, Co. Galway. He assumed by royal license dated
April 24, 1837, the surname and arms of Daly in lieu of his
patronymic Blake, in compliance with the testamentary provisions
of his maternal great-uncle, Hyacinth Daly of Raford.
He married, on April 30, 1864, Lady Anne Nugent, daughter
of Anthony, ninth Earl of Westmeath, and has had issue one
son and one daughter, viz. :
1. Denis (Captain), who married, on June 3, 1899, Kathleen,
   only daughter of Richard Lynch of Petersburgh,
   Co. Galway, and died vita patris in November, 1899,
having had posthumous issue a son and a daughter,
VIZ. :
      (1) Denis, born in March, died in August, 1900.
      (2) Denise (twin with her brother).
2. Anne, who died unmarried in 1897.

Above is listed Andrew Blake's and Mary Daly's son Andrew, who married, but died without issue.
I found his baptism record in the Catholic Parish registers at the National Library of Ireland.
He was baptised in Rahoon on 19 June 1842. One sponsor was Malachy Blake. It seems the
Blakes of Furbo were Roman Catholic. Given the proximity of the Blake Chapel to the Furbo
Catholic church, one might have deduced that. A decade or two or so ago, the chapel was damaged.
I'm unsure if the act was political, looting, or was just vandalism.

As mentioned earlier, John Henry Blake, originally of Furbo, married late in life, in St Andrew's
Catholic Church, Westland Row, Dublin. This is the church where one of the Sherwood girls said
she was to have been confirmed, on 15 March 1860. An event that, for her, never occurred, given
her trek the day before from Dublin to the Galway Train Station.

Appendix IX
The Bunburys

Thomas J Bunbury's (1793-1874) seat was Lisbryan House, Co Tipperary. Earlier generations seemed to be referred to as Bunbury-Isaac, and were active in Carlow. He successfully petitioned in 1844 to establish a Spiddal post office. Eventually passengers could ride the mail wagon from Galway to Spiddal for 1s 6d. From remarks of his, one can date Thomas J Bunbury's arrival in Spiddal to ca 1831.

On the 1822 Spiddal Relief Committee was T L Dundas. This indicates that he held property in the area, likely on the east side of Spiddal. Thomas Laurence Dundas (1788-1845) was born in Midleton Co Cork, and had a maternal grandmother named Jane Greene née Bunbury. Her father was a Thomas Bunbury of Shronell, Tipperary. Some of TL Dundas's siblings were born in Cork, others were born in Tipperary. Thomas J Bunbury and TL Dundas are somehow related, seemingly cousins of some sort.

It seems that the Thomas and Mary (née Bernard) Bunbury summered in Spiddal. Newspapers of the day, often had little social section. One paper had one called "Table Talk." In these sections the gentry would announce their move from one estate to another of their estates. It was important to them, at any given point in time, that other gentry knew where they were in residence. The estates on the east side of Spiddal were sometimes referenced as something like the 'marine residence', even though strictly speaking, the residences weren't "on" Galway Bay. There is some oral history about a big rock on the shore, that Mrs Bunbury liked to come down to and picnic on. Mike P Ó Conaola tells me;

> On that rock also is a pool of seawater that gets replenished regularly by the Atlantic Ocean. As children we oftentimes used it to dip into it's lukewarm water before venturing into the sea proper. The pool was and is called 'poll bhean bhun.' Translated literally as 'Mrs Bunbury's Hole' or Mrs Bunbury's Pool.

Seán Ó Neachtain mentioned to me that he once found mackerel in the pool.

Thomas & Mary Bunbury had a daughter, Susan Catherine Bunbury, born in 1837. In 1876, she married John Palmer, a flour merchant, of Foster's Place, Galway. He died within a year, and was memorialised in St. Nicholas' Church. Landed estates compilations of the time put Susan Bunbury Palmer's Spiddal 'Manor House' estate at 954 acres. Some fraction of this acreage (perhaps all of it), was the estate previously owned by Sir Robert Staples. At about this time, there also was a Thomas Palmer in Galway, undoubtedly related to John Palmer. My guess, probably brothers, or father and son. In 1876, Thomas Palmer was on the Galway Board of Commissioners.

My maternal Great[3] Grandfather, Martin Conneely, alleged that, on 4 May 1861, a car(t) operated by John Daly, in the service of Thomas Palmer, a brewer of Dominick St Galway, broke the axle of Martin Conneely's car(t). I assume Daly was hauling kegs of porter. The collision took place on the road by Park. Martin Conneely was awarded damages of 5 shillings.

Susan Catherine Palmer is in Spiddal for the 1901 and 1911 Irish Censuses. The steward of her Manor House estate was Bartley O'Donnell. Bartley O'Donnell was the informant at the 94-year-old Susan Catherine Palmer's 13 Sept 1931 passing. His son Patrick was the heir to the bulk of the Manor House estate.

Appendix X
Sir Robert Staples

Sir Robert Staples' ancestor, Thomas Staples of Bristol, arrived in the North ca 1610, as part of the Ulster Plantation. In 1628 he was created the first Baronet of Lissan in the County of Tyrone and Faughanvale in the County of Londonderry.

The Bunburys were preceded in Spiddal by Sir Robert Staples (1772-1832), the 8th Baronet. His main estate was Dunmore House, Durrow, Queen's County (Co Laois). Martin Morris's 1846 fishery testimony has Sir Robert Staples in Spiddal circa 1816. Sir Robert Staples died in 1832, unmarried, but with an illegitimate son Edmund Staples. Edmund inherited the Dunmore Estate after his father's suicide. The Staples Baronetcy passed to another (legitimate) branch of the family.

Thomas Bunbury indicated that the Bunburys arrived in Spiddal around 1831, suggesting that perhaps they acquired Sir Robert Staples' east-side Spiddal holding after his 1832 death. However, given TL Dundas's maternal Bunbury connection, one could say the Bunbury connection to Spiddal goes back to before 1822. How the Dundas – Staples – Bunbury holdings meshed is unclear.

In the 1853 VOB, Edmund Staples Esq was listed, with his name then crossed out, as possessing a significant hunting and fishing lodge, in the Derrynea townland. His name was overwritten with the name; "Hon Richard Hely Hutchinson." The (circa October) 1853 assessor's notes were written as if Edmund Staples Esq still occupied the property:

> Remote Situation, but desirably situated for Angling and Field Sports,
> the purposes for which Mr Stables [Staples] keeps it. --- He seldom occupies
> it for more than three or four months a year.

From the assessor's building measurements, it was a significant complex. It was assessed at nearly £19 (before downward adjustments).The Landed Estates Database states that Staples was leasing the property from George Cottingham. Around this time, the was a George Cottingham who seemed to be a County Galway coroner. Within the VOB, for September 1853, the Field Books list Staples controlling 1122 acres of land in Derrynea, basically the whole townland. The VOB cover the period 1824-1856, and don't show Edmond Staples as having any Spiddal Village area property.

Victims of the 2nd Tully eviction gathered at the Lodge in February 1848, to provide testimony.

By the latter part of the 19th Century, it was referred to as "Costello Lodge." After the 1912 Titanic sinking, it became the part-time refuge for the surviving passenger turned recluse, J Bruce Ismay, former Chairman of the White Star Line. Apparently he wasn't entirely reclusive. A maternal cousin of mine remembers his paternal grandmother recounting how Ismay visited the Derroe primary school, and handed out sweets.

Costello Lodge burned in 1922 and was rebuilt in 1925.

Appendix XI
The Lynches

For the Lynches, I've partly relied on *The Genealogy of the Anglo-Norman Lynches who settled in Galway* by Paul McNulty. Prior to Cromwell, it seems there were two property holding Lynch branches from Spiddal to Barna.

Both descended from Thomas Lynch, Provost of Galway--1274, via his two sons:

James----- (Castlecarra, Clogher, Dughiska, Partry, Petersburgh)

William----(Barna, Bordeaux, Lavally, Southampton)

The story (from *Burke's Landed Gentry*) is that the Lynchs came into Barna via an heiress, Anne O'Halloran, who married William de Lynch. There is an 1850 reference to an O'Halloran Castle that was in Barna. Samuel Lewis' 1837 *Topographical Dictionary of Ireland* (page 639), has the O'Hallorans, much earlier in time, controlling lands bordering Lough Corrib. In 1641, we have a Edmund Halloran in possession (page 7) of the Lippa townland. In his 1914 article *The O'Flaherty Country*, E W Lynam sums up the sad decline of the formerly powerful O'Halloran clan:

......In 1587 the O'Hallorans of Ohery [Ross] were driven out by Morrogh na Dtuagh [O'Flaherty]. Seven years later Dermot Duff O'Halloran, of Barna, head of the clan, had to mortgage much of his lands in Barna and Rinvile [Renvyle] to Galway merchants. Between 1612 and 1638 the various O'Hallorans of Rinvile sold their holdings, including the castle, to the O'Flaherties............

........In 1638 Stephen Lynch of Galway seized the castle and lands of Barna for payment of a debt of £410. He sold them to the Fitzmarcus Lynches of Forbogh [Furbo], who had been watching their chance for many years, and now at last became the Lynches of Barna. The last O'Hallorans of Barna sold their lands in 1709, and though their name is still common in Iar-Connacht, they have sunk to the level of the people whom they conquered in the thirteenth century.

From Paul McNulty's work, we see (above) that the *William* branch of the Lynches got around. In the Pauillac commune of Bordeaux is Chateau Lynch-Bages, known to English aficionados as *Lunch-Bags*, according to Hugh Johnson.

Appendix XII
Edward Martyn

Edward Martyn: An Irish Catholic Eccentric
A Machine-Readable Version

Thomas MacGreevy

Original Source: The Father Mathew Record. Dublin. April 1943. p.2.

Edward Martyn
An Irish Catholic Eccentric

By Thomas MacGreevy

He was "*contrairy*" in everything. So orthodox a Catholic that he had to have written permission from Rome to read books which were on the Index, he yet spent years of his life putting over on an Irish public which remained good-naturedly indifferent, the dramatic works of Henrik Ibsen, a Norwegian Lutheran who used the technique of the Parisian well-made play to state the dubiously interesting problems of one group after another of unbelievably solemn small-town egotists.

A convert to Home Rule and Sinn Féin, he insisted on remaining a member and habitué of the Kildare Street Club, and for all his nationalism, he had so little sense of history that he could only see the Civil War as a manifestation of a native instinct for producing subversive minorities which he, who was not of them, thought he perceived in the Irish people.

The most lovable of men, he tended, sooner or later, to part company with those who were originally associated with him in the various enterprises, political and cultural, in which from patriotic motives he interested himself -- and like an old-time patron usually helped to finance.

The explanation of this last characteristic would seem to be that he was more interested in his own preconceived idea of the Irish nation than in the nation itself. It was therefore inevitable that he should sometimes find himself at odds with other enthusiasts whose theory or practice did not fit in with his. In other words, he was a nineteenth century idealist. He was of his time, not in front of it, a man of ideas rather than understanding, of talent rather the genius. But unquestionably of sufficient talent to make a mark on the history of his country. Most of the men who figure in public life make no mark at all on history. A Pádraig Pearse or a James Connolly, drawing inspiration from a whole nation, consciously incarnating its perhaps only half-conscious sense of direction at a moment of crisis, marks a turning-point in a country's destinies. A greater number affirm their influence sufficiently strongly for it to remain memorable though not epoch-making. These are the men of talent. Edward Martyn was one of them. And if at a given moment he failed to reconcile the lesser misunderstandings that existed between the mass of his countrymen and himself, they, at least, never failed to recognise that on the larger issues he was according to his lights, a man of outstanding rectitude and goodwill.

And what were his lights? Secularly they were those of the small group of more liberal landlords who accepted the sociological ideas of the nineteenth century. But unlike the majority of these, Edward Martyn was brought up in the religion of the mass of the people, the Catholic religion. And he took his Catholicism seriously. Indeed he was more than a little of a saint. But if it be correct to say that a man's life in relation to the community is fulfilled only in so far as he helps to realise the needs of the community -- and history suggests that it is correct -- then it would seem that in secular matters, where the point of departure was that of a man not of the people, Edward Martyn's influence must almost inevitably tend to be ephemeral, whereas the enterprises he undertook in connection with religion, where he was at one with the people, might be of more lasting value. And so it has turned out.

To-day we associate Edward Martyn's name, not to much with the beginnings of the Abbey Theatre, or with Sinn Féin or the Gaelic League or the Feis Ceóil or the Irish Literary Theatre -- all of which he encouraged and materially helped -- as with, first and foremost, the Palestrina Choir at the Pro-Cathedral and then with the modern Irish stained glass revival. An ever-increasing number of people are aware that it was he who initiated the movement for the establishment of the Irish stained glass industry which was to take definite shape as An Túr Gloine, The Tower of Glass. Out of that was to come the whole series of greater and lesser masterpieces by Michael Healy, over fifty of which remain in Ireland. And from that fine start came the broader development that was to include the stained glass work of Wilhelmina Geddes, Harry Clarke, Hubert MacGoldrick, Evie Hone, Richard King and others who, it is not an exaggeration to claim, have placed Ireland amongst the very first countries of the contemporary world in the production of stained glass art. Without attempting to minimise the extremely valuable part, artistic and financial, played by Miss Sarah Purser in the early days of that venture, it is still true to say that had it not been for Edward Martyn who initiated the idea it would never have been undertaken at all.

Even more important to Edward Martyn, however, was the Palestrina Choir at the Pro-Cathedral. Liturgical music was, he said, himself, the chief interest of his life. And it is thanks to him and to that great Irishman, Archbishop Walsh of Dublin, who with infinite understanding and patience saw Martyn's scheme through from conception to realisation, that, for forty years now, the Palestrina Choir has provided such opportunity as was never before available to the Irish laity of hearing all the music of the Liturgy worthily sung by a trained body of singers. Sunday after Sunday and feast after feast; above all, perhaps, Easter after Easter, the wonderful music of the Liturgy is rendered by the Choir (of "at least eight men and twenty boys" as the foundation agreement laid down -- though usually a good many more), under the still admirable direction of Dr. Vincent O'Brien, whom Martyn and Dr. Walsh first appointed. There we hear the sublimest compositions in all music, the anonymous ancient chants that were already old and consecrate in the days of Gregory the Great, nearly fourteen centuries ago, and the later settings of the inspired words by known masters like Pierre de la Rue, Pier Luigi Palestrina, Orlando di Lasso and Vittoria.

From the establishment of the Choir on, Martyn was the most faithful attendant at High Mass in the Pro-Cathedral. Half-crippled with arthritis, one would see him making his way slowly up the aisle. And how pleased he was if, afterwards, one ventured to make an appreciative remark about the music or the rendering of it. He really loved his choir, as many less musically learned Irishmen than he have come to love it since. Even in matters of the rendering of church music, however, he had very decided views. I do not know whether he ever argued with Dr. O'Brien on the subject, but I do remember how, in his helpless and lovable way, he fulminated to me against the Vatican Choir for what he considered its excessively "operatic" methods, as we happened on each other coming out from the first of the concerts of sacred music it gave in Dublin about twenty years ago. I did not know whether he was right or wrong, but I dared to say that a setting of some stark passage from the Liturgy -- I think it was the *Dies Irae* -- by Vittoria was the most awe-inspiring piece of music I had ever heard. But no! As rendered by the Vatican Choir Edward Martyn would have none of it. And he pottered off grumbling.

He was the same in everything. He knew how things ought to be done, and if they were not done his way they were wrong. But he was as modest in his behaviour as he was tenacious of his principles. And he seldom quarrelled. He declared his views and if he failed to win agreement for them he busied himself with something else. For everything he ever took up he made sacrifices. He always gave money. But he gave more than money. He gave time, thought, energy, advice. He wrote articles, he attended committee meetings. For the Irish Literary Theatre he wrote plays. He was ready to talk till all hours of the night with anyone who came to see him in his little flat beside the Club. Young people interested in any political or cultural scheme susceptible of national application were always encouraged. I remember the plain room with its bare furniture and the solitary thing in the way of a picture, an unframed colour-print of the *Madonna of the Eucharist* by Ingres, propped up on the chimney-piece. There the great men of the great generation, that of the first quarter of this century, had all, at one time or another, gone to talk over some aspect of the nation's life with the generous, saintly, patriotic old crank.

Like most of them, but in his own way, he gave in death as he had given in life. Though he was only moderately rich, his generosity had been proverbial. In his will he left money to the Gaelic League as well as to many charities. The Palestrina Choir had lived mainly on his original endowment. At his death he made provision for entertainments to be given to his singers twice a year. There was a small gift for every tenant who had bought his holding from him under the Land Purchase Acts. His bequest to the St. Vincent de Paul Society carried a clause to the effect that the charitable purposes on which it was spent must be Irish ones. The few fine pictures he owned -- they included a Degas and a Monet -- went to Ireland's National Gallery. The idea of pompes funèbres did not interest him and he directed that instead of being buried in the family vault his body was to be taken to the Cecilia Street Hospital, for dissection by the medical students, among the other corpses that are provided from the workhouse infirmaries. So it was done. That was the end of the earthly life of the "*contrairy*" Christian and patriot. But his goodness in all things remains an inspiration. For all his vagaries, of few men is it as plainly evident that he lived and died, as the simple phrase has it, to God and Ireland true.

Appendix XIII
The Loughaunbeg Naval Mine

There is some question about whether the mine was German or British. Some (but not all) reports said that what could have been Geman iconography was found on some of the debris. Descriptions of the mine survive, but, there are complications. Some reports have the mine as barrel shaped, although one report describes a more pear-shaped device. At the war's outset, the German Navy had an effective moored barrel mine that the Royal Navy lacked. Obtaining and disassembling a German mine, the Royal Navy was impressed enough that they copied the German design. The Germans used a castable explosive, hexanite (typically 60% TNT and 40% hexanitrodiphenylamine).

The Germans designated their mine EMA (Elektrische Minen type A). The EMB was a higher yield version. Both versions of the moored mine were 34 inches in diameter and 46 inches long. It was the standard German WWI moored contact mine.

The EMA mine weighted 560 lbs with 330 lbs being hexanite, while the EMB weighted 760 lbs with 485 lbs being hexanite. With the anchor, the EMA unit weighed one ton (200 lbs more for the EMB). The mine had two lugs that could be mistaken for handles. One lug is visible in the photograph. These mines could be deployed from ships or submarines.

The spikes the accounts mentioned were called Hertz Horns. There were five of them (seven on the EMB), four along a circle around the mine near the top, and one centered on top. They were metal tubes with a glass ampule of sulfuric acid inside. When the horn and ampule were crushed, the acid flowed, creating a wet battery, which generated a spark.

Disassembled WWI German
EMA/EMB Moored Contact Mine
(Credit: Schleswig-Holstein ordnance
disposal team teaching materials)

Of the various accounts, the one making the most sense is that someone removed a screw(s) holding one of the Hertz Horns. Then out came something that resembled a bicycle inner tube.

That tube contained the explosive tetryl, a crystalline powder sensitive to friction, shock, and spark. Breaking the ampule (creating a spark), or sharply shaking the tube, one of which a fisherman apparently did, accomplished the same deadly thing. Tetryl's detonation would trigger the hexanite.

At the end of WWI, the Germans stockpiled a number of these mines, some of which were deployed in the early days of WWII, possibly again in Galway Bay in September 1939. In 1939, the Germans were incapable of using submarines to deploy these mines. One can infer from the above photograph credit that, to this day, these mines still turn up, mainly in the Baltic and North Seas.

Appendix XIV:
Remarks on Some References

The crucial online document archive is;

DIPPAM (Documenting Ireland: Parliament, People, and Migration)
https://www.dippam.ac.uk/

Much of the discussion of the famine relief in and west of Galway occurs in the Fifth, and Sixth and Eighth Series of "Papers Relating To Proceedings For Relief Of Distress, And State Of Unions And Workhouses In Ireland:"

http://www.dippam.ac.uk/eppi/documents/12269/page/295710   *(Fifth Series, 1848)*
https://www.dippam.ac.uk/eppi/documents/12269/page/296418   *(Sixth Series, 1848)*
https://www.dippam.ac.uk/eppi/documents/12269/page/297496   *(Seventh Series, 1848)*
https://www.dippam.ac.uk/eppi/documents/12598/page/156788   *(Eighth Series, 1849)*

One gets a feeling for the Irish situation from 1840 through 1846, and part-way into 1847, from:

Poor Law Commissioners: Thirteenth Annual Report With Appendices
https://www.dippam.ac.uk/eppi/documents/12367/pages/305246

For the 1848 *EPPI* document #12269, the metadata states that there are 6132 pages in the file. But I couldn't get beyond page 2044. I found a hack, and discovered that the 6132 page file is a triplicate of the fifth, sixth, and seventh series, numbering 2044 pages. 2044 pages times 3 = 6132 pages. Thus, there is no need to proceed beyond page 2044.

The following reference list is not exhaustive. For many links in this document, such as the one for the *Griffith's Valuation*, typing the hyperlink name into a search engine will get one there, or close to there. Another approach for the devilishly complicated web addresses is to type in the lead segment of the address, and perhaps the next segment, to get to the website in question. Then use the site's internal engine, or table of contents, to snoop around.

EPPI References			
Text Page	EPPI Document	EPPI Page	Comment
9	13139	161179	1851 Census Summary (includes the 1841 Census Data)
12	12367	305230	Irish arriving in Liverpool 13 Jan- 20 Apr 1847
14	9960	219414	Galway Elections, 12 April 1827 Report
46	11161	256782	1 Dec 1837 Poor Law Bill
46	12269	301951	1841 Galway Poor Law Union Electoral Division Populations
66	12269	297513	Gregory Clause & Family Relief
69	12394	306668	Thomas Bunbury writing to Lord John Russell
69	12367	305252	Thirteenth Annual Report of the Poor Law Commissioners
71	12350	304528	Spiddal Fever Hospital Certificate
75	12269	296603	Barley and Indian Meal Bread, Workhouse Oven
75	12233	294366	Bread made from Rye and other meal
75	12269	296466	"

			EPPI References
Text Page	EPPI Document	EPPI Page	Comment
75	12269	306942	Beet-root & Parsnip Bread
75	12269	307141	Soup Boilers
76	12269	296191	Connemara Paupers in the Workhouse
77	12269	296199	Capt Hellard's Illness
77	12269	297484	Galway Poor Law Union Statistics on Outdoor Relief
78	12269	297739	"
78	12598	157113	"
78	12269	296596	Killanin Relief District Split into 3 Districts
78	12269	296606	Gentry in Poor Rate Arrears
78	12269	296605	The Tax Collector Pat Martin's Assault
80	12269	296596	AB Martin Writing to Galway Vice-Guardians about Arrears
91	12367	305249	Workhouse Dangers
91	12269	296203	Tully Evictions
150	16068	193655	Sheep Depredation by Dogs

The template is: *http://www.dippam.ac.uk/eppi/documents/12269/page/295710*

For the gentry, the genealogies mainly come from *Hardiman* and *Burkes Landed Gentry*:

Hardiman's History of Galway:The History of the Town and County of the Town of Galway: The History of the Town and County of the Town of Galway; Clachan Publishing, 2020 (paperback); ISBN-13: 978-1909906518

A Genealogical and Heraldic History of the Landed Gentry of Great Britain & Ireland, Volume 1; 1847
https://books.google.com/books?id=YdIKAAAAYAAJ&printsec=frontcover#v=onepage&q&f=false

A Genealogical and Heraldic History of the Landed Gentry of Great Britain & Ireland, Volume 2; 1871
https://books.google.com/books/about/A_Genealogical_and_Heraldic_History_of_t.html?id=H65CAAAAYAAJ

Also see The UK Genealogical Archives; https://ukga.org/search.php?action=loadDB&DB=33

BLAKE FAMILY RECORDS - 1300 TO 1600 by Martin J Blake
First Series; London; Eliot Stock 1902
https://drive.google.com/file/d/1OKjNz2VcdLORn4TlbRfLngu_3-PHmgm_/view?usp=sharing

BLAKE FAMILY RECORDS 1600 TO 1700
Second Series; London; Eliot Stock 1905
https://archive.org/stream/blakefamilyrecor00blakuoft/blakefamilyrecor00blakuoft_djvu.txt

Also useful is Burke's East Galway;
http://burkeseastgalway.com

Page 8
Down Survey
https://downsurvey.tchpc.tcd.ie/

The O'Flaherty Country by W. Lynam Irish Quarterly Review Vol. 3, No. 10 June 1914, pp 13-40
https://www.jstor.org/stable/30092464

Page 9
Griffith's Valuation
https://www.askaboutireland.ie/griffith-valuation/

Page 10
The O'Flaherties and their interactions with the Anglo-Normans
The O'Flaherty Country by W. Lynam Irish Quarterly Review Vol. 3, No. 10 June 1914, pp 13-40,

Page 11
Laws in Ireland for the Suppression of Popery (Penal Laws);
http://www.law.umn.edu/library/irishlaw

Eighth Year of Anne; "8 Anne Ch3 Sec 39;"
http://moses.law.umn.edu/irishlaws/8Annc3s27-37.html#8Ac3p214s37

Eviction tally for Lord Campbell's April 1852 Barna eviction:

THE TEDIOUS BUSINESS OF UNWANTED TENANTS: GALWAY AND MAYO IN THE 1850s by Pádraig Lane
Journal of the Galway Archaeological and Historical Society; Vol. 60 (2008), pp. 126-135
https://www.jstor.org/stable/20720183

Page 12
Lord Campbell's 10 Shillings
Connemara After The Famine Journal of a Survey of the Martin Estate, 1853; Thomas Colville Scott
Edited with an Introduction by Tim Robinson, The Lilliput Press (1996); ISBN-13 : 978-1874675693

https://www.advertiser.ie/galway/article/126352/connemara-after-the-faminadraig

Page 13
Landed Estate Court (Vol 11, 1861, go to page 330)
https://www.google.com/books/edition/Irish_Chancery_Reports/_hoWAAAAYAAJ?

Page 14
Galway Elections, 12 April 1827 Report, Mayhem and Death;
https://archive.org/details/op1250133-1001/mode/1up?view=theater
https://www.dippam.ac.uk/eppi/eppi_lc_subjects/2113

https://www.advertiser.ie/galway/article/125934/the-turbulent-life-of-col-richard-martin-mp-in-three-acts

Page 15
Evie Hone
https://www.irishtimes.com/news/ireland/irish-news/evie-hone-remaining-stations-of-cross-on-display-in-galway-museum-1.1570783

Page 16
The Shape of The Killannin Parish by Hilary Kiely
https://www.oughterardheritage.org/content/place/killannin/the-shape-of-killannin-parish

Page 17
Cill Éinde Registeries;
https://registers.nli.ie/parishes/0641

Memorials of the Dead
https://archive.org/search?query=creator:
%22Association+for+the+Preservation+of+Memorials+of+the+Dead+in+Ireland%22

Page 18
Connaught Journal; Father Fahy & Father Fahy in Moycullen
www.irelandoldnews.com/Galway/1840/JUL.html
https://moycullen.galwaycommunityheritage.org/content/topics/the-famine/an-gorta-mor-i-maigh-cuilinn-1845-1850

Page 20
Representative Church Body
https://www.ireland.anglican.org/cmsfiles/pdf/AboutUs/library/registers/ParishRegisters/PARISHREGISTERS.pdf

Tim Robinson
Connemara, A Little Gaelic Kingdom, by Tim Robinson, pg 264; Penguin Books 2011, ISBN 978-0-141-04959-5

Page 21
Moycullen Census;
https://moycullen.galwaycommunityheritage.org/content/uncategorized/blake-census

Page 27
Geohive;
https://www.geohive.ie/

Page 28
Cill Éinde - Céad Bliain, editor; Eoin O Droighneáin;
Publisher: Comhlacht Forbartha An Spidéil Teoranta, 2007   ISBN 13: 9780955750007

Lord Killanin's Cill Éinde Reminisces
https://www.coisfharraige.ie/cumann-forbartha/stair-chois-fharraige/st-endas-spiddal-by-lord-killanin/

An Túr Gloine;
https://www.artbiogs.co.uk/2/organizations/tur-gloine

Cill Éinde's Stations of the Cross & Stained Glass
(Ethel Rhind, Catherine O'Brien, George Walsh, Phyllis Burke)
Gazetteer of Irish Stained Glass: Revised New Edition, 2021,
Editors; Nicola Gordon Bowe, David Caron & Michael Wynne, Irish Academic Press ISBN-13 : 978-1788551298

Page 29
Voices of Ireland by Raymonde Standún & Bill Long; Island Press ISBN-13: 978-1848408746
https://www.newisland.ie/nonfiction/voices-of-connemara

Page 31
Ian Cantwell; Memorials of the Dead: Counties Galway & Mayo (West)
http://www.iancantwell.com/GalwayMayoMemorials.html

Page 32
Cré na Cille
by Mairtin Ó Cadhain   Translated by Liam Mac Con Iomaire and Tim Robinson,
Yale University Press 2017   ISBN-13 : 978-0300227062
https://yalebooks.yale.edu/book/9780300227062/graveyard-clay/

Page 33
Spiddal Graveyard 1898;
https://archive.org/details/journalforyear04asso/page/n225/mode/2up

Page 34
Adrian Martyn & The Kirwins of Galway and the Battle of Aughrim
https://adrianmartyn.ie/
https://www.genealogy.com/forum/surnames/topics/kirwin/29/

Index to Prerogative Wills of Ireland, 1536-1810, Sir Arthur Vicars, F.S.A., Publisher: Edward Ponsonby, 1897
https://archive.org/details/indextoprerogati00vica/page/n3/mode/2up

Prerogative and diocesan copies of some wills and indexes to others, 1596 – 1858
http://census.nationalarchives.ie/search/dw/home.jsp

Extract of Stephen Martin's Will
Findmypast.com; Ireland, Inland Revenue Wills & Administrations 1828-1879
The Patrick Blake mentioned is likely not the infamous Patrick Blake of the Great Famine era, but an earlier one.
See Appendix VII.

Catholic Qualification Rolls 1700-1845
http://census.nationalarchives.ie/search/cq/home.jsp

James Hardiman; *The History of the Town and County of the Town of Galway*
https://books.google.com/books/about/The_history_of_the_town_and_county_of_th.html?id=Lv8HAAAAQAAJ

Page 37
Church of Ireland Parish Registers
https://www.ireland.anglican.org/cmsfiles/pdf/AboutUs/library/registers/ParishRegisters/PARISHREGISTERS.pdf

https://www.ireland.anglican.org/cmsfiles/pdf/AboutUs/library/registers/ParishRegisters/JKL/KillanninParishRegisterList.pdf

Page 39
Census of Ireland 1851 : part V: tables of deaths, volume I; volume II (tables and index), containing the
"Table of Cosmical Phenomena, Epizootics, Famines, and Pestilences, in Ireland"; pages 41-333, at
https://ia600207.us.archive.org/19/items/op1247882-1001/op1247882-1001.pdf

Page 40
Spiddal-Moycullen Road Project
https://www.nationalarchives.ie/search-the-online-catalogue/advanced-search/#!/details/111053909

Page 42
Dr James Andrew Veitch; https://www.dib.ie/biography/veitch-james-andrew-a8799

Page 44
Francis Comyn and Caroline, the Baroness von Stenz vs Mrs Little
Comyn vs Little; *Journals of the House of Lords (JHL), Vol 97 1865* JHL, Vol 101, 1869, Also on Google Books

Page 46
Poor Relief (Ireland) Act, 1838
https://www.irishstatutebook.ie/eli/1838/act/56/enacted/en/print.html

Page 48
Soupers and Jumpers: The Protestant Missions in Connemara by Miriam Moffitt 2008
The History Press; ISBN-13 : 978-1845889241
https://www.thehistorypress.co.uk/publication/soupers-and-jumpers/9781845889241/

Page 50
GENUKI Database; British Coastguards 1841 – 1901;
https://www.genuki.org.uk/big/Coastguards

Page 51
John Horrocks Ainsworth and the Irish Connection and The Irish Industrial Exposition of 1853
https://friendsofsmithillshall.co.uk/wp-content/uploads/2014/04/Friends-Bulletin-21.pdf

https://www.google.com/books/edition/The_Irish_Industrial_Exhibition_of_1853/HwY-D1IgYL4C?hl=en

Page 53
Phelan, Mary (2013) Irish language court interpreting 1801-1922. PhD thesis, Dublin City University
https://doras.dcu.ie/17739/

Page 57
Good News from Ireland by the Rev John Garrett; Hatchard and CO, 187 Piccadilly London
Dublin; Hodges, Smith and CO; 1863
Copy in the British Library and on Google Books:
https://www.google.com/books/edition/Good_News_from_Ireland/NZcuDGYjvKQC?
hl=en&gbpv=1&dq=good+news+from+Ireland&pg=PA110&printsec=frontcover

page 60
Margaret Lappin
https://www.geni.com/people/Margaret-Lappin-nee-Kain-Kane-Keane-Mrs-Domestic-Servant-then-
Wife/6000000018950574954

Page 61
Architectural Drawing Project;
https://www.ireland.anglican.org/news/7104/architectural-drawings-project-moves-west

Interior Plan for St Joseph's Anglican Church, Spiddal
https://archdrawing.ireland.anglican.org/items/show/5114

Pages 63
Edward Krumm at the Galway Train Station;
https://www.advertiser.ie/galway/article/116605/a-violent-night-in-galway

Irish Military Archives;
www.militaryarchives.ie/collections/online-collections/bureau-of-military-history-1913-1921

Micheál Ó Droighneáin on the Spiddal Raids
https://www.militaryarchives.ie/collections/online-collections/bureau-of-military-history-1913-
1921/reels/bmh/BMH.WS1718.pdf#page=16

Page 64
Anglican Killannin Parish Records
https://www.ireland.anglican.org/cmsfiles/pdf/AboutUs/library/registers/ParishRegisters/JKL/KillanninParishRe
gisterList.pdf

Page 67
1824 Statistical and Agricultural Survey of Co Galway by Hely Dutton
https://archive.org/details/astatisticaland00duttgoog/page/n7/mode/2up

Page 68
A History of the Irish Poor Law by Sir George Nicholls, John Murray Publisher, Albemarle Street, London; 1856
https://www.gutenberg.org/files/56957/56957-h/56957-h.htm

Pages 74-75
Irish grain and alcoholic beverage exports to Britain during the Great Famine by Christine Kinealy
https://www.historyireland.com/food-exports-from-ireland-1846-47/

Corn vs Corn Meal
The Great Hunger Ireland 1845-1849, by Cecil Woodham-Smith, 1963 Penguin Books, ISBN 978-0-14-014515-1

Ireland's Hunger, England's Fault? by Cecil Woodham-Smith; The Atlantic, January 1963
https://www.gutenberg.org/files/14412/14412-h/14412-h.htm

Nixtamalized Corn; Hominy, Sent to Ireland
https://www.bostonglobe.com/2020/02/05/magazine/it-is-not-an-everyday-matter-see-nation-starving/

The History of the Great Irish Famine of 1847, with Notices of Earlier Irish Famines.
By the Rev John O'Rourke, P.P. M.R. I.A. Third Edition Dubin James Duffy and Co., LTD., 15 Wellington Quay 1902
https://www.gutenberg.org/files/14412/14412-h/14412-h.htm

Page 76
The Wallscourts;   https://www.genealogics.org/getperson.php?personID=I00087162&tree=LEO

Page 79
Thomas Redington;   https://www.dib.ie/biography/redington-sir-thomas-nicholas-a7598

Page 96
Francis Skeet's Blake of Gortnamona and Tully Genealogy;
https://archive.org/details/historyoffamilie00skee/page/n3/mode/2up

Page 98
Louisa Catherine Beaufort; *Irish Scraps to Amuse my dear Admiral from LCB* May 27, 1857
Trinity College Dublin Digital Collections:
https://digitalcollections.tcd.ie/concern/works/47429d36q?locale=en

Louisa Beaufort's Diary of her Travels in South-West Munster and Leinster in 1842 and 1843
Magda Loeber & Rolf Loeber, Analecta Hibernica, No. 46 (2015), pp. 121, 123-205;
https://www.jstor.org/stable/24592521?read-now=1&seq=23#page_scan_tab_contents

Page 106
Erin's Hope (Several years of issues, starting from 1879, are included)
https://www.google.com/books/edition/_/v2wEAAAAQAAJ?hl=en&gbpv=0

Page 109
Spiddal Orphanage;
https://www.advertiser.ie/galway/article/4528/an-unseemly-brawl-over-god-and-scripture

Page 114
Erratum
John Lynes, mistakenly thought by me to be Elizabeth's child, actually was born to Henry Lynes and Catherine Padmore. A pregnant Elizabeth Lynes returned to England in 1873. Arriving in Canada in 1874 to conduct his inspection, it seems Andrew Doyle heard her sad story second-hand, and sought her out upon returning to Britain to confirm the story. Doyle found Elizabeth Lynes in the able-bodied women's ward of the Wolverhampton workhouse, "waiting to be confined of an illegitimate child." On 17 June 1875, Charles Lynes, son of the "spinster" Elizabeth Lynes of the Wolverhampton Workhouse, was baptized in an Anglican ceremony. Elizabeth Lynes was twice abused; first in Canada in 1873 at age sixteen, and then in Wolverhampton late in 1874 at age seventeen.

Page 117
Dublin Fire Brigade Ambulance;
https://databases.dublincity.ie/logbook/april26.html#

Page 117 (continued)
Abraham Vantreen Arriving in Canada—1906;
https://canadianbritishhomechildren.weebly.com/ellen-smyly.html

St Werburgh's Church;
https://www.findagrave.com/cemetery/859743/memorial-search?page=1#sr-130468060

Page 118
Abraham Vantreen's Military Service
http://www.canadiangreatwarproject.com/searches/soldierDetail.asp?ID=172920
https://canadianbritishhomechildren.weebly.com/ellen-smyly.html

John Vantreen; In the 1921 Canadian Census and His Grave Marker
https://www.bac-lac.gc.ca/eng/census/1921/Pages/item.aspx?itemid=1713712
https://www.findagrave.com/memorial/147445187/john-thomas-vantreen

Page 127
Dr W Peard's; A Year of Liberty or Salmon Angling In Ireland
Horace Cox, 346, Strand W.C., 1867, London
https://books.google.com/books/about/A_Year_of_Liberty.html?id=1rVGAAAAIAAJ
Also in the Harvard College Library.

Page 132
Humble Works for Humble People: A History of the Fishery Piers of County Galway and North Clare, 1800-1922.
by Noël P Wilkins; Irish Academic Press; 2017 ISBN-13 : 978-1911024910

Ceibh an Spideil 1867-1871
https://www.coisfharraige.ie/cumann-forbartha/stair-chois-fharraige/ceibh-an-spideil-1867-1871/

Page 133
Dumhach na Leanbh (Dune of the Babies)
https://www.coisfharraige.ie/cumann-forbartha/wp-content/uploads/2019/04/Dumhach-na-Leanbh-Tuairisc-le-MI-Gibbons.pdf

Page 138
Captain Pulteney Murray;   https://www.whobegatwhom.co.uk/ind213.html

Page 141
The Rev John Darley; http://www.darley.ie/history

Page 147
Commonwealth of Massachusetts Passenger Manifest Lists (1848-1891)
https://www.sec.state.ma.us/ArchivesSearch/Passengermanifest.aspx

Forgetting Ireland by Bridget Connelly, 2003; Minnesota Historical Society ISBN-13 : 978-0873514491

Catholic Colonization on the Western Frontier by Shannon, James P. Yale University Press, New Haven, CT, 1957

Immigrant's Condition
https://storage.googleapis.com/mnhs-org-support/mn_history_articles/35/v35i05p205-213.pdf

Blacksod Bay;   http://www.blacksodbayemigration.ie/

Page 151
Compulsory Purchase
https://www.europeana.eu/en/item/574/_c247tf43h
https://hansard.parliament.uk/Commons/1898-02-23/debates/cc26efda-594e-467c-be3b-280eaa78e22c/CongestedDistrictsBoard(Ireland)(CompulsoryPurchasePowers)Bill

Page 152
Royal Commission On Congestion In Ireland;
https://archive.org/details/op1255387-1001/page/68/mode/2up?view=theater

Page 156
Frank NcNally on the last Earl of Clanricarde; Irish Times 10 August 2021
https://www.irishtimes.com/opinion/end-of-the-line-frank-mcnally-on-the-dubious-legacy-of-the-last-earl-of-clanrickarde-1.4644017

Land Annuities
https://www.irishtimes.com/opinion/de-valera-not-averse-to-breaking-international-agreements-1.4354511

Page 157
National Inventory of Architectural Heritage
https://www.buildingsofireland.ie/buildings-search/building/30327002/spiddal-house-bohoona-east-spiddal-county-galway

Page 158
Potatoes of Historical Interest in Ireland;   Department of Agriculture, Fisheries and Food 2008
https://archive.org/details/potato-varieties-of-historical-interest-in-ireland

Page 161
Against the Tide by Dr Noël Browne, 1986, Gill Books, ISBN-13 : 978-0717114580

39 George III c15.;   https://play.google.com/books/reader?id=H3xaAAAAYAAJ&pg=GBS.PA194

The 1819 Attempt to Repeal the Window Tax
https://api.parliament.uk/historic-hansard/commons/1819/may/05/motion-for-the-repeal-of-the-window-tax

Page 162
The Poor-Law Medical Service Of Ireland. The British Medical Journal, vol. 1, no. 525, 1871, p. 78.
www.jstor.org/stable/25228775.

Page 167
WW II Coastal Look-out Posts;
https://coastmonkey.ie/protecting-our-neutrality-ww2-lookout-posts/
https://www.lookoutpost.com/fromabove/lop49-spiddal/

Look-Out-Post Logbooks
https://www.militaryarchives.ie/collections/reading-room-collections/look-out-post-logbooks-september-1939-june-1945

Page 168
Sinking Of The Neptune
https://www.advertiser.ie/Galway/article/97399/the-sinking-of-the-neptune

Page 180
The Martins of Ross, Compiled by Seymour Clarke, Inverness: Printed at the "Northern Chronicle" Office, 1910
https://www.familysearch.org/library/books/records/item/188441-the-genealogy-of-the-martins-of-ross?offset=44
https://drive.google.com/file/d/1QskSkJJyldqP1FOsujhuZXZjOCRAmN-O/view

Genealogy of the Family of Martin of Ballinahinch Castle, in the County of Galway, Ireland
by Archer E S Martin, Winnipeg The Stovel Company 1890
https://archive.org/details/cihm_09842/page/n5/mode/2up?view=theater

Page 180 (continued)
Nimble Dick Martin and Birch Hall
The O'Flaherty Country by W. Lynam Irish Quarterly Review Vol. 3, No. 10 June 1914, page 33
https://www.jstor.org/stable/30092464
http://places.galwaylibrary.ie/place/51961
https://www.townlands.ie/ga/galway/moycullen/kilcummin/oughterard/curraveha/

The 20 Acre Bog Riot of 1837
'The Battle of Rushveala': Origin and Outcome of a Faction Fight at Oughterard, Co. Galway, on 8 December 1837
by James Mitchell. Journal of the Galway Archaeological and Historical Society Vol. 55 (2003), pp. 72-85.
https://www.jstor.org/stable/25535758

Page 181
The Comyns
http://www.limerickcity.ie/media/nmas%2003%2001,%2002%20Notes%20on%20the%20Comyn%20pedigree.
%20By%20David%20Comyn.pdf

Page 183
THE NAME AND FAMILY OF LORD MORRIS OF GALWAY AND SPIDDAL
THE IRISH LAW TIMES AND SOLICITORS ' JOURNAL VOLUME X X XI. - 1897
https://books.google.com/books?
id=aFMtAQAAMAAJ&pg=PA55&source=gbs_selected_pages&cad=2#v=onepage&q&f=false

Page 185
Hereditary Peerage for Baron Morris;
https://www.thegazette.co.uk/London/issue/27202/page/3751

Page 189
Catholic Baptismal Record of the son of Andrew Blake of Furbo
https://registers.nli.ie//registers/vtls000634200#page/98/mode/1up

Page 190
Thomas Bunbury and the Spiddal Post Office, *Aspects of Galway Postal History 1638-1984* by Jimmy O'Connor
Journal of the Galway Archaeological and Historical Society Vol. 44 (1992), pp. 119-194
https://www.jstor.org/stable/25550154

Page 192
The Genealogy of the Anglo-Norman Lynches who settled in Galway by Paul B McNulty
Journal of the Galway Archaeological and Historical Society, Volume 62, 2010, pages 30- 50
http://www.tara.tcd.ie/bitstream/handle/2262/86882/Genealogy_of_the_Ang-CSP_Proof-11-07-13.PDF?
sequence=1

A Week in the West of Ireland by Anonymous; Dublin: Hodges and Smith
https://books.google.com/books?
id=nl9ZAAAAcAAJ&printsec=frontcover&source=gbs_ge_summary_r&cad=0#v=onepage&q&f=false

A Topographical Dictionary of Ireland by Samuel Lewis London : S Lewis and Co, 1837
https://www.askaboutireland.ie/reading-room/digital-book-collection/digital-books-by-subject/geography-of-
ireland

Page 196
Moored German Barrel Mine:
https://phys.org/news/2018-08-hazardous-contaminated-sites-north-baltic.html

Underwater German Ordnance; Mines:
https://www.ibiblio.org/hyperwar/USN/ref/OP-1673A-Ger-Mines.pdf